PORT SECURITY MANAGEMENT

PORT SECURITY MANAGEMENT

KENNETH CHRISTOPHER

CRC Press
Taylor & Francis Group
Boca Raton London New York

CRC Press is an imprint of the
Taylor & Francis Group, an **informa** business

Auerbach Publications
Taylor & Francis Group
6000 Broken Sound Parkway NW, Suite 300
Boca Raton, FL 33487-2742

International Standard Book Number-13: 978-1-4200-6892-4 (Hardcover)

Library of Congress Cataloging-in-Publication Data

Christopher, Kenneth.
    Port security management / Kenneth Christopher.
       p. cm.
    Includes bibliographical references and index.
    ISBN 978-1-4200-6892-4 (hardcover : alk. paper)
    1. Watercraft police. 2. Harbors--Security measures. 3. Harbors--Management. I. Title.

    HV8080.W38C47 2009
    363.12'3--dc22
                                       2009004454

Visit the Taylor & Francis Web site at
http://www.taylorandfrancis.com

and the Auerbach Web site at
http://www.auerbach-publications.com

Contents

For Jeanne, Kris, and Lucas,
who in one way or another
were all inconvenienced by my work.

Preface

In 1996, after eighteen years in South Florida law enforcement, I had my career developed. In the informal police organizational lexicon of the time, *career development* was a euphemism for a less-than-desirable assignment that most ambitious, midlevel police managers (like me) would view as having limited potential for advancement. I was transferred from a fairly pleasant staff job in police headquarters doing planning and research to a uniform patrol command that included the Port of Miami. The seaport? Isn't that where night watchmen work?

When I teach Human Resources Management to college students, I tell them that the difference between training and career development is that you train employees to perform tasks required by their current job, and you develop employees by educating them to assume and take on new responsibilities. Little did I know back then how unprepared I really was to take on the tasks associated with managing law enforcement, and later, security, in a port facility. Though I had enough training and experience to successfully command police officers in the field, my entrée to the inner workings of a major world seaport opened up an entirely new perspective of the word *management*. It is one thing to plan, organize, and coordinate activities related to most standard local law enforcement responsibilities. Burglaries, robberies, accident investigations, and even the shootings and police chases have certain predictabilities in terms of the people, equipment, procedures, and finances needed to accomplish the typical police mission. But as I gradually assumed more and more responsibilities for the security function at the Port of Miami, I came to appreciate a certain premise: to manage security effectively in a port facility—to achieve results securing a dynamic port facility operation—you have to understand the *business* of maritime commerce.

In all, I spent ten years at the Port of Miami, and during that time the world changed dramatically. The term *homeland security* hardly existed before September 11, 2001, and now, seven years later, it dominates the public policy and economic agendas of world governments. The push for enhanced attention to critical infrastructure security and the focused concern on threats emanating from both domestic and foreign terrorist groups have fostered new challenges for organizations to maintain comprehensive security regimens that integrate with national and international strategies for homeland security. As we witnessed after September 11, the transportation sector, and aviation in particular, was subjected to unprecedented scrutiny and the imposition of regulatory prescriptions that have changed the way we travel and do business. Historically, maritime sector security has not been as heavily regulated as aviation. After September 11, the development of a worldwide maritime security convention, the International Ship and Port Facility Security Code, and the push for increased security of worldwide commerce and shipping presaged a heretofore unknown dynamic in the management of a port facility: the need for security to be a central component in the business of running a seaport. This was my career development at the Port of Miami.

The idea and the structure of this book come directly from my experiences in learning how to manage security effectively in a port facility. Through the countless meetings, discussions, and planning sessions I led or participated in as the port labored to develop a comprehensive security umbrella, I developed one fundamental paradigm about managing security in a port: nothing good gets done without collaboration and cooperation. This is the central theme running throughout the pages of this book. Volumes could be filled with technical details about security hardware, but the real knowledge to be gained does not come only from studying fencing materials and lighting standards. To be sure, those are important issues in security, and this book does discuss many important physical and procedural security issues. But the larger understanding and focus of this book is about developing working collaborations with the diverse actors from government and business, whose own organizational missions, while certainly focused on a secure port, sometimes collide in the development of efficient methods and best practices for port security.

This book is an effort to provide both practitioners and educators with a framework for managing port security that assumes little prior knowledge of the industry. This is management from the perspective of a novice who enters the complex interface between land and sea known as a seaport. I have written this book for the contract security provider who is considering port users as potential clients. It is written for the young Coast Guard ensign who has just been assigned to command a port security unit. It is written for the police commander who has just been transferred to a new assignment at the port. It is for the cargo terminal manager who has just learned that a team of government agents has shown up for an unannounced inspection of a cargo warehouse for compliance with a state or national security law. In sum, this book is written for anyone with a vested interest in both a secure *and* prosperous port facility who wants to develop insights into how best to tackle the management of security.

Kenneth Christopher

Acknowledgments

In so many ways, this book is a product of my association with the many fine professionals I had the pleasure of working with and learning from over the years during my associations with the Port of Miami and the Miami-Dade Police Department. It is impossible to name everyone, but several deserve recognition for their contributions, directly or indirectly, to my efforts here.

My sincere gratitude goes to former Port of Miami Director Charles Towsley, who re-energized and grew port operations when he arrived, and provided steady and confident leadership through the turbulent times after September 11. His recognition of the evolving importance of merging security into all facets of the business of running a seaport set the tone for the capital development and business improvements necessary for the growth and prosperity of a world-class seaport. Thanks also goes to Khalid Salahuddin, the deputy director at the Port of Miami, whose endless patience in managing conflict and knowledge of business and government administration provided guidance in balancing security with the practical realities of growing the port's business. My former colleague, Marie Di Rocco, a previous security chief at both the Port of Miami and Miami International Airport, was a trusted partner whose knowledge and experience in managing transportation security were instrumental in developing confidence in the security program at the Port of Miami. Thanks must also go to Louis Noriega, chief of Information Technology (IT). His ability to make complex IT systems understandable was invaluable in crafting technology solutions for port security. His vision of the convergence of IT, business, and security is charting new ground in the port environment. Thanks also to Donald Waugh for helping understand the integration of security into the design of port infrastructure. I salute the many hardworking security officers and supervisors I had the pleasure of working with, especially John Stephens, Fred Wong, Juan Gonzalez, Vernal White, Craig Proctor, and Silfredo Garcia.

Finally, a special thank you goes to Leticia Stewart, a role model for outstanding public service. Her many contributions to the port's security plan, documentation, and organization, as well as her ability to multitask and coordinate multiple projects with an unflappable professional demeanor, were a blessing.

During my career with the Miami-Dade Police Department, I was fortunate to work with and learn from many excellent law enforcement professionals. There are so many people that had a hand in helping me to be a good officer, supervisor, and manager, but I especially want to thank a select few who innately understood the value of collaborative management: Bob Swan, Jimmy Green, Jim Linville, Charles Miller, Michael Gruen, Ken Bernatt, Dick Roberts, and Loxley Arch, whose counsel to "always read from the top of the page to the bottom of the page" I still carry to this day. Thanks also goes to the many police officers and supervisors who worked their share of hot, humid, busy days and nights under my command over the years. I especially want to recognize some who provided dedicated service during some difficult times at the Port of Miami, mostly in the background with fairly little recognition: Gervasio "Herbie" Fundora, George Birlidis, Jorge Brito, Norberto "Maverick" Gonzalez, Mike Santos, Kathleen Sullivan, Rudy Vazquez, Mike Owens, Don Mills, Bill Eades, Brian Benson, James O'Riley, Glen Fonteciella, and particularly Lieutenant Mauricio Rivera. Lieutenant Rivera is an expert in motivating teams and a role model for leadership who understands how to get a job done from start to finish.

I also had the pleasure of learning from several outstanding security and maritime professionals. Among those are Bob Beh, vice president for Surveillance and Security, and his staff at Carnival Cruise Lines; and Captain A. Newhoff, manager of security for Royal Carribbean International and Celebrity Cruises. Their commitment to professionalism and collaboration in managing mutual security issues was invaluable. For their assistance, thank you also to Thomas Morelli, former program manager, Port and Cargo Security; and Raymond Barberesi, former director, Office of Ports and Domestic Shipping, Maritime Administration, U.S. Department of Transportation. Also, thank you to Bill DeWitt of SSA Marine, a strong advocate and voice of reason for best practices in maritime security.

From Auerbach Publications and CRC Press of the Taylor & Francis Group, thanks to senior editor Mark Listewnik for reaching out and motivating me to complete this project. Thank you also to Catherine Giacari, Tara Nieuwesteeg, and Amy Blalock for their work and assistance to me.

Thanks go to my Park University Criminal Justice faculty colleagues, Greg Plumb, Carol Getty, John Hamilton, and Michael Eskey, for their support and the opportunity to teach and share knowledge with our students.

Thank you, Nelson Oramas, for opening the door.

Finally, I want to thank my family for providing the foundation and support upon which all my work rests.

About the Author

Dr. Kenneth Christopher holds a bachelor's degree in criminal justice and master's and doctorate degrees in public administration. He is a graduate of the Administrative Officers Management Program at North Carolina State University and the Executive Contemporary Education for Leadership Program at the University of Miami. Dr. Christopher served twenty-six years in law enforcement, most recently as a captain with the Miami-Dade Police Department. From 1996 to 2006, he held progressively responsible police and security management positions at the Port of Miami. In 2005, he was appointed Chief of Seaport Security Enforcement and Facility Security Officer, responsible for the Port Facility Security Plan, leadership for the civilian security staff, and the coordination of security and law enforcement operations at the world's largest passenger cruise port.

Currently, Dr. Christopher is assistant professor and program coordinator for criminal justice at Park University, which provides educational services to 26,000 students on over forty campus centers across the United States and through distance learning from its home campus in Parkville, Missouri. He has held teaching positions at Lynn University in Boca Raton, Florida, and St. Thomas University in Miami, Florida.

Previously, Dr. Christopher worked with the U.S. Maritime Administration and the Organization of American States as a curriculum developer and instructor in the Inter-American Port Security Training Program. He has consulted on and developed educational programs and curricula in port security, criminal justice administration, security administration, terrorism and domestic preparedness, police management, and organizational behavior. His current interests include cooperative leadership strategies for port security management, human resource needs for intelligence in homeland security, and international service learning for individual and community safety and security.

Dr. Christopher is a member of the Academy of Criminal Justice Sciences, the American Society for Industrial Security (ASIS) International, and the Midwest Academy of Management. He has been an invited speaker at international and national conferences on maritime and homeland security, including SecurePort, the Institute for Defense and Government Advancement, and ASIS International's Asia-Pacific Security Conference.

The author invites comments and questions regarding this book and is interested in any ideas and observations that contribute to more effective management practices in the port security environment. The author may be contacted at:

Kenneth Christopher, D.P.A.
Department of Criminal Justice
Park University
8700 NW River Park Drive
Parkville, MO 64152

PART I
HISTORY AND ORGANIZATION OF PORT AND MARITIME SECURITY

1

INTRODUCTION TO PORT SECURITY MANAGEMENT

1.1 The Global Transportation System: The Context for Port Security

Seaports are a critical component of the global transportation infrastructure but historically have not been subject to comprehensive governmental regulation and security oversight. The terrorist attack of September 11 was a paradigm-shifting event for transportation systems' security in general. For the maritime sector, that event has prompted dramatic shifts in the focused perspectives on security now required by anyone even remotely affiliated with the management of port security, as well as the vessels, conveyances, and people transiting them. In Figure 1.1, a container ship is seen departing a port for its next destination, a common occurrence, but one that illustrates the crucial dependence much of the world places on the ability to move commodities securely using many nations' ports and waterways. Before the specter of global terrorism grew in the world's consciousness in the late twentieth century, the notion that this fairly routine activity might be vulnerable to significant harm was mainly a concern that occupied the minds of security and law enforcement professionals. What scrutiny has been given to this vessel, its crew, and its cargo as it moves around the world from port to port? What is really inside those metal boxes that move from warehouse to truck to train to ship to port? How closely have the activities of the men and women who transferred the containers onto this vessel been monitored? Questions like these must be posed by those managing the security of the world's transportation systems and infrastructure as they confront new, significant, and viable threats. While these managers have always had the responsibility to ensure the safety and security of the passengers, crew, and goods being moved, world events in the last ten to fifteen years now cause us to critically examine how well the security of our maritime and port infrastructure is being managed. Within this context, this book will provide a basic introduction and user's support guide to managing security at a port facility. Given the complexities of a still-evolving homeland security strategy, this book is written for those professionals, educators, and students who have responsibilities or interests in securing transportation infrastructure associated with the maritime sector in general, and port facilities in particular.

The goal of *Port Security Management* is to provide maritime industry professionals, government law enforcement and regulatory officials, and especially port operators,

02/03/2003

Figure 1.1 Container ship leaving port.

employees, users, and stakeholders with a basic awareness and understanding of security management in the port facility environment. The text is presented as a tripartite composite of port security management within a framework of organizational structure, risk, and vulnerability analysis, and the management of security operations. The first part of the book is concerned with illustrating a historical and organizational perspective on maritime and port security. Seaports, as passenger transportation and cargo delivery systems, are unique from a historical perspective because they developed as a function of geographical interfaces between one form of transportation, the seagoing vessel, and another, the land conveyance. Developing initially as enterprises built and operated on land owned by private, military, and/or commercial interests, the layers of security now deemed so essential in a homeland security environment were not necessarily embraced early on by commercial port interests. The evolution of organized security processes in the maritime sector can be understood as a product of increasing governmental and commercial concerns about the criminal exploitation of seaports, the growing use of vessels for the smuggling of contraband and other illicit activities, and the rising threat of global terrorism in the late twentieth century.

Second, the management of risk assessment is presented within the context of the unique vulnerabilities within the maritime and port environments. The important relationships between risk analysis, facility security planning, and coordination among port stakeholder business and security concerns provide the framework for understanding the pivotal role of the port security manager in coordinating the diverse interests of port users. The third and most comprehensive component of this text addresses the ground-level issues, tasks, and responsibilities that must be managed by port security, in concert with the port director and his or her staff. The structure for this discussion is based on the Port Facility Security Plan, the cornerstone for the construction of the port's security program. Component aspects include personnel and physical security systems and processes, access control, security force management, and vessel and cargo operations. The text explores issues related to the growth of multiuse port facilities for recreation, hospitality, and external business and commercial interests in those ports with interconnected relationships in many regions, cities, and towns. The important and complex role of technology in security, especially as related to computer and information security, intrusion detection, and biometrics, provides the reader with current perspectives on balancing physical and human resources in port protection systems. Finally, the need to develop contingency and emergency operations plans and to work effectively with federal, state, local, and private enterprises in coordinating both routine and emergency response mechanisms enables the reader to build a well-balanced perspective for working with all parties to achieve productive outcomes.

The primary reason why a book like this is important is that it provides a basic foundation for understanding the need for developing a *culture of security* in the port facility. Since ports have developed as open systems designed to interact efficiently with external commercial environments, there has been only minimal examination of the coordinating role played by port management in terms of security integration processes. The overwhelming governmental public policy response to September 11, 2001 demands effective leadership, management, and coordination of security operations in the port facility. Whether a small or large port, a cargo or passenger facility, it is imperative for port managers and security professionals to efficiently integrate the security function into each and every aspect of port operations. Disparate port functions such as engineering, finance, marketing, human resources, media relations, passenger operations, cargo operations, and many others coalesce within the framework of an organizational culture, emphasizing public confidence in the stability of operations by way of efficient and effective security controls.

Port directors and port security managers play pivotal roles in managing the complex interrelationships of the port stakeholders necessary to maximize productivity, while concurrently generating a safe and secure port environment. Now more than ever there is a need for a basic framework for understanding the relationship between risk and vulnerabilities at seaports, and specific ways in which port users can help to reduce the risks associated with those vulnerabilities as part of the port's overall security infrastructure. By encouraging a culture of security through an appreciation of the management constructs necessary for both effective and efficient port security, this book provides resource-minded industry officials, government agents, port professionals, educators, and students with tools to effectively identify and execute a management strategy for port security.

1.2 A Renewed Security Concern about Threats to Shipping and Commerce

In the maritime sector, concerns about incidents of violence and crime against world-wide shipping have taken on renewed emphasis because of the global threat of terrorism. Although acts of piracy at sea are not a new phenomenon, the ability of criminal and terrorist agents to attack relatively defenseless commercial shipping assets and crews outside the purview of law enforcement and security is a significant issue for world security. Table 1.1 shows that while worldwide acts of piracy against shipping in 2007 were down about 20 percent from 2004, there have been significant increases in the numbers of piracy incidents occurring in critical regions of the world, such as on both the western and eastern coasts of the African continent. While world maritime interests have recognized and responded to the threats of piracy in Asia and the Americas since September 11, the world is seeing a growing threat to shipping in many regions of the world that provide global conveyance routes for important natural resources, such as oil from the Middle East and Africa.

In the first quarter of 2008, forty-nine attacks against shipping by pirates at sea were reported worldwide, up by 15 percent from the same period a year earlier. Nigeria ranked number one with 20 percent of all attacks on vessels by pirates, likely attracted by Nigeria's oil wealth. Most of these attacks occurred at sea off Lagos, the economic and financial capital of Nigeria. India and the Gulf of Aden ranked as numbers two and three. Attacks in India have been primarily against small vessels, and in the Gulf of Aden attacks have involved the hijacking and taking of vessels to ports on the eastern coast of Somalia (International Chamber of Commerce 2008). In 2007, thirty-one attacks on ships were reported off the coast of Somalia, compared with just two in 2004. Pirates are reported to be using more weapons than in the past, with at least one report of a grenade launcher being used (Economist.com 2008). In February of 2008, Somalia's

Table 1.1 Acts of Piracy 2004 and 2007

REGION/COUNTRY	2004	2007	% CHANGE
Asia (Total)	205	110	-46.3
--Indonesia	94	43	-54.3
--Malacca Strait	38	7	-81.6
--Bangladesh	17	15	-11.8
--Rest of Asia	56	45	-19.6
Africa (Total)	65	107	+64.6
--Nigeria	28	42	+85.7
--Somalia	2	31	+1450
--Rest of Africa	35	34	-2.9
Americas (Total)	45	21	-53.3
Rest of World	14	25	+78.6
Total	329	263	-20.1

Data Source: Economist.com. Piracy: Peril on the high seas. 2008, April 23. Economist.com. http://www.economist.com/research/articlesBySubject/displaystory.cfm?subjectid=7933596&story_id=11079332 (accessed May 18, 2008).

Transitional Federal Government formally requested assistance from the United Nations Security Council for assistance in combating piracy in its territorial waters. The United States has noted the increase in incidents of piracy off the eastern coast of Africa and has been working with other UN member states—most notably, France—in drafting a UN Security Council Resolution that will authorize states to take steps to assist the Somali government in deterring, preventing, and suppressing acts of piracy and armed robbery off the Somali coast (U.S. Department of State 2008).

In 1948, the relatively young United Nations held a conference that adopted a convention establishing the International Maritime Organization (IMO), the first international body with a mission centered on world maritime affairs. Initially organized to consider issues of safety, and later the threat of marine pollution from ships (particularly pollution by oil carried in tankers), it has most recently devoted considerable time, energy, and resources to issues of world maritime security. "It has always been recognized that the best way of improving safety at sea is by developing international regulations that are followed by all shipping nations . . . but it was not until the establishment of the United Nations itself that these hopes were realized" (International Maritime Organization 2008, par. 13). Today, the IMO is a specialized agency of the United Nations, with 167 member states based in the United Kingdom and three hundred international staff.

In its 2002 guidance to ship owners, operators, shipmasters, and crews, the IMO published advisory information on preventing and suppressing acts of piracy and armed robbery against ships. The IMO advisory outlined risk prevention measures and alternative responses to acts of piracy and robbery, and emphasized the need to report such attacks, even the unsuccessful ones. In the wake of September 11, the worst case of international terrorism in modern times, the IMO has obviously raised concerns for maritime interests that the threat of terrorism could be extended to threats against shipping at sea and in ports around the world.

Terrorists' effective use of and threat to maritime assets was also demonstrated in the November 26–29, 2008 Mumbai, India terrorist attacks. Small teams of attackers, armed with conventional weapons, infiltrated the commercial center of Mumbai using small inflatable vessels after sailing from Karachi, Pakistan by cargo vessel, and hijacking an Indian fishing trawler (Rabasa et. al. 2009). The coordinated attacks against relatively soft targets, including an explosion at the Mazagaon docks in Mumbai's port area (Kerala Online 2008), lasted 60 hours and resulted in 172 deaths and over 300 injuries. The attackers' ability to enter Mumbai undetected and hold a major world city captive emphasizes the real threat facing localities dependent on the maritime sector.

Another example of the new and vigorous threat-environment being confronted by world maritime interests is the case of the Liberation Tigers of Tamil Eelam (LTTE). Bound by nationalism and ethnic identity, the LTTE, also known as the Tamil Tigers, initiated a conflict with the Sri Lankan government in 1976. Claiming to represent the Tamil minority in Sri Lanka, the LTTE has been reported to have as many as ten thousand members in active support of their cause of establishing an independent Tamil state. The LTTE uses a guerilla strategy, including the use of terrorist attacks in armed conflict with the Sri Lankan government. To date, some sixty thousand people have died in the civil war (GlobalSecurity.org 2008a). On October 19, 2006, the LTTE was responsible for a seaborne suicide attack in Galle, a top holiday destination on the southwestern tip of Sri Lanka. Disguised as fishermen in five small vessels, the attackers approached the town's naval base. Three of the attackers' crafts exploded at sea, damaging Sri Lankan naval vessels. Two vessels made it to shore, and the attackers engaged the naval base force in a gun battle. The at-sea explosions and land attacks led to the deaths of one hundred people, mostly sailors, and injuries of 160 others. Significantly, the LTTE is used as an example of how one group, dedicated to its cause, has been able to amass the capability to cause significant damage and continued future threats to maritime and port interests. The methods and tactics of ethnic terrorism used by the LTTE in its campaign against the Sri Lankan government, particularly the military, naval training, and attack tactics, have become a major concern for worldwide security experts. The use of small vessels in attack scenarios against larger, slower ships has illustrated a critical vulnerability faced by ships coming in and out of ports around the world.

As witnessed with the 2000 suicide attack on the U.S. guided missile destroyer USS *Cole* in the Port of Aden, the small vessel threat against shipping is real and is seen as a crucial motivator for new security regimens for ports around the world. The Yemen Ports Authority operates the Port of Aden, on the Gulf of Aden at the southern tip of the Arabian Peninsula, a critical location at the southern entrance to the Red Sea along one of the world's major trading routes through the Suez Canal. Aden's history as a seaport and center of trade goes back several thousand years. In the eleventh and twelfth centuries, Marco Polo visited Aden as part of his exploration of trade routes to India, China, and Southeast Asia. He described "how ships transfer their cargoes to smaller boats in the harbor, 'sail for seven days along a river' (presumably the Red Sea), and then transfer the goods to camel-back and send them overland on a 30-day trip to the Nile and thence to Alexandria and the Mediterranean" (Lunde 2005, par. 18). In modern times since the 1800s, Aden became an important regional fueling port, providing coal and water for steamers. With the opening of the Suez Canal in 1869, Aden's strategic location helped it grow into a major ship bunkering facility, as well as a tax-free shopping and trading port. Today, the primary commodities imported into the Port of Aden include rice, sugar, wheat, flour, and cement. Its major exports are salt, fish, cotton, and iron scrap. In 2007, 590 vessels called on the Port of Aden, handling a total cargo volume of approximately 3.4 million tons (Port of Aden 2008).

These numbers certainly do not place Aden anywhere near the top fifty ports worldwide in terms of cargo volume. For example, the Port of New Orleans, which ranked fiftieth worldwide in cargo volume in 2006, handled approximately seventy million tons, according to the American Association of Port Authorities (2008). In worldwide comparison, the Port of Aden is not a major center of shipping and trade, but it is a port with certain political and military strategic significance. At Aden, the strait of Bab el Mandeb separates Asia from Africa and connects the Red Sea to the Indian Ocean via the Gulf of Aden. Disputes over the control of this important choke point, between Eritrea and Yemen over the Hanish Islands, and between Yemen and Saudi Arabia over border issues, have often become violent. As it does for the Suez Canal and the Strait of Hormuz, the U.S. Navy, at the direction of the U.S. Central Command, is responsible for protecting the Bab el Mandeb choke point at Aden. It is partly for this reason that the USS *Cole*, a U.S. Navy guided missile destroyer, came to be in the Port of Aden on October 12, 2000.

In the late 1990s, the U.S. Navy sought a new port in the Middle East to conduct refueling for its vessels deployed in the region. The navy had been using Djibouti, a country in eastern Africa, as a refueling port, but became interested in an alternative port in the region when political conditions in Djibouti destabilized and the perceived threats to U.S. Navy assets increased. During the early and mid 1990s, the United States and Yemen had no diplomatic relations, but as Yemen emerged from a civil war, it was seen as a less risky alternative to the deteriorating conditions in Djibouti. Pursuant to a U.S. Defense Energy Support Center survey of the Port of Aden in 1998, a refueling contract was bid out and awarded, and the navy commenced refueling its ships in Aden (GlobalSecurity.org 2008b). While moored in the Port of Aden, the *Cole* was attacked by a small, motorized vessel on a targeted suicide-bombing mission. The attack craft approached and struck the *Cole* on its port side. The explosion created a forty-by-sixty-foot gash in the ship and resulted in seventeen deaths and thirty-nine injuries to navy personnel on board. At the time of the attack, the *Cole* was in the midst of a scheduled refueling operation.

In its 2001 report, the U.S. Department of Defense's USS *Cole* Commission Report stated emphatically that the attack on the *Cole* "demonstrated a seam in the fabric of efforts to protect our forces, namely in-transit forces" (U.S. Department of Defense 2001, p. 2). Several of the commission's findings emphasized the critical need for the managers of the nation's antiterrorism and force protection assets and personnel to focus more directly on processes associated with risk management. The commission specifically articulated the need for an interagency, coordinated approach to improving security to protect U.S. forces transiting other nations. It also stressed that antiterrorism and force protection programs must be "adequately manned and funded to support threat and physical vulnerability assessments of ports, airfields and inland movement routes that may be used by transiting forces" (U.S. Department of Defense 2001, p. 6). The fact that this significant act of global terrorism occurred in a port during a routine ship refueling operation illustrates the vital importance of the risk management process in port security management and planning.

1.3 Public Policy and Port Responsiveness to Commerce

In its traditional context, public policy is made by a legislature in the form of laws, which are enforced by the executive branch. In the United States, the Congress, states, and local governing bodies legislate in complicated areas where expert knowledge of programs is essential. This expertise is typically supplied by administrative officials who specialize in particular areas. For example, U.S. federal legislation designed to ensure the safety of the air-traveling public is often driven by the recommendations emanating from National Transportation Safety Board air crash investigations or by research from the Federal Aviation Administration. The laws and regulations that surface as public policy establish fees that can be charged, set standards of service, and control the activities of industries in the public interest. Private organizations are not typically subject to outside scrutiny. They exist to satisfy their clients. Internal operations are their own business and not that of the general public. It is when the activities within the private sector intersect with the general well-being and safety of the public that government steps in to effect controls in managing private sector operations. Much of public policymaking in government must be accomplished with the collaboration of numerous private groups and individuals. Public–private partnerships are essential for progress in achieving social goals. As evidence, one only need study the history of New Deal legislation in the wake of the Depression of the 1930s, or the War on Poverty in the 1960s, to see how effective public programs can only succeed with the cooperation of private sector entities. Much public policy is formalized as an outcome of the public and/or private sector's conception of the appropriate values, which are then translated into effective programs and funding. The problem with values in society is that they may be in conflict. For example, a police department may see a value in stopping and questioning every person in a neighborhood that has a rising crime rate, but the values embedded in the Fourth Amendment of the U.S. Constitution proscribe against searches and seizures that are unreasonable. The political system is therefore the societal mechanism for resolving questions of values. Since in the United States, as in many regions of the world, the government operates in both a political and a capitalistic system, its role includes controlling for the externalities that impact society. In other words, the government is responsible for ensuring that the side effects of market transactions do not harm the public good. Thus, the government requires controls on vehicle emissions that pollute the environment, though these controls effectively raise the cost of automobile production and transportation in general. This is the framework for law and order and economic stability.

The essential reason for a port's existence is to ensure the ability of the maritime industry to transact business. Without the ability of the industry to function competitively, there is no reason for the port to exist. Ships bound for a particular port may seek alternative harbor if the berthing conditions are unfavorable to the organization's business model or to shorten the transportation circuit and lower costs. Not unlike a traveling motorist's search for a night's sleep at a highway motel, many ships can proceed to the location that suits their cost structure, comfort needs, and security posture. Experienced managers and organizational leaders come to understand the need for security in the business environment. Security, which used to receive consideration as a necessary but uncomfortable overhead expense, is now seen as not only a necessary component of business but a value-added feature that can maximize profits through the mitigation of risks and costs associated with harm. In the recent past, an emerging paradigm has identified security as a component feature of many aspects of organizational productivity. A port facility's very existence is bound by two necessarily intertwined goals: (1) being responsive to the commercial needs and economic interests of the maritime industry, and (2) providing a safe and secure harbor for the transaction of the business operations of shipping and trade. In this business, security can no longer be guided by a myopic vision of port security as an ill-trained assortment of night watchmen jangling a set of keys and shaking the terminal doors in the middle of the night. In a time when the transportation of traded goods and the carriage of passengers has come onto the radar of extremists who desire to inflict maximum casualties in the pursuit of a narrow, destructive vision of the world, those in the business of securing port facilities must comprehend security in new and redefined ways. At the same time, those responsible for designing and implementing the security plans for these intersecting hubs of global trade must also be tuned in to a port's role in sustaining the livelihoods of not only the people who work there but the prosperity of the businesses, governments, and societal organizations that derive benefits from an economically competitive seaport. Thus, a port's responsiveness to commerce in the maritime sector must be guided by security plans and processes that provide the umbrella of safety in ways that ensure continued port productivity and growth. This is not an easy task, to be sure, and it will take port leadership that is committed to the vision of security and prosperity to move in the desired directions.

At many ports facing energized governmental security regulation and business efficiency demands, security has become such a compelling imperative that many port users are frustrated. Maritime businesses and port interests responsible for the movement and storage of cargo, as well as cruise lines and ferry operations responsible for the safe transportation of paying passengers, understand the need for security and have spent a lot of money to enhance their own security in the wake of the September 11 terrorist attacks. New international, national, state, and local laws and regulations were forged in the aftermath of September 11, which demanded a heretofore unheard of level of security in and around port facilities and throughout the maritime industry. Because these new standards in some cases prescribed specific requirements for ports, such as standardization of security plans, new security infrastructure, and new access control protocols, the ability of ports to co-opt the security improvements made by its own users demanded a reassessment of the entire process of security provision. For example, in the state of Florida, a comprehensive set of security standards implemented in 2001 for the state's fourteen deepwater ports required, among other things, that the governing port agency staff all restricted access area gates, despite the fact that a commercial port user/tenant may also be employing a security force to control access to the same area. Even though the requirement is designed, with perhaps good reason, to hold the port agency accountable for the ingress and egress of authorized individuals, legal constructs sometimes limit ports' flexibility in allowing the users to implement strategies that have the same objective—a safe and secure port.

The frustration that many port and maritime business professionals experience as a result of the renewed emphasis on port security is natural. Ports historically were designed to provide easy access for far-off businesses and shipping to land markets. Security, in the form of restricted access controls, conveyance inspections, identification checks, and personnel searches, slows down commerce. On another level, these same business interests understand the need for security in the technologically competitive open market of today's modern port environment. It would be folly to allow unrestricted access to the assets of the port and shipping interests. So, why the frustration? The answer lies within the framework of public policy and its impact on the risk management and security-planning processes. In an era when critical infrastructure security has become a driving force in public policy, government decisions to impose sometimes drastic security regimens may be seen as inhibiting commerce and playing into the game plans of extremists and terrorist seeking to do economic harm.

The challenge for all—government, business, and security—is to recognize and implement risk management and security-planning processes that engage the ports and their end users cooperatively in driving security at ports. The movement toward a convergence approach to security, one where port security managers can engage the diverse actors in the port in collaborative ways, should work to develop a framework of public policy, security regulations, and plans that are flexible enough to allow port tenants and security operations to work in tandem in developing a safe, secure, and economically completive port environment.

1.4 Economic Dependence on Maritime Transportation

For ten days in the fall of 2002, twenty-nine western U.S. seaports, including the ports of Los Angeles and Long Beach, which handle 40 percent of U.S-bound containers, were closed by their owners and operators during a labor dispute. "The lockout disrupted the itineraries of more than 200 ships carrying 300,000 containers, resulting in cargo delays, costly diversions to alternative ports, and unemployment lines as businesses laid off workers and cut production. The cost to the U.S. economy—in the form of delayed shipments and business disruptions—has been estimated to range from $450 million to several billion dollars" (Greenberg et al. 2006, pp. 122–123). This incident, prompted by a regional dispute between industry and labor, illustrates the impact that can befall the economy when disruptions occur in the maritime transportation sector. This is significant considering the substantial growth in the movement of shipping containers around the world in the early twenty-first century. Figures reported by the U.S. Maritime Administration (2005) indicate the following:

- Between 1999 and 2004, U.S. container imports were up by 58 percent, while exports rose by 22 percent.
- By 2004, trade with Asia accounted for 60 percent of all U.S. imports and exports.
- There were 3,375 vessels in the world containership fleet in 2004, 69 percent of which were newly constructed since 1995, with 950 additional containerships in various phases of development.
- The average size of containerships calling at U.S. ports has increased by 26 percent, and the containership capacity calling at U.S. ports increased by 39 percent.

As Table 1.2 shows, there has been substantial growth in the major cargo ports in the United States, much of it since September 11, 2001. The top ten U.S. ports experienced a combined 48.9 percent growth in the movement of cargo containers between 1999 and 2004. These numbers suggest not only that trade has increased but that the capacities of these ports to handle both larger and more container vessels has also increased dramatically.

The fact that the world depends on the free movement of trade by vessels, combined with the significant growth in trade by shipping, suggests that the threat of global terrorism in this economic sector is cause for concern from the perspective of port security management. Scenarios involving the dispersal of radiological materials or nuclear detonation and extended port operational disruptions have been identified as a major risk to the container shipping industry (Greenberg et al. 2006). Indications are that global terrorist organizations such as al-Qaeda are interested in causing economic harm to a targeted country or region as they carry out their plans. As Jackson, Dixon,

Table 1.2   Growth in Container Trade, Top Ten U.S. Ports, 1999 and 2004 (in TEUs[1])

TOP TEN PORTS IN U.S. CONTAINER TRADE	1999	2004	% CHANGE 1999 TO 2004
LA/Long Beach	5,599,524	8,638,986	54.3
New York	2,027,188	2,200,343	56.0
Charleston	1,169,552	1,421,047	21.5
Virginia Ports	908,902	1,302,122	43.2
Savannah	624,497	1,290,178	106.6
San Francisco	943,977	1,221,111	29.4
Houston	713,677	1,097,769	53.8
Seattle	961,847	1,049,105	9.1
Tacoma	581,162	940,638	61.9
Miami	618,436	940,638	52.1
Top Ten Total	14,148,763	21,064,776	48.9

Data Source: U.S. Maritime Administration. 2005.

[1] TEU is an acronym for twenty-foot equivalent unit and is a standard of measurement used in the cargo containerization industry.

and Greenfield (2007, p. 22) have discussed, the economic impacts of terrorism can be understood in three ways:

1. The costs of the attack itself
2. The costs of security in mitigating the threat of future attacks as well as the associated indirect costs, such as increased wait times for security searches
3. The costs resulting from behavioral changes as a result of the fear of future attacks, such as a decreased demand for goods and services (e.g., air transportation)

"In crafting a strategy to target a major national economy, a terrorist group has a variety of options. The desire to inflict economic damages produces pressure to scale up attack operations to generate large immediate costs, take advantage of networks and infra-structures to produce cascading effects, or manipulate substitution behaviors to maxi-mize costs" (Jackson, Dixon, and Greenfield 2007, p. 49). Thus, there is good reason for public policy direction in the maritime and port security realm to be driven by a desire to mitigate, not only the immediate physical threats from terrorism, but the long-term economic threats that could befall the industry, the nation, and world markets.

The policy concerns in maritime security are certainly not limited to the cargo trade. The safety and security of the world's passenger vessel services, whether for rec-reation or for transportation, require similar, and perhaps even higher, considerations from a security management perspective. The attendant threats to commercial port facilities and the risk of monetary losses associated with litigation against commer-cial defendants also gives rise to significant influences on public policy mechanisms to strengthen port and maritime security regimes. A recent study (Greenberg et al. 2006) on maritime terrorism risk suggests the following:

- Cruise and ferry vessels need more protection against terrorist attacks that could kill and injure many passengers and cause serious financial losses.
- Maritime attacks could result in mass casualties, severe property damage, and commercial disruptions.
- Independent commercial defendants may be held civilly liable for damages caused by terrorist attacks.
- Risk-management approaches must include securing nuclear materials at their points of origin.
- Passenger ferry scenarios include on-board bombs and USS *Cole*-style impro-vised explosive device attacks.
- Maritime attacks could target port facilities or inland locations.
- Supply chain disruptions could initiate contractual and tort disputes.

Risk mitigation in this arena is understood as reducing the vulnerabilities of ferries and cruise ships, auditing vessel and facility security plans, improving port security measures concerning passengers and luggage, and implementing procedures for docu-menting crew and staff (Greenberg et al. 2006). In this sense, it is therefore not difficult to understand that the push for new government security regulations in the maritime and port environment is being fostered by legitimate concerns that the industry as a whole must be viewed as critical infrastructure and included in comprehensive planning processes. The dependence of the world on the maritime transportation sectors is precisely why the security management processes must now reexamine port applications and plans that place a high priority in reducing threats to this industry.

1.5 A Renewed Emphasis on Securing Ships and Ports

The practice of managing the security of ports and shipping must be viewed within a new context—as a rapidly changing discipline—especially in the aftermath of the terrorist attacks on the United States in 2001. This field has progressed significantly since World War II, yet the reality is that this evolution of security, and its important new interfaces with business and government, is a critical point of awareness for practitioners. The important dynamic to focus on is the need to develop joint initiatives and relationships between the private and public sectors in securing port interests from the threats of terrorism and criminal activity. Security and law enforcement are facing new threats to critical facilities and urban areas that may not necessarily emanate from enemies abroad. There is in fact some evidence that the more imminent terrorist threat may actually be from within the United States versus from enemies abroad. In 2007, the New York City Police Department published a report written by its intelligence division that suggested the real terrorist threat is not from al-Qaeda overseas but from "homegrown" radical jihadists in the United States. The police agency identified clusters of extremists in the northeast United States operating with ideologies similar to those espoused by the followers of Osama bin Laden. In May of 2007, the Federal Bureau of Investigation (FBI) arrested five foreign-born men described as "radical Islamists" and charged them with conspiring to attack Fort Dix, a U.S. Army installation in New Jersey. The FBI alleged that the men trained at a shooting range in the Pocono Mountains in Pennsylvania and planned to attack the installation with assault rifles and grenades. "Authorities said the group has no apparent connection to al-Qaeda or other international terrorist organizations aside from ideology, but appears to be an example of the kind of self-directed sympathizers widely predicted—and feared—by counterterrorism specialists" (Russakoff and Eggen 2007, p. A01). Given that port and shipping facilities may be targets for extremists, security management in these facilities must give new gravitas to the possibilities that the people who come in and out of ports every day—the truck drivers, vendors, dock workers, secretaries, even security and law enforcement agents—may be using their ability to access critical infrastructure to contemplate or plan harm to a facility.

It is a given in the security profession that the mitigation of risk begins with controlling access to the facility. Are our port facility managers confident that the individuals and vehicles being admitted, whether by land or by sea, have received sufficient scrutiny in terms of criminal background checks, business affiliations, and regulatory compliance? Not long after September 11, when more attention was directed to how well (or not so well) seaports were being secured, an International Maritime Bureau report suggested that maritime certificate fraud was a growing threat to the international maritime community. The possibility that terrorists could pose as legitimate ships' crew members surfaced in view of the apparent ease of obtaining forged crew travel documents. "'Background checks of incoming foreign registered ships' crew lists by U.S. authorities may not be totally revealing of potentially undesirable visitors among a ship's crew," said Vincent Cannistraro, former chief of operations for the CIA's Counterterrorism Center (Watkins 2002, par. 6–9). Some especially significant figures compiled by a 2001 IMO report indicated that of thirteen thousand false certificates identified, 90 percent of cases were reported in the Philippines. Perhaps most distressing: "in 10 of the 13 countries visited, it was evident that forgery was more than a backroom business . . . It was typically well-organised, with effective links to maritime administrations, employers, manning agents and training establishments" (Watkins 2002, par. 12–13). It should come as no surprise that the impetus for government policies mandating more stringent maritime, port, and employee documentation and access requirements is the fear that those individuals who might do harm to people and assets in this environment should not have ready and certain access to facilities.

Probably the most significant outcome of the public policy direction focused on enhanced ship and port security has been the establishment of the U.S. Transportation Worker Identification Credential, or TWIC, program. TWIC was authorized by the passage of the Maritime Transportation Security Act (MTSA) of 2002. The program, administered by the Transportation Security Administration and the U.S. Coast Guard, requires the issuance of a tamper-resistant biometric credential for workers who require unescorted access to secure areas of ports, vessels, and outer continental shelf facilities and for all credentialed merchant mariners. Applicants for a TWIC must provide their fingerprints, name, date of birth, address, phone number, alien registration number (if applicable), photo, employer, and job title. Background checks will be conducted to review criminal history records, terrorist watch lists, immigration status, and outstanding wants and warrants. Originally, it was estimated that about a million workers including longshoremen, truckers, port employees, and others would require a TWIC (Transportation Security Administration 2008). As of early 2008, the U.S. Coast Guard was estimating that up to 1.5 million workers could need TWICs (Bain 2008). The full implementation of the TWIC program, originally scheduled for September of 2008, has been pushed back to April of 2009 due to the increased estimates on the number of enrollees and the complicated and extensive systemic requirements for vetting and credentialing such a large and diverse work-force. Nevertheless, the push to a unified credentialing system, one that may provide another layer of access control security for ports and shipping, is evidence that security managers in ports must contend with and respond to the collective public policy drive toward greater security in the maritime sector.

1.6 A Need for Partnerships between Government and Business in Managing Port Security

The momentum for comprehensive and focused management of port security has been strengthened by governmental policy response to the threats posed by terrorists and other criminal elements to the maritime transportation sector. Although no business operating in this environment wishes to turn a blind eye to the growing security needs, the complexities of commercial enterprises in this sector demand sound management practices for planning the security of port facilities. There are no unlimited budgets for security managers. At many ports in the United States, there are no tax dollars funding operations that may solely be driven by the revenues taken in by the port. As a business must continue to operate and thrive to support its shareholders, clients, and customer base, a realistic approach to planning port security must transcend a fortress mentality. A balanced approach, one that develops and employs rational methods to risk mitigation yet remains cognizant of both common sense and compliance with governmental policies, is essential. In making improvements to securing an efficient global supply chain, one study (Willis and Ortiz 2004) has suggested three interconnected strategies:

1. Government-driven policies strengthening the global container supply chain
2. Multi-sector efforts to improve container shipping system security
3. Research and development on new technologies for low-cost, high-volume remote sensing and scanning

These are logical strategies and have immediacy for port security managers. Our local, state, regional, national, and international economies depend heavily on the continued operational efficiency of the global maritime transportation industry. Because ports are crucial nodes in this system, it is certain that the closure of a port for any reason could have dramatic effects on the economy. Consider the example of Port Fourchon, located on the Gulf of Mexico at the end of Louisiana Highway 1—the only road access to the port from the rest of the United States. "Port Fourchon services approximately 90 percent of all deepwater drilling activity in the Gulf of Mexico. In addition, nearly $63 billion worth of oil and natural gas is directly tied to the port, area offshore platforms, and the highway system, which is used to serve all the offshore entities" (Cheramie 2008, par. 6). A recent economic impact study emphasized the importance of Port Fourchon to the national economy: ". . . if Port Fourchon had a 3 week loss of service for any reason, it would equate to a national economic impact of $9.9 billion in sales loss, $2.9 billion in household earnings loss, and over 77,000 jobs loss nationally. These figures are based on $66 barrel of oil" (Greater Larouche Port Commission 2008, par. 4). At the time of this writing the price of oil was $127 a barrel (Bloomberg.com 2008). The need for well-thought-out and effective government–business partnerships in managing the security strategies in this environment could not be greater.

1.7 A Strategy for Port Security Management

The basic theme of *Port Security Management* is to help those who have a role or interest in the security of a port facility to understand and educate themselves about managing the challenges within the context of both internal and external organizational issues. This book is essentially about what it takes to provide good management in port security. It is not meant to be a treatise on the maritime industry in general, nor a compendium of cargo security techniques or practices. Rather, this book offers a fundamental strategy for understanding what it takes to implement and manage a sound security plan in a port environment. In this introductory chapter, the focus of discussion has been on laying the foundation for port security management by understanding ports as critical components of the global transportation infrastructure. The decision-making roles that security managers have are very powerful in this industry. A decision to build a new fence, to curtail operating hours at an access control point, or to restrict certain people or vehicles from entering particular areas can have powerful consequences for a business operating on a thin profit margin. In this arena, security managers will find that building consensus and productive working relationships with port stakeholders are crucial. These will be necessary to maximize resources and maintain stable, secure port conditions that will give confidence to government authorities and corporate owners that the port is a safe environment to be in.

The discussion thus far has been an opening for the examination of ideas and concepts associated with port security. In proceeding chapters, the discussion will identify pertinent security issues, build toward an understanding of risk assessment, and provide the components for developing supportable security plans for a port facility. The text ahead will explore various issues, trends, programs, and strategies that are being used or considered in many ports and can be adapted by security managers in various types and sizes of port facilities. The discussion will examine policy responses to terrorism and homeland security. What are the issues and solutions related to hazard identification, risk management, and vulnerability analysis that can be applied to port settings? What other organizational approaches have been developed in responding to homeland security requirements and mandates? What is the expanding role of law enforcement in responding to the national and international threat of terrorism? How does the security manager comply with government mandates and balance security planning with costs and their impact on free trade? Our continuing emphasis will be on developing government and business partnerships engaged collaboratively to manage emerging threats and on determining the problem-solving strategies that can be used to develop preparedness initiatives.

References

American Association of Port Authorities. 2008. World port ranking 2006. http://aapa.files.cms-plus.com/Statistics/worldportrankings_2006.xls (accessed May 6, 2008).

Bain, Ben. 2008, January 24. TWIC card needs double since initial estimates. FCW.com. http://www.fcw.com/online/news/151419-1.html (accessed May 30, 2008).

Bloomberg.com. 2008, June 1. Energy prices. http://www.bloomberg.com/energy/ (accessed June 1, 2008).

Cheramie, Doug. 2008, June 1. In-depth study of LA-1 planned by feds. *Tri-Parish Times.* http://www.tri-parishtimes.com/articles/2008/05/20/business_news/225_52_bridge.txt (accessed June 1, 2008).

Economist.com. 2008, April 23. Piracy: Peril on the high seas. Economist.com. http://www.economist.com/research/articlesBySubject/displaystory.cfm?subjectid=7933596&story_id=11079332 (accessed May 18, 2008).

GlobalSecurity.org. 2008a. Military: Liberation Tigers of Tamil Eelam. http://www.globalsecurity.org/military/world/para/ltte.htm (accessed May 24, 2008).

GlobalSecurity.org. 2008b. Port of Aden. http://www.globalsecurity.org/military/facility/aden.htm (accessed May 6, 2008).

Greater Larouche Port Commission. 2008, April 17. Economic impact study provides evidence Port Fourchon is critical to the nation's economy. Press Release. http://www.portfourchon.com/explore.cfm/20080417economicimpactstudy/ (accessed June 1, 2008).

Greenberg, Michael D., Peter Chalk, Henry H. Willis, Ivan Khilko, and David S. Ortiz. 2006. Maritime terrorism: Risk and liability. Center for Terrorism Risk Management Policy. Santa Monica, CA: Rand Corporation.

International Chamber of Commerce. 2008, April 16. Piracy figures up by 20% for first quarter of 2008. http://www.icc-ccs.org/main/news.php?newsid=109 (accessed May 18, 2008).

International Maritime Organization. 2002. Piracy and armed robbery against ships. MSC/Circ.623/Rev.3. London: International Maritime Organization.

International Maritime Organization. 2008. Introduction to IMO. http://www.imo.org/ (accessed May 17, 2008).

Jackson, Brian A., Lloyd Dixon, and Victoria A. Greenfield. 2007. Economically targeted terrorism: A review of the literature and a framework for considering defensive approaches. Center for Terrorism Risk Management Policy. Santa Monica, CA: Rand Corporation.

Lunde, Paul. 2005. The explorer Marco Polo. Saudi Aramco World. http://www.saudiaramcoworld.com/issue/200504/the.explorer.marco.polo.htm (accessed May 6, 2008).

New York City Police Department. 2007. Radicalization in the west: The homegrown threat. http://sethgodin.typepad.com/seths_blog/files/NYPD_Report-Radicalization_in_the_West.pdf (accessed May 15, 2008).

Port of Aden. 2008. Port of Aden history. http://www.portofaden.com/History.htm (accessed May 6, 2008).

Russakoff, Dale, and Dan Eggen. 2007, May 9. Six charged in plot to attack Fort Dix. *Washington Post.* http://www.washingtonpost.com/wp-dyn/content/article/2007/05/08/AR2007050800465.html (accessed May 26, 2008).

Transportation Security Administration. 2008. Transportation Workers Identification Credential (TWIC). http://www.tsa.gov/what_we_do/layers/twic/index.shtm (accessed May 30, 2008).

U.S. Department of Defense. 2001, January 9. *USS Cole* Commission Report. http://www.fas.org/irp/threat/cole.pdf (accessed May 6, 2008).

U.S. Department of State. 2008, April 22. UN Security Council resolution on piracy: Taken question. Office of the Spokesman. http://www.state.gov/r/pa/prs/ps/2008/apr/103894.htm (accessed May 18, 2008).

U.S. Maritime Administration. 2005. Containership market indicators. http://www.marad.dot.gov/MARAD_statistics/2005%20STATISTICS/Container%20Market%20Indicators.pdf (accessed May 15, 2008).

Watkins, Eric. 2002, February 6. Shipping fraud heightens terror threat. *BBC News.* http://news.bbc.co.uk/2/hi/asia-pacific/1804146.stm (accessed May 18, 2008).

Willis, Henry H., and David S. Ortiz. (2004). Evaluating the security of the global containerized supply chain. Santa Monica, CA: Rand Corporation.

2
MARITIME AND PORT SECURITY
A Manager's Perspective

2.1 Understanding the Port Environment

As a security manager contemplates reducing risks in a target environment, the first challenge is understanding the unique nature of that environment. Consider the daunting task facing a police officer, newly graduated from the police academy and assigned to patrol in an unknown sector of the city or county. How effective that officer will be in reducing the threat and fear of crime in the community will certainly depend on coming to know every facet of community life: the geography, the socioeconomic conditions, the demographics, the politics, the level of support to be expected from businesses and citizens, and the nature of the organizational culture within which the officer will need to interact. Much like that police officer, a manager tasked with effecting security plans within a port must become educated in the complexities of the maritime sector.

Ports can range from the small marina primarily servicing a recreational lakefront boating community to the Port of Singapore, which at any given time may have as many as a thousand vessels transiting its facilities. Ports can be used strictly for civilian use, commercial purposes, or to provide national security for a country's surface and submarine navies. The value of a port to a government in terms of military significance can increase substantially during periods of conflict or heightened national security. Ships of war, such as aircraft carriers and guided missile destroyers, require significant land-based resources for maintenance, provisioning, and staging. Beyond that, in times of war, ports become strategic centers for the transportation of supplies, raw materials, and human resources. Ports can be owned and operated by private, commercial interests or be part of the complex bureaucracy of a local, state, or national government. Many ports are operated as *landlord/tenant* operations, whereby the controlling port authority provides the land-based resources, such as dockworkers, terminals, and equipment for shippers, who pay rent or fees for their use during ports of call. Often times, there are complex rules, regulations, and fee structures, or tariffs, in place which provide the organizational structure for port operations. For the new port security manager, coming to understand and grasp the nuances of the port environment will make for a solid foundation for initiating risk assessment and security planning.

Ports primarily managed for the handling of cargo or raw materials will have facilities and equipment such as container yards, cargo sheds, storage tanks, pipelines, cranes, loaders, and towing vehicles. Figure 2.1 illustrates the transfer of cargo containers between vessels and land facilities, a common activity at many of the world's commercial ports. Ports that are managed primarily for the handling of passengers will have facilities and staff to handle both people and/or vehicles transferring on to and off of vessels such as ferries, recreational vessels, and passenger cruise ships. The term *seaport* is often used to describe a port that primarily serves ocean-going vessels. A *river port* is one that handles vessels trafficking on rivers such as barges and transport vessels that are capable of operating in shallower waters. *Inland ports* on lakes, rivers, and canals may have access to larger bodies of water. *Fishing ports* are primarily used to service and manage a fleet of vessels engaged in the fishing industry. A *dry port* describes a facility used to store cargo containers or break bulk cargo. These locations may be connected to a port by rail or road access. Due to the strategic locations of ports and the intersection of land and sea, they often sit on prime real estate that is controlled by a port administration or authority with jurisdiction over port operations and management. Ports often have limited flexibility in growing capacity due to unique geographical features or development limitations in place in the community in which the port is situated. In many port facilities, the provision of services and utilities for both ship and port operations requires the placement of critical infrastructure,

Figure 2.1   A gantry crane transfers a 40-foot cargo container between the port and the vessel.

such as the electrical power substation shown in Figure 2.2. Thus, a security manager in a port facility may have much more than the vessels themselves to consider in terms of risk mitigation.

The passenger cruise sector of the maritime industry has witnessed unprecedented growth over the past thirty years. The average annual passenger growth rate has been 8.1 percent since the 1980s, with a hundred million passengers having taken a deepwater cruise of two or more days. Most of the passenger growth has been generated within the last ten years, with 36 percent within the past five years alone (Cruise Lines International Association 2008a, par. 1–2). The cruise industry's total economic benefit to the U.S. economy was $35.7 billion in 2006. "The cruise industry's growth is also reflected in its expanding guest capacity. Nearly 40 new ships were built in the 1980s, and nearly 80 new ships debuted during the 1990s. By the end of 2008, over 100 new ships will have been introduced since 2000" (Cruise Lines International Association 2008b, par. 2–3).

In managing port operations and growth, property administration strategies must include systems for supporting the port's core business needs. The port director and his/her staff are responsible for creating competitive advantages for the port users. Port operations associated with efficient ingress and egress of both land vehicles and seagoing vessels are crucial to the synergies that must exist to efficiently transfer cargo and people. The port director must not only improve the port's operational efficiency but

Figure 2.2   An electrical power substation situated at a port facility illustrates part of the complex infrastructure present in many ports.

address client needs to make the most of existing logistical infrastructure (American Association of Port Authorities 2006). The importance of this major sector of the economy, not only to the United States but to the world at large, cannot be understated. According to a 2008 report by Masters:

- Twenty percent of U.S. national income comes from merchandise trade through seaports.
- Ninety percent of the world's goods move through shipping containers.
- There are 108 million cargo containers in worldwide circulation.
- The container-port throughput is 500 million containers per year.

The intermodal nature of the cargo shipping business suggests that transportation costs for merchandise have gone down as the world has bought into the cargo container shipping system. "The efficiencies associated with global specialization inevitably lead to increasing interdependence. This poses certain vulnerabilities which could be exploited by terrorist groups. The security challenge is to protect the nation from terrorism without unduly restricting the flow of international commerce" (Masters 2008, p. 1).

2.2 Security Management within the Context of History

All social organizations must consider their security relative to the environments they operate in. Businesses must assess their competitive viability within the context of employee and customer safety, operational resiliency, and their ability to interact successfully in the marketplace. Even a social organization as basic as a family must constantly assess the threats in its environment. Residences must be secured against the threats of cold, heat, storms, burglary, and vandalism, and internal systems such as the electrical and plumbing must be maintained and upgraded as they age. A new baby in the house must be protected from any number of safety threats: hazardous materials, electrical outlets, swinging doors, stairways—the list goes on.

Organizations that have operated in relatively stable environments for long periods of times without problems may not be focused on threats lurking in the background. There may be signs and symptoms of potential harm, but complacency may have set in because times have been good. With the growth of technology and the ability to conduct business globally, the world has seemingly become a much smaller place. The relative security that people and organizations may have felt in the past has been shaken by the recognition that threats can surface from previously unknown places. Before the hijackers of September 11 deliberately crashed stolen airplanes into buildings, an airplane hijacking event was usually regarded as an extortion effort. The security strategies and plans in place to mitigate the threat of an airplane hijacking perhaps did not consider that the threat could be more than just an effort to wrangle money, concessions, or political capital from a corporation or government. The reality of commercial airplanes being converted into weapons of mass destruction to deliberately kill innocent people has provoked a consciousness that security planning processes must be energized to.be more responsive to changing environments. This is really not so unusual from a security manager's perspective, because history shows that the practice of security has one pronounced constant: security management is an ever ongoing activity, one with plans requiring constant evaluation and revision.

The word *security* can actually be understood as a stable, relatively predictable environment in which an individual or group may go about its business without disruption or harm and without fear of disturbance or injury. Security can also be viewed as a system or orderly method for establishing conditions and procedures for stability. The system of security is arranged so that all aspects of the organization are functioning as planned. Security can also relate to peoples' comfort levels with respect to their environment. This *sense of place* describes a feeling people have as they interact with their environment. To what extent do people become involved in protecting themselves from perceived threats? The answer may depend on the settings they find themselves in. These settings change constantly, as do the security threats and risks to safety, which exist everywhere. How safe do you feel when you: leave your home? drive your car? ride the bus? walk in a department store? sit in a baseball stadium? enter a skyscraper? ride an elevator? board a ship? As the environmental conditions change, a person's sense of place changes, and the degree to which people increase or decrease their security plans changes. The sense of place is important to security management because it goes to the heart of the security mission in a given organization. If the mission of an organization is to provide a safe and secure environment for people to operate a business, then the security manager's task is to establish a secure sense of place for the relative community. For example, crime rates and people's perceptions of crime or fears about specific criminal activities are a factor in assessing security needs because they influence the sense of place. People will raise their defenses when they know that the risk of being in a certain neighborhood or setting is greater than in others. It becomes important for the manager to understand these dynamics and to integrate security concerns at various levels in the organization in order to meet the mission challenges.

When studying past civilizations, there is evidence of similar experiences of how the sense of place has contributed to security management and planning. There are many cases of how people who might have once felt secure suddenly found themselves at risk because of new or changing environmental conditions. For example, there is evidence that during the Mycenaean Age in Greece, from around 1600 to 1100 BC, large fortress-like palaces were constructed, designed no doubt to enhance the security of the inhabitants by protecting them from invaders or perhaps from warring opponents intent on subjugating the populace. One such facility was the 215,000-square-yard Mycenaean fortress of Gla, located on an island in Lake Copais. Little is known about the reasons for its construction and eventual destruction, but it had a twenty-six-foot-high mud-brick rampart, surrounded by a two-mile-long wall of burnt brick and bitumen. In modern times, we might compare the fortress of Gla to a piece of fortified critical infrastructure, a high-security government installation, for instance. The fortress of Gla used what is known today as *crime prevention through environmental design* (CPTED) risk-mitigation strategies to dissuade possible perpetrators from violating the security of the facility. In other words, it used the built environment effectively to reduce the fear and incidence of harm to the community. The sense of place is improved by a facility design and plans that eliminate or reduce the chance of harm. Crime-prevention programs and strategies today often employ CPTED principles to take advantage of environmental conditions to improve security. A classic example is a CPTED strategy called *territorial reinforcement*, in which users assert control over an environment by defining property lines and distinguishing private spaces from public spaces using landscape plantings, pavement designs, and natural fences such as shrubbery, trees, and water. Many public and private facilities today have design features that assert territorial control of the environment. As feudal barons once constructed moats around castles to fortify their defenses, security planners today use similar concepts to fortify the sense of place around modern facilities. The effort is designed to not only reduce the risk of given threats, but to lead to behavior that encourages people to keep an eye out for one another in what is hopefully a safer, and more livable, community.

Certainly, the ancient Greeks, Egyptians, who designed and built the great pyramids to bury their dead with their treasures, and the Romans, known for the development of early locks and keys, recognized the relative importance of incorporating security into the development of management systems in the conduct of commerce and trade. After the Norman invasion and domination of England by William the Conqueror in 1066, feudalism, though not recognized by this term until the 1600s, provided a substantial level of security for individuals and groups. As the king was able to grant land and develop a cadre of loyal knights, the political, military, and economic systems it fostered helped to strengthen people's ties to the central authority. As in ancient times, this is evidence that societies adapted management systems using their surroundings to mitigate the risks associated with their environment, such as predators, thieves, opposing forces, and the like. During the Middle Ages in Europe, the movement of an agrarian people to the cities, with the increased urbanization of the population, created conditions of considerable poverty and hardship. With no public law enforcement agencies in existence, crime rose in many cities. In England these conditions prompted the development of the night watchman, or *wait*, "an English town watchman or public musician who sounded the hours of the night. In the later Middle Ages the waits were night watchmen, who sounded horns or even played tunes to mark the hours. In the 15th and 16th centuries waits developed into bands of itinerant musicians who paraded the streets at night at Christmas time" (Encyclopedia Britannica Online 2007). Other developments during this time included the formation of private police agencies, individual merchants hiring men to guard their property, and the hiring of agents to recover stolen property. In 1829, Sir Robert Peel, the British Home

Secretary, fostered the creation of the "Bobbies," a strong, unified, professional police force, with the Metropolitan Police Act. The purpose of reorganizing the London police was to decentralize police efforts and encourage each community to take the responsibility for its own security. Again, this is evidence that a response to environmental conditions to eliminate or mitigate the risks, in this case rising crime, required the organization to develop management of security as part of its structure.

In America, police and security systems began to develop in the British tradition, which had a distinctly community dimension. The notion of community-oriented policing, which has become one of the prevailing models of American policing today, often refers to the saying "the police are the public, and the public are the police," which is rooted in the English tradition of justice that every able-bodied freeman was a policeman. Early colonial America followed the patterns that colonists had been familiar with in England. The need for mutual protection in a new land drew them together in groups much like those of earlier centuries. The American models of policing and security, however, developed differently from the British. The decentralized pattern of early-American police placed considerable power in the ward and precinct politicians. American police organizations first began to develop in the larger northern cities as an outgrowth of the system of night watches. The development of private security in the United States followed no predictable pattern. For example, in New York City, little effort was made to establish formal security agencies until the beginnings of a police department were established in 1783. It was private agencies, such as Wells Fargo, Pinkerton, and Burns, that provided contract security services to industrial facilities across the country as industrialization picked up speed in the nineteenth century.

Proprietary, or in-house, security forces hardly existed prior to the significant growth of defense-related production facilities in the 1940s and the need to secure them. The movement for increased security services came as businesses undertook expanded operations that in turn needed more protection. The 1900s saw growth in many industrial and economic sectors, which motivated the push toward increased protection of property and personnel: retail establishments, hotels, restaurants, theaters, warehouses, trucking companies, industrial companies, hospitals, and other institutional and service functions. From the 1950s to the late 1970s, the United States witnessed a steady increase in crimes of all types. While the volume of violent crime offenses remained relatively unchanged, the property crime offenses rose by about 2 percent each year. Society has relied almost exclusively on the government to prevent and control crime, but rising crime rates, increased costs, and public budget shortfalls have challenged law enforcement agencies' abilities to be responsive to all threats. For this reason, private security plays a major, if underappreciated, role in controlling the risks to people and property in society. It is not difficult to see evidence of the presence of private security forces in most everyday venues: hospitals, shopping malls, schools, factories, transportation facilities, even amusement parks. Despite the development of new technologies such as digital closed-circuit television and biometrics, security practices that have been in place for decades, such as a guard watching an access door, still predominate. The basic theories of protection have changed little over the past centuries, but the challenges faced by society and its organizations continue to evolve, with the threat of terrorism taking precedence within the past few years.

Today, the threat of acts of terrorism has become a driving force for the strengthening of the security of much of our infrastructure, and seaports have received an unprecedented level of scrutiny, at least if one considers the historically unregulated environments that most ports have operated in. Global acts of terrorism now highlight the diverse vulnerabilities of seaports and emphasize the importance of strong protective measures and activities designed to deter terrorist acts. In addition to terrorism, seaports are vulnerable to a variety of international and domestic criminal activities. The smuggling of drugs, weapons, and illegal migrants through seaports represents a constant threat to safety and security. Other forms of criminal activity include environmental crimes, cargo theft, and the unlawful export of controlled goods, munitions, stolen property, and drug proceeds.

2.3 The Maritime Sector and Security

At its basic level, a port is the developed interface between waterborne vessels and land adjacent to a body of water, whether a lake, river, bay, or ocean. It can be a facility for managing the transfer of cargo, raw materials, and/or people between the land and the water. Historically, as explorers ventured farther away from their land bases in search of wealth or conquest, the worldwide value of shipping routes and ports to the economies of nations took on greater and greater importance.

Christopher Columbus's arrival in the West in 1492 contributed to the instability of relations between Spain and Portugal, two of the world's major seafaring nations at the time. The lands "discovered" by Columbus, who was sailing for Spain, were claimed by Portugal pursuant to decrees issued by the Pope in the mid-1400s. The King and Queen of Spain brought the dispute with Portugal to Pope Alexander VI, a native of Valencia who was friendly to the Spanish monarchy. In 1493, the Pope settled the dispute between Spain and Portugal with a papal bull, the *Inter caetera*. Pursuant to a line he drew down the Atlantic Ocean, the Pope granted everything west of it to Spain, including the Pacific Ocean and the Gulf of Mexico, and everything east of it to Portugal, including the South Atlantic and the Indian oceans. This decision, widely interpreted as being favorable to Spain, effectively initiated colonization and the spread of Catholicism in the New World. At its most basic level, the *Inter caetera* can be interpreted as a global effort to affect some level of security regulation within the maritime sector. Because shipping was the only means of transportation across water, the papal decision to give control of ocean regions to one major sea power over another certainly emphasizes the value that world leaders placed on maritime assets, such as ports, and their associated organizations. It is security management at its most fundamental level: an effort to manage risk within a given operational environment, in this case an effort to control the risks of conflict and competition between nations.

Before the modern era, seaborne commerce was handled by mercantile groups who operated in ports in the countries lying along the sea routes their ships traveled. These mercantile groups would develop relationships with indigenous traders in these ports not only to obtain merchandise to trade but also to distribute the goods they brought in. "Monarchical or feudal administrative units in countries along the sea-routes encouraged the growth of seaborne commerce whenever it was considered to be advantageous to them. Foreign traders were provided with facilities in most countries in return for the payment of taxes and customs duties" (Seeriweera 2008, par. 1–2). Naturally, those ports that were able to prosper and develop capacities to handle increased shipping, as well as changes in shipping technology, were the ones that grew to have economic, political, and military strategic importance for the nations and authorities that controlled them. The four-hundred-year slave trade from the African continent to locations in the Western Hemisphere is one historical, if not notorious, indicator of the value of port facilities to the economies of the world. Captured indigenous people to be shipped across the ocean as slaves were often held at points in west African locations frequented by European traders. These embarkation points included port towns, forts, and castles that changed hands among European and African powers. Most of those captured and forced into slavery came from the Congo region. It is estimated that ten to fifteen million African captives were processed through these west African ports in what is now Senegal, Sierra Leone, Liberia, Upper Guinea, Lower Guinea, Congo, and Angola (Slavery in America 2008). In Europe, London, Bristol, Liverpool, and Greenwich were major slave-trading ports (Antislavery.org 2008).

2.3.1 Freedom of the Seas

Beginning in the seventeenth century, the world's nations essentially operated under the Freedom of the Seas doctrine, or *Mare Liberum*, as advanced in a 1609 treatise by the Dutch jurist Hugo Grotius. *Mare Liberum*'s major position was that the world's oceans were a resource that all nations could use as they liked. The doctrine limited each country's maritime jurisdiction to a relatively narrow three-mile strip of water along a nation's coastline. The rest of the world's oceans were open to all nations and could be claimed by none. This principle was complemented by another Dutch argument, the "Cannon Shot" doctrine. In a 1610 fishing dispute with England, the Dutch argued that a coastal state had sovereignty over the waters adjacent to its coastline "as far seawards as a cannon can fire a cannon ball," the theory being that a nation could effectively control that portion of the sea over which it could effectively fire a cannon shot—about three miles (Schafer 1997).

In 1793, Secretary of State Thomas Jefferson claimed a territorial sea out to three miles for the United States. At least one characterization of the developing world's interpretation of the freedom of the seas is ". . . the freedom to fish, the freedom to navigate, the freedom to lay submarine cables, the freedom to overfly and other freedoms that might be recognized by the general principles of international law" (Mani 2002, p. 4). Industrialization and economic growth into the 1900s raised concerns about the depletion of fishing stocks and threats to the oceans posed by ship pollution and hazardous materials cargo, which led to calling into question the freedom of the seas doctrine. In addition, competition for the vast resources available in the world's oceans contributed to the advancing agendas of public and private interests to curtail other nations' use of the seas.

2.3.2 *International Convention for the Safety of Life at Sea*

In 1914, the first version of the International Convention for the Safety of Life at Sea (SOLAS) was adopted in the aftermath of the *Titanic* disaster. The RMS *Titanic*, a British ocean liner, the largest passenger steamship of its time, was on its maiden voyage from Southampton to New York, when on the night of April 14, 1912, it hit an iceberg and sank early the next morning. Of the 2,223 passengers and crew, 1,517 people perished, many because of the limited number of lifeboats on board the vessel. This disaster, still regarded as one of the worst peacetime maritime disasters, presaged changes in maritime practices and ship design, such as the establishment of ice patrols, 24-hour radio watches, and lifeboat regulations.

In 1945, President Harry S. Truman unilaterally extended U.S. jurisdiction over all natural resources on its continental shelf. Though a response to pressure from domestic oil companies, it started a trend.

> In October 1946, Argentina claimed its shelf and the Epicontinental Sea above it. Chile and Peru, in 1947, and Ecuador, in 1950, asserted sovereign rights over a two hundred-mile zone, thereby hoping to limit the access of distant-water fishing fleets and to control the depletion of fish stocks in their adjacent seas. The hazard of pollution was ever-present, threatening coastal resorts and all forms of ocean life. The navies of the maritime powers were competing to maintain a presence across the globe on the surface waters and even under the sea (United Nations, Division for Ocean Affairs and Law of the Sea 2008, par. 3–5).

Since the 1950s, nations of the world have been advocating a twelve-mile territorial limit in their ability to control the waters adjacent to their coastlines. In 1983, President Ronald Reagan proclaimed a U.S. Exclusive Economic Zone, an area between twelve and two hundred miles offshore; in 1988, he proclaimed a twelve-mile territorial sea for the United States.

The SOLAS Convention came to be regarded as an important international treaty concerning the safety of merchant ships. After the adoption of the 1914 form, successive amendments were made in 1929, 1948, and 1960. The 1960 convention was the first major task for the IMO after its creation as far as modernizing maritime regulations and maintaining currency with technical developments in the shipping industry.

The 1974 convention has been updated and amended many times and is often referred to as SOLAS, 1974, as amended (IMO 2007). The convention addresses minimum standards for ship construction, equipment, and operation. Flag states ensure compliance, and contracting governments may inspect ships of other contracting states.

2.3.3 United Nations Convention on Law of the Sea

Additional evidence of global efforts to effect regulations within the maritime sector was the United Nations Convention on the Law of the Sea (UNCLOS). Also known as the Law of the Sea Convention and the Law of the Sea Treaty, UNCLOS is an international agreement that resulted from the third United Nations Convention on the Law of the Sea, 1973–1982 (United Nations 2008). Even though the Freedom of the Seas doctrine prevailed well into the twentieth century, many countries began to extend claims over offshore resources. Concerns relating to the depletion of coastal fish stocks by long-distance fishing fleets, the threat of pollution from ocean-going ships and oil tankers, and the growing naval presence of many nations' military organizations around the world contributed to a global consensus that the world's oceans were being exploited and manipulated. These incidents and trends, and the ones in the following example, illustrate the conditions prompting international consensus to further secure the maritime domain:

> From oil to tin, diamonds to gravel, metals to fish, the resources of the sea are enormous. The reality of their exploitation grows day by day as technology opens new ways to tap those resources.
>
> In the late 1960s, oil exploration was moving further and further from land, deeper and deeper into the bedrock of continental margins. From a modest beginning in 1947 in the Gulf of Mexico, offshore oil production, still less than a million tons in 1954, had grown to close to 400 million tons. Oil drilling equipment was already going as far as 4,000 metres below the ocean surface.
>
> The oceans were being exploited as never before. Activities unknown barely two decades earlier were in full swing around the world. Tin had been mined in the shallow waters off Thailand and Indonesia. South Africa was about to tap the Namibian coast for diamonds. Potato-shaped nodules, found almost a century earlier and lying on the seabed some five kilometres below, were attracting increased interest because of their metal content.
>
> And then there was fishing. Large fishing vessels were roaming the oceans far from their native shores, capable of staying away from port for months at a time. Fish stocks began to show signs of depletion as fleet after fleet swept distant coastlines. Nations were flooding the richest fishing waters with their fishing fleets virtually unrestrained: coastal States setting limits and fishing States contesting them. The so-called "Cod War" between Iceland and the United Kingdom had brought about the spectacle of British Navy ships dispatched to rescue a fishing vessel seized by Iceland for violating its fishing rules.

Offshore oil was the centre of attraction in the North Sea. Britain, Denmark and Germany were in conflict as to how to carve up the continental shelf, with its rich oil resources.

It was late 1967 and the tranquillity of the sea was slowly being disrupted by techno-logical breakthroughs, accelerating and multiplying uses, and a super-Power rivalry that stood poised to enter man's last preserve - the seabed.

(United Nations 1998, par. 7–12.)

As a result, UNCLOS was operationalized in 1994, a year after Guyana became the sixtieth state to sign the treaty. It defines the rights and responsibilities of nations in their use of the world's oceans, establishing guidelines for businesses, the environ-ment, and the management of marine natural resources. The treaty provides provi-sions for signatory nations to mutually manage activities on, above, and beneath the ocean's surface, addressing the following:

• Navigational and transit issues
• Regulation of deep-sea mining
• Redistribution of wealth to underdeveloped countries
• Marine trade, pollution, research, and dispute resolution
• Twelve-mile territorial sea limit
• Two-hundred-mile exclusive economic zone
• Definitive limits on the oceanic area over which a country may claim jurisdiction
• Innocent passage, including nonwartime activities of military ships
• Restrictions and regulations of intelligence and submarine maneuvers in ter-ritorial waters

To date, 155 countries and the European Community have joined in the conven-tion. Notably, the United States has signed the treaty, but the U.S. Senate has not rati-fied it. In the early 1980s, the Reagan administration objected to the treaty, primarily over powers given to the UNCLOS multinational authority related to the regulation of and competition for ocean-bed mining resources, which was seen as inconsistent with American free-market principles. UNCLOS was in many respects, though, viewed positively, and "on March 10, 1983, President Reagan announced that the United States would recognize the rights of other states in the waters off their coasts, as reflected in the Convention so long as the rights and freedoms of the United States and others under international law are recognized by such coastal states" (Rubin 1994, p. 1). This position illustrates that although not all parties may agree on all aspects of a security convention, there is recognition that some level of security regulation is in all parties' best interests.

2.3.4 International Ship and Port Facility Security Code

The IMO is a worldwide convention on maritime issues established in 1948. As dis-cussed, the world maritime community has been subjected to very little in the way of international regulations related to shipping and seaport security. In 1948, an international conference in Geneva adopted a convention establishing the IMO. The IMO represented the first major international initiative to establish cooperation among governments concerning regulations affecting international shipping. The IMO has been able to effect standards in use around the world that regulate maritime safety, navigation, and the prevention and control of marine pollution from ships. Global fears of the terrorist threat after September 11 spurred the IMO to critically review its agenda concerning vessel and port facility security, and resulted in the adoption of the International Ship and Port Facility Security (ISPS) Code.

The ISPS Code created minimum standards for port facility and vessel security for countries that are signatories to the IMO convention. Increases in crime, piracy, smuggling, and terrorism led to increases in regulations affecting the security of vessels and seaports. As a new security regime for international shipping implemented in July 2004, the ISPS Code is designed to counter acts of terrorism, drug smuggling, cargo theft, and other forms of cargo crimes. It establishes an international framework for cooperation between most of the world's governments, government agencies, and the shipping and port industries to detect security threats.

2.3.5 U.S. Maritime Transportation Security Act

The United States enacted the Maritime Transportation Security Act (MTSA) of 2002 in response to calls for enhanced security for vessels and in the nation's ports after the tragedy of September 11. Designed to model and implement the ISPS Code within the United States, the MTSA requires U.S. seaports to conduct vulnerability assessments, which are necessary to determine the nature and type of threat or risk for each particular port facility. Based on the assessment, ports must develop Facility Security Plans (FSPs) to mitigate the threats. The goal of the MTSA is a national maritime transportation security planning system. The strategy behind MTSA is to create a national security infrastructure at the nation's seaports. Because seaports are a vital link in the nation's economic and transportation systems, the absence of a comprehensive standard of security among the nation's seaports represented a significant vulnerability. FSPs are now required at each port facility and are subject to review and oversight by the Department of Homeland Security (DHS), a new cabinet agency created in the aftermath of September 11. It combines federal agencies with diverse enforcement and regulatory responsibilities to better manage security concerns. The U.S. Coast Guard has primary responsibility, as a DHS member agency, regulating port security, including review and approval of Port FSPs.

2.4 September 11: A Paradigm Shift toward Enhanced Security in Maritime and Ports

On September 11, 2001, nineteen hijackers affiliated with al-Qaeda, a terrorist organization organized by Osama bin Laden, hijacked four civilian jetliners within the

United States. Three of the jets were deliberately flown into prominent U.S. buildings: two into the World Trade Center in New York City, and one into the Pentagon
in Washington, D.C. The fourth jet crashed in Pennsylvania. Over three thousand
people were killed in this attack, which ominously demonstrated that commercial aircraft can be successfully used as weapons of mass destruction. Could oil, natural gas,
or other hazardous cargo-laden ocean-going vessels also be used as such weapons by
terrorists against seaports and the communities they serve? Increasingly, the response
from government officials charged with public policy responsibilities has been "yes,"
and the public policy movement has been toward increased regulation and oversight
of security planning in the maritime and port sectors.

Historically, the global maritime industry has been subject to relatively little regulation concerning vessel and seaport security. That paradigm has changed significantly
with increasing levels of criminal activity, piracy, international smuggling, and global
acts of terrorism. Recognized international standards for seaport security have not
existed until relatively recently. The term *security* has meant different things to different organizations. With the heightened sense of urgency and concern that has developed in the wake of recent acts of global terrorism, measures aimed at neutralizing
ports' vulnerabilities to criminal activity have become more focused, with a concerted
global effort to strengthen maritime and port security around the world.

In October 1985, four armed members of the Palestinian Liberation Front hijacked
the Italian cruise ship *Achille Lauro*, which was carrying four hundred passengers
and crew in the Mediterranean Sea. The hijackers demanded that Israel free fifty
Palestinian prisoners. They killed a disabled American tourist, Leon Klinghoffer,
and threw him overboard in an act that drew worldwide attention and revulsion.
The hijackers surrendered after two days of negotiations with Italy, Egypt, and the
Palestine Liberation Organization, in exchange for a pledge of safe passage. They
were taken into custody by Italian authorities after their Egyptian jet was forced to
land by U.S. fighter planes. After the hijacking of the *Achille Lauro*, political pressure
from the United States spurred the IMO to develop measures to protect passengers
and crews aboard ships (Center for Research on Population and Security 1986). In
October of 2000, the U.S. Navy guided-missile destroyer USS *Cole* was in the Port of
Aden, Yemen, for a routine fuel stop. A small craft carrying four- to seven-hundred
pounds of explosives approached and struck the port side of the destroyer. The explosion caused a forty-by-sixty-foot hole in the port side of the ship. The attack, carried
out by suicide bombers, was organized by al-Qaeda. Seventeen people were killed,
and thirty-nine were injured. In another, more recent terrorist event in 2002, the
Limburg, a French oil tanker carrying oil from Iran to Malaysia, was rammed by a
small boat with explosives in the Arabian Sea. The attack resulted in one death and
the spillage of ninety thousand barrels of oil.

In 2004, Gary Bald, acting assistant director of the FBI's Counterterrorism Division,
testified before the Senate Judiciary Committee's Subcommittee on Terrorism,

Technology, and Homeland Security. Addressing the topic of seaport security and the FBI's work with the U.S. DHS, the U.S. Coast Guard, and local port authorities, he testified about the difficulty of protecting ports, given the complex and open nature of their operations. "The United States' economy depends on the free flow of goods through these waterways, but with the free flow of goods comes the inherent risk of terrorist attacks. Ports, because of their accessibility to both water and land, together with the chemical and natural resource storage facilities that are often located within close proximity, are inherently vulnerable" (FBI 2004, par. 1–2). Research into the economic impact of a terrorist event in the maritime sector indicates that there would be significant disruption to the national economy in the United States. One scenario involving the Port of Los Angeles/Long Beach "estimated that the direct and indirect economic costs could reach $45 billion under a set of plausible conditions. This scenario envisaged the use of conventional explosives to destroy three bridges and one rail line connecting major port facilities" (Masters 2008, pp. 1–2). Worldwide concerns about the possible use of a dirty bomb, an explosive device designed to disperse radiological material in a populated area, or the use of cargo containers to covertly transport weapons of mass destruction into the United States have resulted in government efforts to mitigate this threat using radiation detection equipment in ports around the world.

The terrorist events and criminal activities that have been witnessed have alerted the world to the fact that vessels, and by association, the ports they access, be they civilian or military, are exceptionally vulnerable to acts of terrorism. Figure 2.3 depicts two passenger cruise vessels, one docked in port as the other slowly navigates the channel to the open sea. While fairly fast and maneuverable on open waters, they are slow moving and a challenge to navigate in the tight confines of port facilities and inland waterways. It is not difficult to imagine threat scenarios against vessels like these, which could cause death, damage, and disruption if they occurred in port. They are evidence of the vulnerabilities ships face while conducting operations in any environment, but especially in the relatively confined spaces of seaports.

Seaports operate within a complex and fluid intermodal transportation system. Ships transport people, containers, bulk cargo, and raw materials to and from ports, which link with railroads, surface transportation, airports, highways, and the cities and regions in which they are situated. Any weak link in the security chain within the larger transportation system represents a higher degree of vulnerability. Since ports are especially vulnerable to acts of terrorism that could kill or injure thousands and cause significant disruptions to the nation's economy and transportation infrastructure, there has been significant movement within the past several years to strengthen the security regimes that ports must manage.

Figure 2.3 Two cruise ships in port.

References

American Association of Port Authorities. 2006. Growth opportunities for general cargo and shallow draft ports: A property perspective. http://aapa.files.cms-plus.com/SeminarPresentations/Pigna.pdf (accessed May 20, 2008).

Antislavery.org. 2008. Slave routes. http://www.antislavery.org/breakingthesilence/slave_routes/slave_routes_unitedkingdom.shtml (accessed May 20, 2008).

Center for Research on Population and Security. 1986. Public report of the Vice-President's task force on combating terrorism, Part 2, U.S. policy response to terrorists. http://www.population-security.org/bush_report_on_terrorism/bush_report_on_terrorism_2.htm (accessed June 27, 2008).

Cruise Lines International Association. 2008a. Cruise industry overview. http://www.cruising.org/press/overview%202006/1.cfm (accessed May 20, 2008).

Cruise Lines International Association. 2008b. Profile of the U.S. cruise industry. http://www.cruising.org/press/sourcebook2008/profile_cruise_industry.cfm (accessed May 20, 2008).

Encyclopedia Britannica Online. 2007. Occupation of medieval wait. http://www.britannica.com/EBchecked/topic/634176/wait (accessed May 16, 2008).

FBI. 2004. Covering the waterfront against terrorist attacks: FBI testifies on seaport security and how concerted law enforcement partnerships protect U.S. ports. http://www.fbi.gov/page2/jan04/ports012704.htm (accessed May 20, 2008).

International Maritime Organization. 2007. International Convention for the Safety of Life at Sea (SOLAS), 1974. http://www.imo.org/Conventions/contents.asp?topic_id=257&doc_id=647 (accessed May 16, 2008).

Mani, V. S. 2002. Exclusive economic zone: AALCO's tribute to the modern law of the sea. http://www.aalco.int/Prof.%20Mani2007.pdf (accessed June 4, 2008).

Masters, Donald C. 2008. Safe ports: A global issue. Homeland Security Innovation Association. http://www.hlsia.org/briefs/Safe_Ports-a_Global_Issue.pdf (accessed May 20, 2008).

Rubin, Alfred P. 1994. Monster from the deep: Return of UNCLOS-United Nations Convention on Law of the Sea. BNET Business Network. http://findarticles.com/p/articles/mi_m2751/is_n37/ai_16315050 (accessed May 16, 2008).

Schafer, Lawrence. 1997. Legal aspects of contemporary marine fisheries: The canon shot rule. http://cdserver2.ru.ac.za/cd/011120_1/Aqua/Marine%20Fisheries/CHAP2/CANON.HTM (accessed June 4, 2008).

Seeriweera, W. I. 2008. Ports in ancient Sri Lanka. http://members.tripod.com/~hettiarachchi/port.html (accessed May 20, 2008).

Slavery in America. 2008. Geography: West African slave ports. http://www.slaveryinamerica.org/geography/slave_ports_1750.htm (accessed May 20, 2008).

United Nations. 1998. United Nations Convention on Law of the Sea (A historical perspective). http://www.un.org/Depts/los/convention_agreements/convention_historical_perspective.htm#Historical%20Perspective (accessed May 16, 2008).

United Nations. 2008. United Nations Convention on Law of the Sea. http://www.un.org/Depts/los/convention_agreements/convention_overview_convention.htm (accessed May 16, 2008).

United Nations, Division for Ocean Affairs and the Law of the Sea. 2008. A historical perspective. http://www.oceansatlas.org/unatlas/issues/governance_crime/unclos/law%20and%20order/ahistori1.htm (accessed June 4, 2008).

3

SECURITY CHALLENGES
FACING PORT OPERATIONS

This chapter is an introduction and familiarization with some of the general and specific security challenges faced by port management, operations staff, and Facility Security Officers (FSOs). Ports are unique environments in that they provide the interfaces between the global maritime trade, transportation networks, and a wide spectrum of facilities and geography. It is this diversity of infrastructure, economics, politics, and function that differentiates security operations in ports from that in other forms of transportation and industry. Consider the challenge facing the port facility with respect to whom and what will be admitted into the port's restricted areas. At the port illustrated in Figure 3.1, the security staff must contend with an assortment of break-bulk cargo being transported by truck into the port for export. What might be in those sacks? Rice? Sand? Hazardous materials? Narcotics? Improvised explosive devices? What does the manifest indicate as contents? Is the vehicle itself a threat? Is the driver? Can the security inspector effectively screen this shipment manually? What threats may be posed to this employee, this port, the vessel onto which the sacks will be loaded, and the port of destination? In considering these questions and issues, management and staff must have a broad foundation for understanding the scope and magnitude of potential threats to seaports. What are the general and specific challenges existing in the operational environment? Developing a practical appreciation for the organizational constructs of threats is a precondition for implementing management approaches for the security challenges in the port environment.

3.1 The Central Challenge: Security Management as a Component of Organizational Improvement

The key to successful and productive outcomes in all types of social organizations is the effective utilization of human and physical resources. The term *management* (or administration) can be understood as the effort to effect changes in organizational outcomes, using cooperative group efforts, in a public or private setting. For example, school administration or management is concerned with the outcomes associated with student learning. Those responsible for delivering the product or service, in this example, education, cooperate in activities associated with effecting changes in student learning. Security administration in a retail setting is geared toward staffing and planning for reducing threats of internal theft and shoplifting. In a transportation

Figure 3.1   A truck loaded with loose bags of raw materials is inspected before being admitted to the restricted access area of a port's cargo terminal. Port FSOs may be faced with developing a variety of security screening methods due to the wide-ranging nature of materials that are shipped around the world. The ability to screen different types of cargo efficiently to deter and detect the shipment of contraband and/or hazardous materials is just one challenge faced by security managers in complex port operational environments.

organization, the security manager must ensure that the organization is staffed and prepared for reducing threats to passengers, traded goods, conveyances, and terminals associated with operations. In port security management, the focus is on the administration of systems and processes necessary to reduce the threats to effect positive changes in organizational outcomes. In one sense, organizations differentiate work into separate parts or tasks. This *division of labor* is an efficient, that is, economical conversion of inputs into outputs. Organizations must also *integrate*, or bring the work of the specialized parts back together into a coherent whole. This is understood as effectiveness or goal achievement. Management is thus the process of coordinating the individual acts of various specialized subgroups of people toward a unified organizational objective to "get the job done."

Leadership is a construct based on the generalization of specific behaviors that lead to certain results, for example, organizational productivity. Leadership has been characterized in many ways: having vision; "walking the walk"; doing the right thing versus doing the thing right; acting in a results-oriented, proactive manner. Organizational management is a series of functions, such as planning, organizing, budgeting, and staffing; but is everyone who plans, organizes, budgets, and staffs a leader? Not all managers are good leaders (and not all leaders are good managers). Leadership often goes beyond simple management. Both require working with and among people to achieve organizational goals, but the nature of the goals or outcomes to be achieved may affect the style of leadership. The manager may need to employ different leadership behaviors, or styles, in different situations. For example, a security manager may come to his/her staff to engage them in a collaborative process of developing new ways to maintain surveillance on a critical piece of infrastructure, for example, a high-security vault. The manager may employ a participative style, one designed to motivate staff's creativity and innovations. In another setting, for example, during a building evacuation in a fire, the manager's style may be more directive and authoritative—no time for engaging dialog—just get the job done. The ultimate objective of all leaders and managers is to empower subordinates to accomplish organizational missions. In this discussion of the challenges facing port security, the central challenge is to understand the complexities of the port organization and its operations, and to enable the security function to contribute significantly to overall organizational improvement. Again, the challenge for security management is to understand and recognize the signals and respond positively.

3.2 The Port Organization as an Open System

To establish a conceptual organizational perspective on the security challenges within the port operational environment, it is instructive to understand the port organization as an *open system*. Katz and Kahn (1978) theorized the social organization as "an energic input–output system in which the energic return from the output reactivates the system" (p. 20). In other words, it is the transactional exchanges, or the continuing inflow and outflow of information and resources that sustain the endeavor. If there is one constant about managing a port, it is that operational decisions are driven by the day-to-day activities of the maritime industry and ancillary organizations. The interdependence of internal port operations with its external environment is what provides the systemic energy for a port to proliferate. Port productivity and success hinge on the ability of a variety of intermodal transportation networks to intersect at a critical piece of geography. Successful security management depends upon a certain flexibility of thought and process in determining the correct mix of protections to be implemented in a given port environment. By cultivating an open systems perspective of seaport operations, the port security manager will be able to think expansively. This should work to engage creativity in identifying stakeholders' practical needs and recommending appropriate security initiatives to protect the economic and safety interests of the businesses and organizations that depend on a secure yet viable transportation system. To assist port management and security in developing an open systems perspective on port operations, Katz and Kahn illustrate several defining characteristics or elements of open systems, which help to conceptualize the linkages between port operations and the external environment.

3.2.1 Importation of Energy

Much as the human body requires air, food, and water to sustain itself, social systems depend on stimulation from the external environment to maintain themselves. As critical modes of transportation, the systemic success of seaports depends on the efficient inflow and outflow of people, vehicles, and materials. Any interruption in the transportation flow will negatively impact the energy flowing into the system. Consider what might happen to a port facility, heavily dependent on a local labor base, if it was suddenly faced with a shortage of qualified employees to move cargo and load and unload vessels. On one extreme, consider how devastating a pandemic influenza might be to worldwide transportation. The medical profession is concerned that the spread of the highly pathogenic avian H5N1 virus, commonly referred to as Avian or Bird Flu, across parts of Asia and other regions is a significant threat to human health (PandemicFlu.gov 2008). In the United States, the concern about a pandemic affecting worldwide populations is so urgent that the government has authorized the spending of $3.8 billion for preparing for, detecting, and responding to a potential pandemic. "In 1918, the first pandemic (sometimes referred to as the "Spanish Flu") killed over 500,000 Americans and more than 20 million people worldwide. One-third of the U.S. population was infected, and average life expectancy was reduced by thirteen years. Pandemics in 1957 and 1968 killed tens of thousands of Americans and millions across the world. Scientists believe that viruses from birds played a role in each of those outbreaks" (Homeland Security Council 2006, p. vii). The World Health Organization (2005) believes that since "most people will have no immunity to the pandemic virus, infection and illness rates are expected to be higher than during seasonal epidemics of normal influenza. Current projections for the next pandemic estimate that a substantial percentage of the world's population will require some form of medical care" (par. 5).

Certainly all organizations must consider their exposure to this ominous risk in planning for continuity of operations, but a port's dependence on labor energy must consider even less extreme possibilities. For example, on May 1, 2008, International Workers' Day (May Day), cargo traffic along the West Coast of the United States was halted when members of the International Longshore and Warehouse Union engaged in a protest of the U.S. war in Iraq. The movement of approximately ten thousand cargo containers in ports in California, Oregon, and Washington was impacted by this one-day labor action (Veiga 2008). A port that depends on the movement of containerized cargo by trucks may be affected by any number of other variables, such as a rise in the price of fuel or new government regulations requiring drivers to undergo criminal history background checks to acquire port access credentials. From the port security manager's perspective, it is critical to have an understanding of the variables that impact the efficient flow of vehicles into and out of the port. This will be a significant factor, because security responsibilities will certainly include precautions for continuity of operations and intensified screening of vehicles during periods of heightened security.

3.2.2 Throughput

Throughput, according to Katz and Kahn, refers to the notion that organizations, as social systems, require stimulation from the external environment to convert energy into productivity. Energy coming into a system is used in processes required by the system to operate. By eating food, humans use the energy converted from sugars and starches to perform work necessary for sustenance. Port operations use people and equipment in a conversion process that enables raw materials, consumer goods, and in the case of passenger vessels, people, to be transported across waters, be they rivers or vast oceans. Energic transformation can also be understood as a process of converting knowledge into action. Thus, the security manager at a port will be concerned with selecting an efficient mix of security personnel with the correct levels of knowledge, skills, and abilities to enable necessary security mechanisms to be implemented. In this regard, human resource management functions such as training and career development of security staff become important considerations in terms of transforming potential security knowledge into concrete action plans. Since security must be understood as a practice that must undergo constant updating, the challenge for security managers in ports is to continually provide throughput energy for the security system in the form of new, revised, and current training practices. Government-initiated port security regulations, such as the MTSA of 2002, stipulated certain required training. In this regard, government training initiatives, such as the 2005–2007 U.S. Port Security Training Exercise Program (PortSTEP), were funded and developed to provide security exercise and evaluation services and solutions for maritime and port security organizations. Even so, the effective port security manager will not wait for government and external organizations to require throughput stimuli but will come to embrace it as an essential strategy in terms of security training, quality improvement, and good management.

3.2.3 Output

Katz and Kahn state that "open systems export some product into the environment," but their ability to continue to do so "depends on the receptivity of the environment" (p. 24). One way to understand this in terms of the challenges facing port security is to think about the byproducts of port and maritime operations. Sometimes, things do not proceed in productive ways. In 1998 and 1999, Royal Caribbean Cruises Ltd., the world's second largest cruise line, pleaded guilty in U.S. federal court to dumping bilge wastes into the ocean while operating passenger cruises out of the United States, and lying to U.S. Coast Guard investigators about it. In agreements with federal prosecutors, Royal Caribbean agreed to pay fines totaling $27 million (AllBusiness 1999). In one of the cases, Royal Caribbean admitted that its "crews routinely pumped oil bilge, kept dummy logs called 'fairy tale' books by the crew, and disassembled illegal sewage pipes bypassing cleaning devices as part of a conspiracy to hide the illegal practices" (New Jersey Fishing 1998, par. 10).

What a case like this illustrates for port security is that the port, to some extent, will have to contend not only with the byproducts of its own output, but also with the fallout that may occur from the output of port tenants, users, and other stakeholders. Organizations and individuals that use ports to transact their businesses may be held responsible or accountable for the negative byproducts of their operations. By association, right or wrong, port facilities may also be subjected to public backlash, economic penalties, or legal actions as the negative effects of external organizational outputs are mitigated. The perceptive security manager will make efforts to identify environmental conditions that might subject the port's target environment to liability or fallout from organizational outputs that may adversely affect port operations. So, while this may not necessarily be a security operational consideration, it is no less a security challenge. The security manager may have to plan for uncertainties, such as public protests, potential lawsuits, reduced business, or hiring extra security staff, which may impact the port in different ways.

3.2.4 Systems as Cycles of Events

Try to consider the port itself as a system with a structure. Port management is responsible for providing a foundation upon which organizational elements can affect the transportation of products and people. This requires resources: infrastructure, capital equipment, processes, and people. When parts of the structure fail to operate or integrate effectively, the system structure fails. Katz and Kahn discuss the concept of systems as cycles of events, referring to the idea that there are chains of events occurring in systems that enable them to function as designed. *Containerization* is a useful way to illustrate this process. Containerization is a shipping system developed in the 1950s that uses standard-sized cargo-carrying containers that can be easily moved from vessels to trucks and trains. Much of what is shipped around the world is shipped in a standard twenty-, forty-, or forty-eight-foot metal container. Container vessels coming into a port must have access to the gantry cranes and specialized moving equipment that can efficiently transfer these containers from vessel to port to market, and vice versa. Nevertheless, there is still a significant world trade in noncontainerized cargo that requires alternative modes of loading and unloading. Figure 3.2 depicts wheeled cargo being off-loaded from the cargo storage area of a passenger cruise vessel in port. It illustrates the fact that many ports must have alternative systems in place with which to manage the trade that comes into the port. In essence, a port that wishes to engage in multiple types of activities (e.g., containerized shipping, break-bulk cargo,

Figure 3.2   Wheeled and palletized cargo being off-loaded from the cargo storage area of a passenger cruise vessel in port.

combined passenger-cargo operations) must develop systems that consider the various cycles of events that must exist to support the activities. As Katz and Kahn suggest, this is a dynamic process. Port security must be prepared to develop processes and mitigate new and changing risks as port management continues to seek operational depth and expand productivity into untapped markets.

3.2.5 Negative Entropy

Entropy refers to the concept from the science of physics that, in stand-alone systems, there is a tendency to move from order to disorder. Consider the following example: "A new deck of cards comes with all the cards in order. Shuffling them mixes up the cards. Now take a deck of cards that's mixed up and shuffle them. The cards do not come back to their original order" (Slaven 2008, par. 4). In discussing organizations as open systems, Katz and Kahn suggest there must be a reversal of this entropic process, that organizations must develop "comfortable margins of operation" to maintain their energic inputs and improve their survival positions (p. 25). Security planning at its core is a process of negative entropy. Port security managers, especially those operating in complex, mixed port environments, will be challenged to be responsive to the tendency to move toward a state of disorder, to anticipate the "unshuffling of the deck." Even a severe thunderstorm can create entropy at a seaport, as unpredictable weather threatens navigation, scheduling, traffic management, and general safety to staff.

Perhaps more importantly, the responsibilities to the port's clients and customers with respect to a changing threat environment will require additional protections against global terrorism and general criminal activity. This cannot be the responsibility of only the government. Security managers must conceptualize their planning activities as a system, that is, an orderly method for protection and safety, which involves considerable overlap of many subsystems. The term *convergence* has emerged recently in the security literature and practice. It refers to a business movement to combine physical security and security management with computer security measures in an organization, which effectively provides a complete security solution (Tyson 2007). In reversing the entropic process, the port security manager will be challenged to operate in a more convergent manner, to understand the development of security plans as the critical merging of security systems with other organizational systems in seamless and, very often, in cost-efficient ways.

3.2.6 Information Input, Negative Feedback, and the Coding Process

Simply stated, systems respond and react to the information and signals that they are programmed to receive. In essence, a Port FSP (Facility Security Plan) is a program mechanism for responding to information inputs affecting the stability of the target environment. How well a system performs is a function of the coding mechanisms that the operators have programmed in. Katz and Kahn tell us that "the reception of inputs in a system is selective . . . systems can react only to those information signals to which they are attuned" (p. 26). Within this context, organizations overburdened with rules, regulations, and procedures limiting staff actions may become fixated on process and paperwork. The downside of a company constrained in this manner is that its ability to effect meaningful policy action is hampered. For example, a security department, overburdened with restrictive personnel rules, may have a difficult time transitioning from a reactive, stationary model to a proactive service model, where personnel administration may need to be more flexible. Organizations must have a satisfactory balance of rules and flexibility to both ensure efficiency and integrate competent discretion in their decision and action processes. This becomes especially critical in bureaucracies that depend upon structure and rules to function capably. In the port environment, bureaucracy can be a double-edged sword. In an effort to ensure mission success, operational staff adherence to strict policy and procedures may inhibit the creativity and flexibility a security manager must strive toward in responding to the information and coding process in the organization at large. Again, the challenge for security management is to understand and recognize the signals and respond positively.

3.2.7 Steady State and Dynamic Homeostasis

Homeostasis, or the maintenance of the stability of a given internal environment, is a system characteristic that security management must be consciously focused on. Of course, the challenge here is that ports, as open systems interacting with external environments, are constantly challenged to maintain this stability. The essential function of security is to stabilize the system; but to manage homeostasis, how should the security function be organized within the larger organization? The continuous inflow of energy into the port's systems, that is, the movement of cargo, people, vehicles, and business, challenges the organization to be responsive when new conditions or threats stress the ability of the system to preserve its essential character. For example, given the operating environment, that of proximity to water, there are many opportunities for systems to fail. Equipment, dock space, utility availability, and other subsystems may be sensitive to changes in weather or other environmental conditions that affect the port's steady state. Port management and security will have to determine the costs and the projected effectiveness of the security organization function balanced against the important question of whether security can truly and totally preserve stability when stresses to the port systems occur.

3.2.8 Differentiation

In understanding an open systems approach to port operations, *differentiation* refers to the idea that as organizations grow and develop, there is a tendency for more and more functional specialization to occur. Consider robotics as an example of this process. During the Industrial Revolution, mass production evolved as the ability to automate fabrication processes became more specialized. Organizations that were able to capitalize their operations by replacing humans with automated processes became more efficient. Similarly, in government, the transition from a politically driven spoils system to an efficiency-driven bureaucratic system symbolized the differentiation of role functions. The growth of different job classifications as human resource managers developed job task analyses processes is an example of this trend. There is a tendency for social organizations to progressively move toward a differentiated growth in the systems used to accomplish tasks. Port security itself can become differentiated as the system looks for more effective and efficient mechanisms for mitigating risk. While there will always be a place for the security officer standing a post somewhere, the fact is that the field is becoming progressively automated. The use of more and more forms of technology—digital video systems, biometrics, computer technology—to perform tasks that were typically performed by human beings is a reflection of the continued specialization of function that security managers must understand.

3.2.9 Integration and Coordination

Given the tendency toward role differentiation and specialization, it should come as no surprise that open systems organizations must be conscious of the integration and coordination necessary to ensure control and function. In this respect, management and leadership are crucial. A key issue in port security management in terms of integration and coordination processes is determining the appropriate placement of security in the overall organization. Consider the critical decision that a port director must make as to the organizational level of the Port FSO. Should the FSO report to one of the assistant port directors? Or, would it be better that the security operation be closely accessible to the port director for direct control? The decision on organizational placement of security will depend on how well integrated that function is with the rest of the organization.

Fischer, Halibozek, and Green (2008) suggest that the trend in security organizations is toward growing linkages among security, risk management, facilities management, safety, operations administration, human resources, and internal audits. Security integration will be developed, not simply by placement in an organizational chart, but by the commitment and engagement of the organization's leadership. The port director must assess the degree and nature of the authority given to the security manager and engage the manager in all aspects of the business operation. It is not inconceivable that, in a well-integrated security function, the security manager is directly involved in decision making related to any number of business processes, such as construction, capital development, marketing, public relations, legal affairs, and human resources. The coordinating role played by security in the port will be most pronounced as the security manager works to resolve conflicts among port staff, users, and tenants that stem from security systems and their implementation.

3.2.10 Equifinality

The final open systems characteristic relevant to this discussion of port security challenges is what Katz and Kahn, referring to a principle espoused by von Bertalanffy (1940), call *equifinality*: "A system can reach the same final state from differing initial conditions and by a variety of paths" (p. 30). This suggests that security management has many options available to it in abating threats and in effecting stability in port operations. Regardless of the place the security function occupies in the port organizational structure, there are certain characteristics of the function of security that must be a part of the operation. The following functions have been recommended (Fischer, Halibozek, and Green 2008, p. 71) as operational features of security that should be part of the security subsystem:

- Champion asset protection
- Solve more complex issues with less staff

- Identify risk for the company
- Develop programs to manage risk
- Quantify results to the bottom line
- Develop pilot asset protection programs
- Provide business solutions to security problems
- Reduce insurance premiums
- Use shared resources to manage costs
- Establish common objectives with risk management, internal audit, and information management

As these recommendations illustrate, there are many ways that the Port FSO can diversify security approaches to meet the port's goals and objectives. The trick is in being able to anticipate the functions that are needed and to integrate them into systems planning. Systems can become run-down and lose the qualities that differentiate them from other environments. They maintain themselves by maximizing advantages in their interaction processes to obtain resources. Conflict in this business is often unavoidable, thus the issues for security management become the form, magnitude, and modes of the resolution of conflict.

3.3 Specific Security Challenges in the Port Environment

3.3.1 Terrorism

Terrorist acts of the early twenty-first century are altering the nature of security efforts worldwide. The terrorist attacks on the United States in 2001 modified and heightened fears and concerns with regard to critical infrastructure security and the methods necessary for the safety of the general public. In the United States alone, there are over 360 commercial ports, encompassing about thirty-two hundred cargo and passenger handling facilities. Besides the maritime services they provide, U.S. port operations may include security infrastructure responsibilities related to airports, bridges, tunnels, rail systems, inland river or shallow draft barge terminals, industrial parks, Foreign Trade Zones, world trade centers, shipyards, dredging, marinas and other public recreational facilities (American Association of Port Authorities 2008). Criminal justice agencies (police, courts, prosecutors, corrections) are responsible for coordinating among law enforcement services, public health agencies, citizens, and private enterprises, by identifying methods, processes, and strategies to address the terrorism risk. As public policy is developed to prioritize homeland security issues, government officials must engage cooperatively with port security management to understand the security planning challenges in the port environment.

There are many definitions of terrorism, but simply stated, it is the use of force or violence, or threatened use of force or violence, against people and places to intimidate and/or coerce a government, its citizens, or any segment thereof for political or social goals. Terrorism is a form of psychological warfare. Sun Tzu, a Chinese military strategist who lived from 544 BC to 496 BC and authored *The Art of War*, wrote: "Achieving victory in every battle is not absolute perfection; neutralizing an adversary's forces without battle is absolute perfection" (Giles 1910). In other words, the ultimate victory comes from never having to fight at all. Following this strategy, terrorists attempt to coerce an adversary to obtain a goal without the risks usually associated with direct confrontation. Terrorists choose the target and the type of weapon for a particular reason. Certain weapons or weapon configurations are intended to have a devastating effect on the population of interest. An airplane crash may cause significant death, injury, and damage. An airplane crashed deliberately into an office building by suicide pilots will carry greater psychological impact and cause fear in a wider audience. Terrorists will choose their weapons based on their casualty-producing abilities to get attention. For example, the amount of the plastic explosive Semtex in the device that took down Pan Am Flight 103 over Lockerbie, Scotland, in 1983 was less than one ounce of material. Combined with the location and method of delivery, this fairly small amount of material resulted in the gruesome deaths of 270 people.

Terrorists are fighting an asymmetrical war, a strategy employed by the weaker side in a conflict to compensate for its enemy's strengths. For example, the USS *Cole* was a large warship attacked by a much smaller watercraft. The September 11 hijackers used box cutters to evade Federal Aviation Administration screening and assault the cockpits of the airplanes that were then used as guided missiles. The nature of the terrorist threat is such that managers responsible for critical infrastructure security, such as in ports, must also think in asymmetrical ways in responding to the threat. Combating terrorism requires three basic activities:

1. Crisis Management: Developing plans and methods to anticipate, respond to, and manage unpredictable events which may cause disruption to the stability of the operational environment
2. Consequence Management: Developing strategies and resources to respond to and recover from the effects of harm occurring to the target environment
3. Protective Measures: Planning and providing for activities and resources which will protect resources from harm in the target environment during an injurious event

A comprehensive response to terrorism involves the efforts of law enforcement, intelligence agencies, emergency response organizations, and the military if necessary. Terrorists test the basic political values and structures of democracy, the balance between security and liberty, and the essential criminal justice processes in their abilities to administer and provide social control mechanisms. The basic challenge of terrorism from a security manager's perspective is determining how the port organization can work with external organizations to develop strategies and plans to address the risks of international terrorism.

3.3.2 Weapons of Mass Destruction

Access controls in port facilities are a challenge due to the potential for unauthorized intruders, as well as credentialed staff, disrupting operations, national commerce, international trade, and recreational and tourist-related port business. Ports present an attractive target for terrorists and criminal conspiracies due to their component role in the national and local economies. Port facilities contain important assets and infrastructure that, if damaged, could cause significant loss of life, as well as damage to the facility itself, the economy, and the environment. Port access control will be discussed in more detail in a later chapter, but it is important to consider it here also since part of the mission of access control is to prohibit the introduction of materials and devices into the port that could cause serious injury, death, and property destruction.

Weapons of mass destruction refers to the following:

- Destructive devices that may be explosive, incendiary, or poisonous
- Any weapon involving a disease organism
- Any weapon designed to release radiation or radioactivity at a level dangerous to human life

There are two commonly used acronyms in military and homeland security lexicons used to categorize weapons of mass destruction:

- BNICE: Biological, Nuclear, Incendiary, Chemical, and Explosives
- CBRNE: Chemical, Biological, Radiological, Nuclear, and High Yield Explosive

Biological weapons in the form of viruses and bacteria may inflict disease among people, animals, and agriculture. When dispersed, the biological agents may be inhaled, ingested, or absorbed through the skin. A considerable concern from an emergency management and response perspective is that there may be a delay between exposure and the onset of symptoms. Disease may spread beyond the initial contamination point, and officials may have a difficult time locating the source of the attack. There is a long history of the use of biological weapons in combat. Persian, Greek, and Roman literature documents incidents of the use of dead animals to poison well water. During the French and Indian War, British forces reportedly gave Native Americans blankets that had been used by smallpox victims. The German Army developed anthrax, cholera, and a wheat fungus as biological weapons in World War I (eMedicineHealth 2008). In 2001, not long after the September 11 terrorist attacks, a form of a toxic bacterium of anthrax was mailed to media outlets and U.S. congressional offices, causing five deaths and seventeen injuries. The incidents rattled the consciousness of the United States, precipitated a complex criminal investigation, and illustrated the damage that can be caused by these particular types of weapons.

A nuclear weapon is an explosive device that derives its destructive force from the nuclear reaction of fission or from a combination of fission and fusion. A dirty bomb is a radiological dispersal device that uses a conventional explosive to disperse radioactive material. It is generally believed that the probability of a terrorist group obtaining a sophisticated nuclear weapon, such as those used at the end of World War II, is quite high, but there are significant concerns about terrorist groups developing the capacity to deploy a dirty bomb in populated areas. The U.S. Nuclear Regulatory Commission (2008) believes that most dirty bombs would not release enough radiation to kill people or cause severe illness but that the explosion itself would be more harmful. The larger concern is that the deployment of a dirty bomb, especially in densely populated locations, could create significant fear and panic, contaminate property, and require extensive remediation. A nuclear attack may be difficult to detect because the presence of radioactive material may or may not be obvious. There is enough concern in the maritime sector about the scenarios associated with nuclear weapons of mass destruction that the U.S. government has authorized and funded the development and installation of radiation portal monitors in all U.S. Customs and Border Protection ports of entry. In Figure 3.3, a secondary inspection station has been integrated into this port's cargo transfer facility to follow up on possible positive alerts to the presence of radioactive material in vehicles and in cargo entering the country.

Incendiary weapons are used to cause fire damage on flammable materials and objects. Incendiary devices or bombs use materials such as napalm, thermite, chlorine trifluoride, or white phosphorus. Flamethrowers, Molotov cocktails, fire accelerants,

Figure 3.3 Radiation portal monitors are being deployed in all U.S. Customs and Border Protection ports of entry to detect the presence of radioactive material in cargo coming into the United States.

and fuel-air explosives are types of weapons that are included in this category. Incendiary weapons are relatively easy to obtain and use and may cause significant localized areas of destruction. The concern for security managers in a port environment is that the shipment and industrial uses of hazardous materials presents challenges in terms of being aware of and monitoring the presence and use of materials that could be converted into incendiary weapons. Fueling operations and many industrial uses of these types of materials present the security operation with a responsibility to screen vehicles and personnel for the presence of hazardous materials that could be illegally converted into weapons of mass destruction.

Chemical weapons use a chemical agent to cause injury or death through a physiological reaction. There are a variety of chemical substances that can be deployed such as nerve agents, blister agents, and choking agents. Following are some of the more common substances:

- Sarin: a volatile, but colorless and odorless, liquid; a manufactured organophosphate similar to those used in pesticides. Sarin interferes with a chemical in the body that transmits impulses between nerve cells. The liquid form can be absorbed through the skin. In 1995 the Japanese religious cult group *Aum Shinrikyo* released sarin nerve agents at various points in the Tokyo subway system. The agent was concealed in lunch boxes and bags, which were punctured with umbrellas to release the agent. There were twelve deaths, over a thousand injuries, and about fifty-five hundred people who sought treatment at hospitals.

- VX: another manufactured nerve agent not found naturally in the environment. It was originally developed in the United Kingdom in the early 1950s and was also produced by the United States in the 1960s. Like sarin, it is suspected of being used by Iraq during the 1980s Iran–Iraq war.

- Tabun: a man-made nerve agent invented by the German chemist Gerhard Schrader in the 1930s. German manufacturing processes also developed Zyklon-B gas, notorious for being deployed to kill victims in concentration camps during World War II. Tabun reportedly mixes easily with water and can be used to poison water (Centers for Disease Control and Prevention 2008a).

- Sulfur Mustard: also known as "mustard gas" or by the military designations H, HD, and HT, a blistering agent that was first used in World War I. Exposure to the liquid form may produce second- and third-degree burns. Extensive breathing of the vapors can cause chronic respiratory disease, repeated respiratory infections, or death. Extensive eye exposure can cause permanent blindness. Mustard gas weapons are easy to produce, and get their name from their rotten mustard or onion smell (Centers for Disease Control and Prevention 2008b). Saddam Hussein reportedly authorized the use of sulfur mustard by Iraq against Iranian soldiers and Kurdish civilians in the Iran–Iraq war.

3.3.3 Hazardous Materials

The threat of international terrorism has highlighted the risk posed by hazardous materials that, aside from their obvious threats to environmental safety, can be converted into weapons of mass destruction. On a regular basis, ports are the conduit for legal substances such as chemicals, fuels, and other hazardous materials. The control and security of the transportation and storage of these materials is increasingly a concern for seaports due to the destruction that can be caused by their mishandling or criminal intent. As an example of the concerns for homeland security regarding hazardous materials, consider the 2002 testimony about the Port of Tampa in Florida by James F. Jarboe, FBI Special Agent in Charge, Tampa Division, in addressing the U.S. House of Representatives, Subcommittee on National Security, Veterans Affairs, and International Relations:

> The Port of Tampa is centrally located in downtown Tampa within 10 miles of MacDill Air Force Base. The Port of Tampa is the busiest port in Florida in terms of raw tonnage and stores approximately 50% of the extremely hazardous chemicals in the State of Florida. Of major significance is that the Port of Tampa is noncontiguous property, encompassing more than 2,500 acres of land. Generally, the port represents an appealing target of opportunity for would-be terrorists. The port is immense, accessible from land, sea and air. The port is adjacent to a large population of civilians and vital regional and national infrastructure, including power facilities, water facilities, and Headquarters of United States Central Command and United States Special Operations Command at MacDill Air Force Base. The port contains such hazards as liquid propane gas, anhydrous ammonia, and chloride.
>
> Central Florida also has some of the richest phosphate deposits in the world. The western counties are dependent on this phosphate-based industry. Fifty percent of Florida's hazardous materials are stored within Hillsborough County and 25% within Polk County. Major storage of extremely hazardous substances (EHSs) and other chemicals are located in this industrialized area and are vulnerable to accidental, malicious, and acts-of-nature releases. In 1993, the United States EPA conducted chemical audits of the three anhydrous ammonia terminals located on Tampa Bay. . . The audit revealed that the three terminals represent nearly 92.5 percent of Hillsborough County's total amount of anhydrous ammonia (NH_3) inventories.
>
> Individually, each of the three ammonia terminals pose a risk to the surrounding community and the effect of three facilities, in close proximity with such massive quantities, pose even greater risk. . .
>
> The high volume of maritime traffic in the large ports, both commercial and noncommercial, provide ample cover for the movement of illicit goods. . .
>
> Large bulk and containerized cargo pose a smuggling risk in the major ports of the Eastern and Gulf coasts. . .

(Jarboe 2002, par. 6–13).

The State of Florida, it should be noted, has taken a lead role among state governments in addressing security concerns in its port facilities. Although initially focused on the problem of narcotics being smuggled through its seaports, Florida's comprehensive port security legislation, first passed in 2000, has been responsive to port security concerns and the threats of general crime and terrorism. More recently, in 2006, new port security legislation has updated drug smuggling and terrorism risk mitigation requirements in Florida seaports (Florida Department of Law Enforcement 2008, par. 2).

3.3.4 Internal Criminal Conspiracies

The potential for the formation of internal criminal conspiracies probably represents the most complex challenge for security and law enforcement at seaports. Port employees' unique access to vessels and infrastructure inside restricted access areas places a burden on the port security manager to ensure that only authorized and vetted personnel can maneuver freely around the port. Crime on the docks is not a new phenomenon. In 1953, the Waterfront Commission of New York Harbor (2008) was established in response to pervasive corruption on the waterfront in the Port Authority of New York and New Jersey. The literary and artistic depictions of crime and corruption in the port environment in the 1954 feature film *On the Waterfront* are based somewhat on reality.

Consider the challenges facing port security concerning the potential for criminal activity at one port. In 2004, 4.5 million containers, valued at $114.5 billion transited Port Newark in New York and New Jersey. With over nine thousand employees, the port "has long been used to funnel money to the mob . . . Executive Director Thomas De Maria says mob businesses exact a real economic toll. The shipping lines that operate the seaport terminals get hit with higher labor and maintenance costs, but they pay it to keep the cargo moving. 'The businesses don't absorb that. They pass it on,' he said. 'Essentially it's a mob tax'" (Sherman 2005, p. 2). Concerns about waterfront corruption have taken on renewed urgency, given the concerns about easy access to port assets and infrastructure in an environment of homeland security. In testimony before the U.S. Senate Judiciary Committee in 2003, Interim Director John P. Clark, Office of Investigations, Bureau of Immigration and Customs Enforcement (BICE) said:

> The transportation organization that is paid to smuggle cocaine today may very well be contracted to smuggle instruments of terror tomorrow. By using internal conspiracies, criminals utilize corrupt personnel within the seaport and airport environment to introduce contraband or implements of terrorism into otherwise legitimate cargo or conveyances and to remove it prior to examination by the Bureau of Customs and Border Protection.
>
> In an ongoing investigation targeting internal conspiracies at a major U.S. seaport, BICE Special Agents have uncovered the endemic practice of contraband being removed from international cargo prior to the entry process. Utilizing a variety of investigative techniques

including undercover operations and controlled deliveries to successfully infiltrate the internal conspirators, hundreds of individuals have been arrested and convicted, thousands of pounds of cocaine and hundreds of pounds of heroin have been seized.

(Clark 2003, par. 10–11)

The Organization of American States (OAS) has recognized the challenges faced by international ports in protecting themselves and their associated economies from the threats posed by international criminal conspiracies.

> Effective hemispheric port security requires an interdependent network relationship among trade partner ports and associate countries, as well as adherence to a common international standard of security, to protect the flow of international trade and transshipment cargoes, as well as passenger transportation. Those ports with substandard protective security measures are "weak links" in the trade network and represent a vulnerability to the international marine transportation system.

(OAS 2004, p. 2)

To address the vulnerabilities in the maritime sector in the Western Hemisphere, OAS has advocated the following:

- Enhancing maritime and port security controls through inspection and monitoring, greater resource commitments, coordination of national and private sector programs, and better cooperation among OAS member states
- Fuller enforcement of regulations and penalties for private sector behavior that facilitates transnational crime and corruption in ports and maritime commerce
- More use of regulations, enforcement, and prosecutions against individuals and organizations that penetrate commercial maritime activities for illegal purposes

In Figure 3.4, dock workers at this port have ready access to the cargo hold of vessel that uses a roll-on–roll-off ramp for the transport of wheeled or bulk cargo. The threat of organized criminal conspiracies at ports, where contraband can be hidden in and quickly removed from vessels, such as this cargo ship, is a realistic problem confronting security managers in ports. Organized criminal activities committed by smugglers or other criminal groups, aided by corrupt individuals working in seaports or within the transportation industry, present a unique challenge for port management. Smugglers use industry employees with access to seaport areas and/or specific knowledge of customs activities, law enforcement, security operations, and the nature of the security culture within the port. Conspirators exploit a port's vulnerabilities by controlling and monitoring illegal drugs and contraband concealed inside cargo shipments of legitimate importers, which presents a major security and investigative challenge to interdiction efforts. Another illustration of the international concern about seaports' vulnerabilities to criminal conspirators is the United Arab Emirates (UAE). In 2005, the U.S. Department of State reported that the UAE is a transshipment

Figure 3.4   Dock workers with ready access to interior areas of vessels in port present a challenge for port security, as the port tries to mitigate risks of internal criminal conspiracies converting port assets into tools for smuggling contraband and other illicit operations.

point for illegal drugs from major drug-producing countries in Asia. Although the UAE is not a drug-producing country itself, the high volume of shipping transiting UAE ports makes it vulnerable to exploitation by narcotics traffickers.

Cocaine, marijuana, heroin, and methamphetamine are the primary illegal drugs smuggled into the United States through seaports. Most illegal narcotics come through in shipping containers, but some also come in concealed by passengers and crew on commercial vessels and cruise ships. Smuggling by crew is a problem at seaports where bulk cargo is imported. In 2007, the U.S. DHS reported that the U.S. Coast Guard set a record for drug seizures and arrests. The 93,209 pounds of drugs seized were more than the combined amount seized in the previous two years. Preventing criminal exploitation of the port begins with access control, the most common vulnerability of seaports to criminal activity. In this respect, port security cannot be the province of only one agency or entity. Port security must coordinate and integrate each stakeholder's role and responsibility in ensuring that only authorized employees and visitors are permitted access to critical, restricted areas of the port. The need to control ingress and egress of vehicles, cargo, and people, and to have positive identification of the people who do business or work at seaports, is paramount. Controls on public transportation, such as taxis, limousines, buses, and delivery vehicles accessing the seaport, and the defining of boundaries of public and restricted areas, are related activities associated with managing port access.

3.3.5 Piracy

The risk of armed takeovers of commercial vessels within ports themselves should be of high concern to Port FSOs, but piracy on the open seas remains enough of a problem for international shipping that it should be on the minds and agendas of port security managers. Acts of piracy continue to occur against commercial shipping, and port facilities must be aware of the threat of piracy and take steps to strengthen protections against ships that may be targeted. The areas for the greatest concern for acts of piracy against shipping are waters off Indonesia, Bangladesh, Malaysia, Somalia, and Nigeria. In 2005, the passenger cruise vessel *Seabourn Spirit* was attacked off the Somali coast by a small boat, believed to be operated by pirates, who used machine guns and rocket-propelled grenades. It is estimated that piracy and organized crime targeting cargo vessels and bulk carriers, both at sea and in anchorages, cost over $450 million per year (Goslin 2007, pp. 3–4).

3.3.6 Cargo Theft

The potential theft of cargo in transit is a significant concern that will occupy the time and resources of all individuals engaged in port security, whether as an FSO for the port or as the security manager for a cargo terminal. The FBI (2006) estimates that cargo theft costs U.S. business $15–30 billion each year. Worldwide, the theft of goods in transit likely approaches $50 billion or more annually. Law enforcement agencies estimate that more than half of all cargo theft is not reported, suggesting that the true amount of stolen cargo worldwide probably exceeds $100 billion a year. The fallout is not merely the loss of the cargo itself, but the costs associated with reproduction, reshipment, insurance, lost time and material, and many other internal and external costs to business. Protecting cargo from pilferage and illegal conversion while transiting seaports is a major concern for security. The need to deter theft at seaports has resulted in the development and implementation of processes such as gate pass systems and technological advancements in closed-closed television systems, cargo container scanning, and container integrity monitoring, which can help ports maintain controls on the goods being shipped and stored.

3.3.7 Vandalism

The willful destruction of the property of others constitutes the crime of vandalism. Criminal activities may result in vandalism to seaport property, vessels, and private property owned by port tenants and employees.

3.3.8 Stowaways

Stowaways attempting to enter the country by hiding on board vessels are a concern for both seaports and vessels, which requires cooperation among port facilities, terminal operators, and security personnel.

3.3.9 Poorly Trained Security Personnel

Seaports risk exposure to higher levels of crime and infiltration by internal conspiracies if the personnel responsible for port security have inadequate training. Developing the appropriate knowledge, skills, and abilities among security personnel is an essential component of reducing risks to seaports.

3.3.10 Crimes against Passengers and Crew

Protecting individuals who work and travel on board vessels is a responsibility of not only the vessel but also the seaport. The increasing need for cooperation and coordination between port facilities and vessels with respect to security is also driven by the mutual need to protect the public safety in and around seaports.

3.3.11 General Civil Unrest

In some locations, large facilities such as seaports may become the focal point for civil unrest or protest against government and private enterprises. Seaports have a responsibility to ensure that the security of their facilities and activities do not become compromised by the actions of large groups of people intent on publicizing political or personal messages by using port facilities.

3.3.12 Workplace Violence

Violence in the workplace is a risk concern for seaports because it often occurs in settings where employees deal with the public, exchange money, and deliver goods and services. Prevention strategies include procedures for documenting and responding to incidents and developing communications between employers and employees.

3.3.13 Economic Espionage

Competition within the private sector may result in efforts by some to steal trade secrets or compromise business practices to obtain economic advantage. Seaports may be targeted locations for espionage activities due to the confluence of private sector trade, transportation, and import/export interests.

3.3.14 Commercial Conspiracies

The smuggling of contraband out of a country is a significant risk unique to seaports. The transfer of illegal, stolen, or unauthorized goods through the regular cargo transportation systems can proliferate, because many nations depend on large volumes of cargo shipments to sustain their economies. The movement of controlled goods, munitions, stolen property, drug proceeds, and other forms of trade fraud provide a number of risks for port security management that must be considered in developing mitigation and response strategies for security. In the United States, many non-drug–import crimes go undetected at seaports because only a very small fraction of cargo is physically inspected. This rate may vary at targeted ports and has actually increased significantly since the terrorist attacks of 2001. Challenges related to trade fraud and commercial conspiracies include the following:

- Diversion of imported or in-bond merchandise into the country's commerce
- Textile trans-shipments to avoid quotas
- Undervaluation, double invoicing, or false description of merchandise imported into the country
- Importation, transportation, and distribution of counterfeit goods subject to trade and copyright
- Importation, transportation, and transshipment of items that pose a threat to consumers or the environment, such as tainted or prohibited foodstuffs, medicines, and unapproved drugs

Thus, while the Port FSO will certainly be occupied by the perhaps more immediate threats from terrorism and the needs of homeland security, challenges associated with commercial criminal activities must also receive attention. The truth is, there will be many competing security challenges in the port environment. Port managers responsible for the security organization must develop a broad sense of what constitutes risk. Even a relatively small port must consider its role as part of the larger community and transportation networks it intersects with. Understanding the scope of the challenge is the preliminary step to understanding and managing risk.

References

AllBusiness. 1999. Royal Caribbean pleads guilty to pollution. http://www.allbusiness.com/government/environmental-regulations/291620-1.html (accessed June 29, 2008).

American Association of Port Authorities. 2008. U.S. public port facts. http://www.aapa-ports.org/Industry/content.cfm?ItemNumber=1032&navItemNumber=1034 (accessed June 30, 2008).

Centers for Disease Control and Prevention. 2008a. Facts about tabun. http://www.bt.cdc.gov/agent/tabun/basics/facts.asp (accessed June 30, 2008).

Centers for Disease Control and Prevention. 2008b. Facts about sulfur mustard. http://www.bt.cdc.gov/agent/sulfurmustard/basics/facts.asp (accessed June 30, 2008).

Clark, John P. 2003, May 20. Testimony, United States Senate Committee on the Judiciary Narco-terrorism: International drug trafficking and terrorism – A dangerous mix. http://judiciary.senate.gov/testimony.cfm?id=764&wit_id=2112 (accessed May 23, 2008).

eMedicineHealth. 2008. Biological warfare. http://www.emedicinehealth.com/biological_war-fare/article_em.htm (accessed June 30, 2008).

FBI. 2006. Cargo theft's high costs: Thieves stealing billions annually. http://www.fbi.gov/page2/july06/cargo_theft072106.htm (accessed July 2, 2008).

Fischer, Robert J., Edward Halibozek, and Gion Green. 2008. *Introduction to security.* Amsterdam: Elsevier.

Florida Department of Law Enforcement. 2008. Florida seaports. http://www.fdle.state.fl.us/seaport/ (accessed May 23, 2008).

Giles, Lionel. 1910. Sun Tzu on the art of war, the oldest military treatise in the world. http://www.kimsoft.com/polwar.htm (accessed February 19, 2008).

Goslin, Charles. 2007. Maritime and port security white paper. http://www.sibgonline.com/pub-lic/userlisting/wpaper_upload/16637_13_wp.pdf (accessed May 23, 2008).

Homeland Security Council. 2006. National strategy for pandemic influenza implementation plan. http://www.whitehouse.gov/homeland/nspi_implementation.pdf (accessed June 29, 2008).

Jarboe, James. F. 2002, August 5. Testimony, U.S. House of Representatives, Subcommittee on National Security, Veterans Affairs and International Relations: Homeland security: Facilitating and securing seaports. http://www.fbi.gov/congress/congress02/jarboe080502.htm (accessed May 23, 2008).

Katz, Daniel, and Robert L. Kahn. 1978. *The social psychology of organizations.* 2nd Ed. New York: John Wiley & Sons.

New Jersey Fishing. 1998. Royal Caribbean fined $1 million for pollution. http://www.fishingnj.org/artlinerspill.htm (accessed June 29, 2008).

Organization of American States. 2004. Strategic framework for inter-American port security cooperation. http://www.transport-americas.org/Archived%20Documents-2005/Strategic_Frame_Security/Doc.%2023%20%20Strategic%20Framework%20for%20Inter-American%20Port%20Securi.doc (accessed May 23, 2008).

PandemicFlu.gov. 2008. General information. http://www.pandemicflu.gov/general/index.html#impact (accessed June 29, 2008).

Sherman, Ted. 2005, May 1. Tale of docks and mobsters gets new life: Crime figure's vivid testimony fuels U.S. case. Star Ledger. http://www.wcnyh.org/news/Tale_of_Docks_and_Mobsters_get_new_life.pdf (accessed May 23, 2008).

Slaven, Dave. 2008. Entropy. http://mooni.fccj.org/~ethall/entropy/entropy.htm (accessed June 29, 2008).

Tyson, D. 2007. *Security convergence: Managing enterprise security risk.* Amsterdam: Elsevier.

U.S. Department of Homeland Security. 2007. Goal 2: Protect our nation from dangerous goods. http://www.dhs.gov/xnews/testimony/gc_1170955671500.shtm (accessed July 1, 2008).

U.S. Department of State. 2005. International narcotics control strategy report, volume 1, drug and chemical control, United Arab Emirates. http://www.state.gov/p/nea/ci/79196.htm (accessed May 23, 2008).

U.S. Nuclear Regulatory Commission. 2008. Fact sheet on dirty bombs. http://www.nrc.gov/reading-rm/doc-collections/fact-sheets/dirty-bombs.html (accessed June 30, 2008).

Veiga, Alex. 2008, May 1. Terminal operators say west coast traffic halted. USA Today. http://www.usatoday.com/news/nation/2008-05-01-685093740_x.htm (accessed June 29, 2008).

Von Bertalanffy, L. 1940. Der organismz als physikalisches system betrachtet. *Naturwissen-schaften,* 28, 521 ff., as cited in: Katz, Daniel, and Robert L. Kahn. 1978. *The social psychology of organizations.* 2nd Ed. New York: John Wiley & Sons.

Waterfront Commission of New York Harbor. 2008. Brief history. http://www.wcnyh.org/his-tory.htm (accessed May 23, 2008).

World Health Organization. 2005. Ten things you need to know about pandemic influenza. http://www.who.int/csr/disease/influenza/pandemic10things/en/ (accessed June 29, 2008).

PART II

RISK MANAGEMENT, PLANNING, AND COORDINATION OF PORT SECURITY

PORT SECURITY AS A RISK MANAGEMENT ACTIVITY

4.1 Risk Management: A Foundation for Rational Security

The management of risk in any human endeavor requires careful and objective consideration of the environment within which one is operating. In the business of security, the risk management process begins with understanding the target environment as being fraught with risks that must be identified, assessed, and managed. Figure 4.1 illustrates a routine activity that occurs at ports every day: a tanker truck servicing a vessel at a dock. It could be a fueling operation, a water truck servicing a port utility system, or as in this instance, a waste disposal company removing wastewater from a passenger cruise vessel during turnover in the port. The activity is a routine and necessary port-vessel interface operation. What risks may be associated with it? Did the port receive advance notice of the vehicle's arrival for the day and time scheduled? Do the vehicle driver and passengers possess a port or government-issued credential that positively identifies them and provides advance authorization to be in this particular restricted area? Has the truck been subjected to a thorough screening to establish that there are no hazardous devices or weapons being introduced into the port's restricted access area? Has the vehicle operator provided a manifest of the materials or products being brought into the port? These questions and others present the Port FSO with a risk management foundation for identifying threats and vulnerabilities associated with the business of running a port.

In 2007, the Government Accountability Office (GAO), the investigative arm of the U.S. Congress, assembled a forum of experts from the public and private sectors and academia to consider the specific application of risk management concepts to homeland security. The GAO defines risk management as "a process that helps policymakers assess risk, strategically allocate finite resources, and take actions under conditions of uncertainty (2008, p. 1). Forum participants discussed the role of the organization's chief risk officer in relation to his/her communications with the leadership responsible for implementing risk mitigation strategies. One telling observation from the forum discussion was the realization that the private sector has flexibility in deciding what risks to insure against, while public sector managers are constrained by the public's perceptions about the nature of the threats the environment presents. When asked to rank the importance of the challenges facing risk managers in addressing homeland

Figure 4.1   This tanker truck is parked dockside, adjacent to a large passenger cruise ship being serviced while in port. Vehicles permitted to access the wharves and piers in ports present port security managers with a challenge to ensure there is no risk of harm to the docked vessel from potential threats such as vehicle-borne improvised explosive devices.

security issues, forum participants ranked improvements in risk communications as by far the number one issue facing organizations in strategizing how best to deal with threats in the homeland security environment. Considering the important role communications plays in the port environment, particularly in terms of coordinating risk management strategies among port stakeholders, it comes as no surprise that national leaders in this field agree on the importance of good communications in risk planning and security plan development. The following challenges, ranked by GAO forum participants, from most important to least important, suggest these issues deserve critical attention from port security management in developing a plan for risk management:

- Overcoming political obstacles to risk-based resource allocation
- Improving strategic thinking
- Improving risk assessment practices
- Measuring and evaluating risk reduction
- Enhancing public-private partnerships
- Lacking consensus on a definition of risk management
- Lacking common methodologies at all levels of government
- Developing the next generation of risk managers

Certainly, the message that can be taken from this is that port security is a risk management activity that must consider risk within quite a broad framework. Communications between the staff responsible for quantifying risk, and the leadership responsible for policy direction and implementation, is a crucial piece of the puzzle in constructing the port facility's risk management blueprint.

4.1.1 Convergence

In the last few years, particularly in the aftermath of September 11, the notion of convergence with respect to organizational security has taken on increased importance. The American Society for Industrial Security (ASIS) identifies convergence as a conceptual integration of an organization's security risk management function with the other core business functions (Booz Allen Hamilton 2005, p. 1). In essence, security is not viewed as a distinct and separate organizational role, but as a systemwide function for which all critical business functions must be concerned. The importance of this concept for port security managers is grounded in a realistic approach to managing security at ports. That approach requires security managers to not only understand the core business of the port, but to be thoroughly involved in the strategic management and direction of the port as a productive entity. The importance of embracing a convergent approach to security is that port security managers must understand and appreciate the holistic impact that security measures have on the business of the port. For example, a security manager's decision to increase the level of vehicle screenings related to vessel provisions deliveries can have significant impact on the operational effectiveness of a passenger service operation facing scheduling constraints. Similarly, decisions to increase access controls, impose additional credentialing requirements, or require escorts for visitors can have severe economic impacts on businesses operating at a port. To this end, a port's ability to apply a convergent approach to security should result in positive benefits for ports in refining and developing their physical security plans.

The importance of engaging in a business enterprise approach to security was examined in a 2005 study conducted by the global management consulting firm Booz Allen Hamilton on behalf of several international security organizations, including ASIS. The data gathered from chief security officers, information officers, and security professionals highlighted the security industry's keen focus on, among other things, compliance with governmental regulations and the need to reduce costs as driving influences to convergence. The study indicated that security professionals are increasingly focusing on integrating security activities to add value to the business versus focusing narrowly on implementing security requirements absent consideration of systemwide business interests. "Delivering on convergence is not just about organizational integrations; rather it is about integrating the security disciplines with the business's mission to deliver shareholder value" (p. 1). Within the context of risk management, the importance of taking a convergent approach to managing port security cannot be overemphasized. While many commercial organizations have a variety of operational and staff functions to manage, the maritime sector's economic success hinges on moving goods and people in a timely, cost-efficient manner. Security cannot be relegated to a stand-alone function without consideration of the impact a security plan's implementation might have. A systems approach to risk management will place the port's security manager in a position to interact vertically and horizontally with the port's organizational structure. Many port interests that do not necessarily have security roles, such as marketing, legal officers, public information officers, and information technology staff, must be in a position to work cooperatively with the security organization. This will be particularly important as the port develops and refines its emergency operations and response plans.

4.2 Port Facility Security and the Risk Assessment Process

Port FSOs have a legal and moral responsibility to develop strong FSPs based on a normative assessment of risk in concert with government regulations and maritime interests' business models. Information is crucial to assessing the port facility's exposure to harm. Expertise in assessing the essential areas of risk pertinent to port facilities, for example, accidents, theft, natural disasters, and particularly terrorism, is an essential element of ensuring that risk assessments are accurate and supportable. There is a critical need for accurate data on costs associated with the mitigation of risk in a business environment where economic realities demand that port managers focus clearly on port users' strengths and constraints. There are many alternative strategies for securing a port, yet the costs of mitigating risk exposure have increasingly become a source of conflict among ports, port users, and governmental authorities with a legal responsibility for port security.

One prescription for managing port security efficiently is to model risk assessments rationally by engaging port users and stakeholders more directly in the risk assessment process. A risk management process is a comprehensive identification of the possible harm faced by an organization. It entails a systematic examination of the exposure to risks, including those where people and property may be harmed or where financial losses might occur. What has become problematic in the post-September 11 homeland security environment is a clear understanding of how to assess risk. What are the appropriate sources and uses of information? In a process that involves estimating and measuring the frequency and severity of risks, what strategies will work best to ensure both a strong security posture and adherence to cost efficiencies? Risk management is a process of identifying and developing alternatives to minimize risk exposure. What measures will be used to integrate security requirements and to fund the costs of unavoidable risks? The process entails administering, reviewing, and improving the security program to protect the assets and to minimize costs. In the complexity of the modern maritime environment, it is essential that ports engage both users and interested public and private stakeholders in the risk management process.

As with most businesses, maritime interests must strike a balance between efficiency and effectiveness. The tradeoffs involved when a business is focused on bottom-line efficiencies at the expense of product or service development cannot be underestimated. As Mintzberg and Quinn (1992) stated within the context of organizational strategy, "... when the market is more concerned with product and service features and up-to-date technology, a firm pursuing efficiency can find itself offering a low-priced product that few customers want" (p. 296). A port focused on efficiency at the expense of security enhancements that may offer a higher level of protection may shortchange itself in the long run. Strategic decisions with respect to the pursuit of market share must balance cost reductions against noncost–price marketing effectiveness. Again, Mintzberg and Quinn advise caution in the narrow pursuit of an efficiency strategy indicating "... a firm must guard against going so far that it loses effectiveness, primarily through inability to respond to changes... The challenge is to decide when to emphasize efficiency and when to emphasize effectiveness, and further to design efficiency strategies that maintain effectiveness and vice versa" (pp. 296–297).

Risk assessment modeling in the maritime security environment must follow a similar caution. The post-September 11 terrorist protection paradigm emphasizes a comprehensive, all-hazards risk management strategy. While there continues to be debate about the likelihood of a terrorist incident occurring in specific locations, the question most often considered in developing Port FSPs is not *if* a terrorist incident will occur in the maritime sector, but *when*. Port and maritime business interests are cognizant of the need to protect their assets, but protection strategies must still complement a firm's overall business strategy. In this sense, decisions to implement security plans and processes must be based on assessment models that incorporate both efficiencies and effectiveness.

The primary competing interests in the port environment are quite basic: commerce versus security. To put it another way, there is a need to balance two diverse imperatives: time is money versus security is paramount. For example, within the passenger cruise sector of the maritime industry, there is a realistic and important concern about the negative impact a terrorist event could have on the industry, not just in terms of the deaths, injuries, and destruction that would occur, but for the long-term operational and economic growth of the industry. In 2007, there were 10,287,000 cruise passenger departures from North American ports alone. This represented a growth of 23.2 percent in cruise passenger activity from 2003 (U.S. Department of Transportation, Maritime Administration 2008, p. 11). This segment of the maritime industry continues to develop and prosper as cruise lines build bigger and faster ships and seek additional market share in a growing number of ports that heretofore had not been utilized in this sector (see Figure 4.2). For example, within the past few years, major lines like Carnival Cruise Lines have made it a priority to innovate cruise vacations from new departure ports such as

01/20/2003

Figure 4.2   The growth of the passenger cruise industry since the terrorist attacks of September 2001 has been evidenced by the construction of bigger and faster vessels and the development of new ports of departure in countries around the world. Maritime security executives charged with assessing the port security risks associated with this segment of the industry must balance their security plans in consideration of each industry stakeholder's unique business model.

Jacksonville, Florida, and New York City to enable its faster ships to sail to and from desirable destinations such as the Caribbean and back. By marketing to cruise passengers in new regions of the country, where the benefit is that passengers will not have to travel by air to reach the port, the cruise lines are attracting more and more vacationers who had not previously considered taking a cruise. The importance of this dynamic to Port FSOs and port directors is that this sector of the maritime industry continues to develop new business models and growth, as does much of the cargo trade around the world. While the specter of a terrorist event occupies the minds of many industry security professionals, the practical outcome of the industry's growth is the challenge ports face in managing security processes to minimize the negative effects of security overhead on economic growth and profit margins.

Certainly, effective security measures can be implemented to provide sound protections against many types of harms. The dilemma for port security management is deciding what levels of security can be implemented without having a deleterious effect on budgetary policy and commerce. Besides port management and port users, there are other stakeholders with competing priorities. The U.S. Coast Guard has a legal responsibility to ensure the security of the nation's ports. U.S. Customs and

Border Protection has a concomitant responsibility to secure the nation's borders and protect against intrusions and criminal activity. State and local law enforcement agencies are engaged in missions in which the protection of the nation's ports is an increasing part of their responsibilities. The challenge for port security managers is deciding how best to meet the demands of maritime security constructs and regulators for a layered security approach, while also maintaining a rational perspective in developing a cohesive security plan.

There is an increased need for quality yet simple and cost-effective risk assessment models and strategies. In the wake of new international and U.S. government security initiatives that direct maritime interests to take a lead role in developing and financing complex security plans, Port FSOs and port directors may find themselves seeking answers to the dilemma of how best to construct a security regime that is both practical and economically feasible. In its 2007 report to Congress on port risk assessment, the GAO noted that although the U.S. DHS's 2006 Maritime Infrastructure Recovery Plan articulates a process for restoration of maritime commerce in the wake of a terrorist attack or natural disaster, "it does not set forth particular actions that should be taken at the port level, leaving those determinations to be made by the port operators themselves" (p. 16). The GAO report emphasizes the important relationship between risk consideration and resource constraints in developing responses to security threats and vulnerabilities. There is an understanding that the federal government has provided significant policy guidance for FSOs and maritime security officials, at least with respect to the importance of risk management in developing homeland security plans and response mechanisms. Given the extensive policy direction on homeland security, however, the GAO report goes on to indicate that ". . . little specific federal guidance or direction exists as to how risk management should be implemented" (p. 17). For the port security manager, the requirement for understanding security within the context of risk is a daily task that demands an understanding of a wide assortment of available strategies and tools.

Port security managers must rely on either internal or external expertise to conduct complex, and sometimes expensive, security risk and vulnerability assessments. Federal, state, and local port security regulators are pressing ports to stress good risk assessment in the development of security plan provisions and revisions. For example, in the state of Florida, a 2006 revision to the state's comprehensive seaport security standards law requires the state's fourteen deepwater ports to conduct quarterly risk assessments:

> The seaport director of each seaport, with the assistance of the Regional Domestic Security Task Force and in conjunction with the United States Coast Guard, shall revise the seaport security plan based on the results of continual, quarterly assessments by the seaport director of security risks and possible risks related to terrorist activities and relating to the specific and identifiable needs of the seaport which assures that the seaport is in substantial compliance with the statewide minimum standards.

(Florida Statutes 2006, sec. 311.12(2)(a))

The mandate clearly specifies a port's responsibility to incorporate a rational risk assessment process into ongoing security plan development.

The National Strategy for Maritime Security (NSMS) is the basis of the federal government's strategic direction for protecting the nation's maritime domain in the post–September 11 homeland security environment. It is clear that the United States places great emphasis on the strategic and economic importance of the nation's maritime interests. Ports in this country handle over two billion tons of domestic and import/export cargo each year (Government Accountability Office 2007). The U.S. government is clearly articulating a strong, all-hazards homeland security public policy for the maritime sector that is driving port security managers to consider all manner of natural and man-made threats in their security planning. What is also clear, however, is that the federal government recognizes that there must be a balance between efficiency and effectiveness in operationalizing security strategies for the nation's ports. There is a fundamental understanding that the United States seeks stability in the global maritime economic environment while also emphasizing the prevention of hostile and/or illegal acts in the maritime domain.

Overly restrictive, unnecessarily costly, or reactionary security measures to reduce vulnerabilities can result in long-term harm both to the U.S. economy and to global economies, undermine positive countermeasures, and unintentionally foster an environment conducive to terrorism. Security measures must accommodate commercial and trade requirements, facilitate faster movement of more cargo and more people, and respect the information privacy and other legal rights of Americans (White House 2005, Section IV). Again, public policy advocates in this area are clearly concerned that a normative U.S. strategy for maritime security is essential to remain globally competitive.

Risk assessment is a key component of the federal government's maritime security strategy. The GAO (2007) provides a framework for risk management that port security managers can adapt as they begin to understand the cycle of decision making that revolves around the development of a port's FSP:

- Identify and establish strategic goals and objectives within the context of organizational constraints
- Assess the security risks faced by the port
- Determine what alternatives exist for addressing those risks
- Determine which alternatives to implement
- Implement the solutions and monitor progress and results

This framework suggests that awareness of security risks and knowledge of possible threats to the maritime security environment are the building blocks of effective prevention measures. According to the NSMS, the threats to the maritime environment include those from other nation-states, terrorists, transnational criminals, piracy, environmental destruction, and illegal seaborne immigration. The NSMS recognizes the difficulty of protecting all infrastructure and resources on a constant basis and encourages government to work collectively with the private sector maritime community to conduct risk management assessments to understand the security needs in each particular facility. The NSMS clearly places a responsibility upon private maritime interests to provide the primary means of defense for their facilities and stresses the importance of awareness and threat knowledge for securing the maritime domain. The NSMS characterizes this process as one which maximizes domain awareness in support of effective decision making.

In the port environment, the complexities of interdependent relationships emphasize the importance of good leadership in managing the risk assessment process. As one writer on critical infrastructure risk assessment has indicated, "For those sectors not vertically integrated, ownership of infrastructure assets may span a number of firms, or industries. Whoever is doing the analysis may feel constrained to consider only those assets owned and operated by the analyst or analyst's client" (Moteff 2004, p. CRS-6). This illustrates a crucial complexity about port facilities. As is the case in many ports, assets may be owned by one entity and operated or used by another. Furthermore, waterways, bridges, locks, dams, navigation aids, and the like may not be the direct responsibility of the port entity, but those assets may be considered critical from the perspective of federal, state, and/or local government. For example, a port may operate adjacent to a commonly shared waterway access to the port, without having operational or managerial responsibility for the waterway itself. Governmental security concerns about threats to the waterway, such as might occur with the disabling of a large vessel in the waterway, preventing access to and from the port, may put pressure on the port security manager to consider mitigation strategies for assets not under the port's direct control. The FSO must therefore manage the risk assessment process with an understanding about these interdependency issues and correct for biases associated with the perceived criticality of assets identified as vulnerable in the port domain. As further emphasized in the literature, ". . . the increasing intra- and interdependencies among the various interconnected infrastructures and other systems must also be well-understood and modeled" (Haimes and Longstaff 2002, p. 439). In this regard, Moteff posed two important questions that should be asked by port leadership concerned about vulnerability assessment:

- Are the risk assessment protocols similar across organizational boundaries?
- Is the process considering the level of dependency on assets external to the port?

Basic security risk-assessment modeling is the cornerstone of any security program. Businesses and governments alike utilize risk models to determine security needs. It is logical to propose that ports and related maritime transportation sector business interests co-opt quality, yet cost-efficient, risk-assessment modeling strategies. This is consistent with the framework of the NSMS, particularly in the areas of terrorist threats, transnational crime, and illegal immigration concerns. Port security managers and directors must be more scientific, that is, more rational, in their development of security requirements to protect their interests and to comply with government mandates.

Risk management has historical usage in the insurance industry, for example in the use of actuarial tables to determine life expectancies. In the global maritime sector, risk assessment has taken on increased importance in the post-September 11 environment, particularly subsequent to the IMO's 2004 adoption of the ISPS Code. The ISPS Code contains detailed security-related requirements for governments, port authorities, and shipping companies. In the United States, the passage of the MTSA of 2002 and the continued evolution of mandatory port security regimes presaged the proliferation of risk assessment technologies and models now available to port security managers. Design-basis threat, catastrophe modeling, and levels of probability are just some examples of the models being developed or adapted for use in the maritime sector.

4.2.1 Design-Basis Threat

Using a design-basis threat approach to risk assessment, the security manager will want to conceptualize a profile of the types, compositions, and capabilities of potential threats to the port facility. Once there is an understanding of the likely nature of the threat being faced by the port, the FSO can begin to identify, design, and implement protective safeguards geared toward that particular threat. Design-basis threat as a risk management approach has been used extensively in the nuclear power industry. "The NRC and its licensees use the design-basis threat (DBT) as a basis for designing safeguards systems to protect against acts of radiological sabotage and to prevent the theft of special nuclear material" (U.S. Nuclear Regulatory Commission 2007, par. 1). The Energy Reorganization Act of 1974, which abolished the Atomic Energy Commission and restructured federal governmental oversight of nuclear power, "prescribes requirements for the establishment and maintenance of a physical protection system which will have capabilities for the protection of special nuclear material at fixed sites and in transit and of plants in which special nuclear material is used" (10 CFR 73.1(a)). The ensuing statutory language specifies design-basis threats to be used to design safeguard systems. Even though the statute is specific to the nuclear power industry, the design-basis threats include such things as radiological sabotage by armed individuals and groups, internal threats, land vehicle and waterborne bomb assaults, and cyber attacks. Certainly these threats are not unique to the nuclear power industry. In fact, the threat of a waterborne terrorist attack is one that occupies the minds of many port security officials, risk managers, and law enforcement officials across the maritime sector. Clearly, there are opportunities for facility security managers at ports to co-opt strategies from ancillary industries in developing a risk management strategy unique to a particular port environment.

4.2.2 Catastrophe Modeling

Catastrophe modeling employs computer technology in assessing potential losses that may occur given different threat scenarios. For example, the insurance industry's use of catastrophe modeling in managing risks associated with natural disasters draws from a diverse spectrum of disciplines such as decision sciences, meteorology, seismology, and others to match historical disaster information with current demographic, building (age, type, and usage), scientific, and financial data to determine the potential cost of catastrophes for a specified geographic area. The models use these vast databases of information to simulate the physical characteristics of thousands of potential catastrophes and project their effects on both residential and commercial property (Insurance Information Institute 2007, par. 1). Because there are many sophisticated modeling strategies available, the Port FSO will have to carefully evaluate the types and functionality of software packages on the market.

4.2.3 Levels of Probability

Fryer (2003) reports how Washington state emergency managers are using "a simple formula—'history plus judgment equals forecast'—to determine the probability of a wide range of hazards, from terrorist attacks to tsunamis, wildfires or an explosion at the Umatilla Chemical Depot in Oregon" (p. 2). Risk assessment models may be science-based, but they still require decisions to be made with a certain amount of unpredictability. As the Port FSO begins developing a risk management strategy, organizations that market risk management products and services will become evident. As a testament to the plethora of information and wide variety of services available on the open market, an Internet search engine query using the terms "risk management" and "port" yielded the author over one million results. To be sure, both the maritime and security industries have historically relied upon the expertise of experienced risk managers in understanding the exposure to harm and the need to implement security plans that mitigate that exposure. Post-September 11, particularly in the wake of significant international, federal, and state government oversight of maritime security, the growth in the security industry, with respect to risk assessment products, tools, software, and technology, challenges port security managers to learn all they can to understand what products and services will best suit a particular target environment.

Part of the dilemma for port security managers, especially with respect to assessing the risk of terrorist activity, is determining the probability of a terrorist attack. Post-September 11, the increasing assumption is that terrorist events will occur. The likelihood of a terrorist event is now assumed in many risk assessment models. "The risk of terrorist attacks on critical infrastructure is tangible, but was invisible to policymakers up to 9/11" (Haimes and Longstaff 2002, p. 439). Recommendations for risk assessment models that incorporate understanding of the relationships between terrorism and its outcomes include systematic and quantitative risk modeling strategies. One such device, developed at the University of Virginia, is Hierarchical Holographic Modeling (HHM). HHM can be employed to understand the likely sources of risk and create relevant scenarios templates using a multidimensional model of risk, much like a holographic image.

> The Adaptive Two-Player Hierarchical Holographic Modeling (HHM) Game . . . is a repeatable, adaptive, and systemic process for tracking terrorism scenarios. It builds on fundamental principles of systems engineering, systems modeling, and risk analysis. The game creates two opposing views of terrorism: one developed by a Blue Team defending against acts of terrorism, and the other by a Red Team planning to carry out a terrorist act. The HHM process identifies the vulnerabilities of potential targets that could be exploited in attack plans.

(Haimes and Horowitz 2004, par. 1)

Models such as these, which use computer models for design and operational issues, also rely on human intervention and judgment, since as Haimes and Longstaff indicate: "human behavior dominates in socioeconomically based systems" (2002, p. 439). Tuckey (2005) also discusses methodologies for predicting the risk of terrorism, which "rely on hard data from years of military modeling on the impact of numerous kinds of weapons—both conventional and nonconventional—along with the insights of academics and other counterterrorism experts. . . . However for the most part modelers rely on the expertise of academics who have studied Islamic attack patterns as well as the plans of schemes that did not come off" (p. 17). As this brief review suggests, the dilemma of understanding probabilities associated with terrorism risks can be addressed using available and often sophisticated modeling tools.

For the port security manager, the decisions on the types of risk assessment models to use are crucial ones, requiring an understanding of the methodologies and technologies available. The available alternatives will require the FSO to critically evaluate products and services balanced against available resources—primarily time, staff, and funding. To manage this process efficiently, assistance and input should be sought from those port users and stakeholders who have the most to gain or lose in the process. To that end, consultation and feedback from the business and governmental interests most concerned about an effective security structure at the port will be a valuable component in deciding what type of risk assessment strategy to employ.

4.3 Risk-Based Decision Making

Strictly speaking, risk can be understood as the possibility of harm or loss. It includes an element of uncertainty in the sense that the actual outcomes of security policy and action may be inconsistent with anticipated outcomes. In the basic security environment, organizations consider various types of risk associated with loss or harm.

Risks such as personal injury crimes (e.g., robbery) and property crimes (e.g., burglary, theft, vandalism) have long been the focus of assessment activities associated with crime prevention in commercial settings. Other risks associated with natural disasters (e.g., hurricanes, tornadoes), man-made disasters (e.g., hazardous materials incidents), and human conflict (e.g., civil unrest, labor strife, workplace violence) are considered in many specialized security environments. Today, in the early twenty-first century, organizations considering security needs must assess new risks associated with technology (e.g., computer crime, identity theft) and violence (e.g., terrorism).

Figure 4.3 is a conceptualized understanding of the generalized flow of the risk assessment process and illustrates how risk-based decisions are made within a type of systems feedback loop. The process begins with asset identification. FSOs must understand that a program of protection and mitigation begins with an understanding of each and every asset under their command and control. Once a consolidated list of assets is developed, the security manager engages in a multistep process of identifying and defining the threat(s) associated with each asset. A vulnerability assessment evaluates facility design and layout issues against the types and levels of threats envisioned. A criticality assessment establishes the value of the asset to the continuing mission of the organization. This process leads to a determination of the level of protection necessary for each mitigation measure against the threats identified.

Risk-based decision making entails continuous system-feedback assessments of the impacts of mitigation measures on asset vulnerability and criticality. For example, in many ports, waterside docks and piers are considered necessary assets because they relate directly to the ability of vessels to moor and be serviced. A dock is highly critical to the port's success as a viable commercial function. Docks are vulnerable to a threat of terrorist activity because personnel and vehicles, which may be able to transfer dangerous weapons and devices onto the port, must be able to service a docked vessel. An option for neutralizing the threat that dockworkers could be a conduit for weapons that

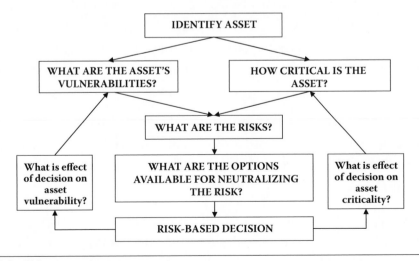

Figure 4.3   Risk assessment process.

could threaten a docked vessel might be to conduct physical screening of every individual and vehicle accessing the dock. The effect of this decision on the dock's vulnerability is that the threat from this potential terrorist attack is reduced. The criticality of the dock is also affected, because enhanced screening may slow down work processes associated with vessel servicing. These assessments must be factored into a continuing risk assessment process, which is enhanced by the flow of information about changing vulnerabilities, threats, and criticality values associated with port assets.

The general purpose of risk assessment is to determine the degree of exposure to hazards or dangers to personnel and property as a preliminary step to identifying preventive measures to minimize risk. The most effective course of action in safeguarding the target environment is to eliminate the source of the risk. Analysis of operations is a component factor of risk assessment. The elimination of risks of criminality, terrorism, and natural and man-made disasters is a function of organizational management, but there may be a government enforcement function (e.g., regulated industries, such as transportation, aviation, energy systems) that provides input to the strategic direction of risk assessment. Risk management is concerned with identifying preventive measures to implement that will focus on minimizing the risks. Risk-based decision making balances the concept of security against three organizational constraints:

- Access: Security measures may restrict use of the facility, which could affect the organization's maximization of its productivity. For example, when heightened levels of security are implemented, facilities may restrict access to certain individuals, companies, or elements.
- Commerce: Security measures may entail direct and indirect costs associated with the business function. For example, costs associated with the procurement of access credentials may be factored into end-user costs.
- Environment: Security measures may require that more capital resources be devoted to security versus commercial use. Thus, a facility may have to incorporate staging areas, screening points, buffer zones, and/or protected zones into the physical plant.

Thus, port security risk assessment is a process that leads the port security manager to make security-related decisions based on a determination of what is an acceptable level of risk. The assessment process entails an examination of three fundamental considerations:

- What types of threats and vulnerabilities does the port facility face?
- How viable are those threats, and what is the extent of the vulnerability?
- What can be done to eliminate or mitigate these threats and vulnerabilities?

4.4 Cost-Effective Risk Assessment

Organizations assessing risk as a prelude to the development of security plans and procedures make decisions that realistically influence the ability of the organization to conduct its core business functions. According to the Federal Emergency Management Agency (FEMA 2003), risk management necessitates that organizations select from one of three choices: "Do nothing and accept the risk; perform a risk assessment and manage the risk by installing reasonable mitigation measure; or, harden the building against all threats to achieve the least amount of risk" (p. 1-44). There are several strategies that port security organizations can integrate into their risk assessment processes that will help FSOs to engage the wider port community in more cost-effective risk assessment.

4.4.1 Recommendations for Developing Efficiencies in Risk Assessment Strategies

- *Use a risk assessment model that considers all stakeholders' interests and concerns.* Seaports are complex and dynamic environments. In many cases, elements of the private sector and government must work cooperatively, anticipating the many strengths and constraints each organization possesses. Port FSOs should engage each interested party in the risk assessment process, using a model that addresses each user's unique business needs.
- *Get buy-in from the seaport community.* The best way forward is the one in which all parties in the process perceive their input as valued and desired. The resolution of conflicting interests and the cooperation of users in a risk assessment process that meets the needs of the seaport community are essential steps in developing efficiencies in security management.
- *Ensure security staff understands risk management.* Part of being efficient is ensuring that the security staff understands the risk assessment process. Management and training activities should be structured so that staff understands the process and can be engaged productively in risk assessment activities.
- *Seaport stakeholders' values must be internalized by security and top seaport management.* Efficiencies in risk assessment will depend on whether or not the seaport is in a position to understand the business and organizational values of its end users. Is port management focused on understanding the strategic directions of its core businesses? To assess security risks properly, the seaport must understand the business of its clientele.
- *When conducting risk assessments, decide to use internal staff or outside experts based on an assessment of strengths, weaknesses, and costs.* In a complex seaport environment, will internal staff be sufficiently knowledgeable of systems and computer models utilized in complex risk assessments? Consider carefully the tradeoffs involved in using outside consultants. If subject matter expertise is

needed, be prepared to justify the expenses to engaged users and stakeholders, as well as senior port leadership.

- *Have frequent meetings with stakeholders, both individually and in groups, to obtain their concerns, answer their questions, and solicit suggestions.* Communication in the risk assessment process is the cornerstone of conflict resolution. The port tenants and users have a stake in the process and the outcome. It is likely that their input and suggestions will enable FSOs to identify factors relevant to the assessment. To the extent that the seaport end users and stakeholders both understand the risk assessment process, and are a viable part of it, port security managers can achieve efficiencies.

4.5 The Security Survey

CAIR is an acronym for understanding the process of assessing risk. It stands for collect, analyze, improve, and reevaluate, and it represents a constant process of understanding the risks in the facility and rationally developing solutions for minimizing potential harm:

- Collect: Information and data about all of the possible security risks inherent in the port facility is collected and organized.
- Analyze: The information on these risks is examined to understand what options and alternatives are feasible for implementation in mitigating each identified risk.
- Improve: Existing security processes, structures, and systems are improved by selecting which risk-mitigating strategies will be implemented.
- Reevaluate: The solutions that have been implemented are checked continuously to ensure the intended outcomes are being met.

System failures, such as breaches of security, will necessitate that the CAIR cycle be repeated for the particular risk. In conducting risk assessments at ports, the FSO's primary goal is a determination of the vulnerability of the port facility's assets to hazards or dangers caused by natural or other forces and using this information to construct a security plan. The CAIR process then is concerned with identifying preventive measures to implement that will focus on minimizing the threats to the port facility. To begin the risk management process at the port, the FSO must conduct a security survey. Security surveys have four essential components: identify assets, establish criticality, determine vulnerability, and determine probability.

4.5.1 Identify Assets

This first step involves constructing a general and specific layout of the port facility to identify important assets and infrastructure that are critical to the port, as well as those areas or structures that, if damaged, could cause significant loss of life or damage to the port's organization, facility, local economy, or environment. The determination of what a port asset or port infrastructure is will vary, depending on the type of port business, organization, or facility, but will generally include buildings, roads, transportation networks, equipment, intermodal connections (e.g., pipelines, railroad access), user assets (e.g., vessels, road vehicles, stevedore equipment, shipping containers), support systems (e.g., information, communication, and management systems), and power and water distribution systems. A complementary aspect of this asset identification step is the articulation of the location of all access points to the facility. In small ports, this may only entail a localized survey of adjacent roads and waterways. In large ports, especially those serving a complex urban, regional, or national economy, asset identification and access point articulation may entail more sophisticated surveys that consider intersections of the port with highways, bridges, road and rail connecters within the larger metropolitan area. In fact, if the port is engaged in significant commercial interfaces (for example, a significant passenger cruise industry with dedicated links to airports), the port security manager may need to conduct joint security surveys with counterparts in airports, rail depots, truck transfer stations, and similar organizations.

4.5.2 Establish Criticality

Once a comprehensive understanding of the port's assets and infrastructure is developed, the second step of the port security survey focuses on establishing the criticality of each asset. The FSO must answer this question: What is the value, impact, or cost of any asset, should it be lost as a result of natural or other forces? By establishing priorities of criticality, that is, assigning priorities to those areas most critical to the port's survival, an objective assessment can be made for devoting precious security resources to those assets deemed essential for port operations and viability. Conversely, the noncritical areas will receive lowered priority for protection. The survey must verify actual conditions and procedures relative to each asset, and the survey results must be shared with port management and affected port tenants/users to arrive at consensus as to the prioritization of security concerns. Obviously, the assessment must identify the actual threats to the critical assets and infrastructure in order to prioritize security measures.

4.5.3 Determine Vulnerability

Vulnerability refers to how prone a particular person, asset, system, function, or process is to injury, death, damage, loss, or disaster. In a general risk management environment, we might consider a particular structural asset's vulnerability in relation to its survivability if it were subject to fire, storms, earthquakes, and other natural or man-made disasters. From a more specific homeland security or emergency management perspective, we may consider vulnerability in terms of how likely it is that a disaster may occur and that an organization or individuals may experience negative impacts from the event, such as injuries, death, property damage, and financial losses (McEntire 2009, p. 15). The vulnerability assessment will identify weaknesses in physical security, structural integrity, protection systems, procedural policies, communications systems, transportation infrastructure, utilities, and other areas within a port facility that may be a likely target. In determining the vulnerability of port assets and infrastructure, the primary question to be answered is: What is the degree of vulnerability of the asset to damage or attack? The answer to this will be determined by an inspection that must look at the following:

- Physical and operational weaknesses
- Peak versus off-peak activities
- Relative sizes of assets (e.g., small verus large buildings)
- How the assets are used (e.g., high public traffic versus restricted)
- Exposure to natural forces (e.g., weather, environment, hazardous materials)
- Exposure to terrorist activities (e.g., piracy, geography, ideology, political landscape)
- What actually goes on in the business (e.g., cash handling, baggage conveyance, container movements)
- The weak points in security (physical and human)
- The history of losses (e.g., crime reports, accidents, weather events, fire, security incident reports, insurance losses, lawsuits, workers compensation injuries, media reports, industry and trade data, government reports, academic research)
- The potential for internal conspiracies (e.g., illegal narcotics, cargo theft)

4.5.4 Determine Probability

The fourth and final component of the security survey is a determination of the probability or likelihood that a particular event or occurrence will compromise security of the port facility. In determining probability, the logical way forward is to make reliable estimates based on past data and experience. Consider the potential threat in terms of its likelihood of occurrence. The plan for security in relation to the threat is to improve "the ratio of favorable events to unfavorable events, or to reduce the ratio of unfavorable events" (Broder 2006, p. 26). In other words, if one perceived threat in a port environment is a fire aboard a passenger cruise vessel while it is docked at a port terminal, reliable estimates of the potential risk can be obtained by looking at historical data on fires aboard vessels and experiences of the passenger cruise industry. The probability of such a fire occurring in the facility can then be expressed. The likelihood of the event actually occurring will be reduced by the deployment of security strategies such as systems (e.g., alarms, monitors, fire suppression), processes (e.g., ship staff training in fire prevention, passenger orientation to combustible conditions), and materials (e.g., use of fire-retardant materials on cruise ships), to name a few. While it is not feasible or wise to discount the likelihood of any injurious event occurring in a port, the rational planning process that considers probability in the security survey provides for objectivity in the risk management planning process.

4.6 The Quantification of Risk

Once the four components of the security survey have been completed, port management can objectively assess the risks to the port and begin to conceptualize and initiate the FSP. The process is essentially a systematic evaluation of the port's security strengths and weaknesses, measured against identifiable threats, leading to a risk-profile baseline and evaluation as to where the port facility lies in reference to security. Risk assessment is, in some respects, a subjective process, but can be a quantifiable activity if undertaken systematically. Figure 4.4 illustrates the formulaic components of the risk quantification process. Consider the following example within the context of the four-step security survey process:

Identify the Asset. Suppose the port operates a passenger cruise terminal facility. It consists of a terminal building with associated intermodal connections for passenger and baggage movement, processing of ticketed passengers, boarding systems, embarkation processes, docks and associated utility systems, and equipment for provisioning and maintenance. The port identifies the terminal as an essential asset, critical to the port's viability.

Establish Criticality (C). In establishing the criticality (e.g., value, impact, or cost, if lost) of the terminal, for security planning and prioritization purposes, one could estimate the harm on a scale from 0 (*insignificant harm; no impact on port operations*) to 5 (*grave harm; permanent shutdown of port operations*). Consider the scenario of a damaging fire that might cause a shutdown to part of the terminal facility and a significant expenditure of resources to keep at least some of the terminal operations going while repairs are made. In this case, the Criticality (C) factor may be 3 on the scale.

$$R = C \times V \times P$$

Where

R = Risk

C = Criticality

V = Vulnerability

P = Probability

Figure 4.4   Quantification of risk.

Determine Vulnerability (V). Assume the terminal is vulnerable to fire. A numerical rating scale can be constructed that considers both the impact of the harm on the port and the availability of resources in mitigating the fire's impact. For instance, using a scale with values from 0 to 5 (*no impact* to *high impact*), one could estimate the impact of a fire in each of these three areas: human impact (HI), property impact (PI), and business impact (BI). One can also construct a numerical scale with values from 0 to 5 (*none* to *strong*) to consider the strength of both the port's internal resources (IRS) and external resources (ERS). Using these numerical ratings, the most vulnerable areas will be those with the highest total.

$$\text{Vulnerability (V)} = \text{HI} + \text{PI} + \text{BI} + \text{IR} + \text{ER}$$

$$\text{High V} = 25$$

$$\text{Low V} = 0$$

Consider the following scenario: If the terminal fire only destroyed property, with no human impact—that is, no deaths or injuries to people—then the HI value would be none, or 0. There will likely be a business impact due to loss of revenue from use of the terminal, and a property impact due to construction or repair costs; thus, the BI and PI values could both be high, or 5 for each. Next, consider the port's internal and external resources. If internal resources included a well-trained security guard force, with firefighting expertise and capabilities, then the port's IR value might be considered strong, or 1. If the port's external resources were adequate (e.g., a quick, on-port fire department response capability), then the port might calculate a moderate ER value, or 3. Thus, values have been determined to calculate vulnerability for the terminal given a fire threat scenario:

$$V = \text{HI} + \text{PI} + \text{BI} + \text{IR} + \text{ER}$$

$$V = 0 + 5 + 5 + 1 + 3$$

$$V = 14$$

Determine Probability (P). What is the frequency of the threat occurring in the port facility? In other words, in this example, what is the likelihood that a fire will destroy the terminal? There will be a need for some research here to assess this realistically. (For example, records maintained by the port, city, and/or state, or perhaps industry research on ports worldwide, could be reviewed to identify past incidents or trends associated with the particular risk.) Make an educated assessment based on the best data available. Again, construct a scale (see example, Table 4.1) to assess the probability of each threat occurrence. For instance, based on the research, one might assess the likelihood of a terminal fire as occurring once every ten years. Using the scale in Table 4.1, the Probability (P) factor would be very low or 1.

Table 4.1   Probability Scale

PROBABILITY	DEFINITION	SCALE
None	Will never occur ·	0
Very Low	Likely to occur once every 10 years	1
Low	Likely to occur once every 5 years	2
Medium	Likely to occur once every year	3
High	Likely to occur several times each year	4
Extreme	Likely to occur on a regular basis	5

There are now C, V, and P factors to plug into the Risk (R) calculation:

$$R = C \times V \times P$$

Where

$$R = \text{Risk}$$

$$C = 3$$

$$V = 14$$

$$P = 1$$

$$R = 3 \times 14 \times 1$$

$$\mathbf{R = 42}$$

By itself, the R value of 42 is unclear because it must be assessed relative to the port's other identified assets and threat scenarios. In assessing and quantifying risks, the port security manager must employ a comparable methodology assessing all identified assets and considering both physical and human resources. Risk values for individual assets in the port facility can be used to balance each asset against alternative protective measures identified to reduce the port's exposure to various threats and scenarios. Using the terminal fire example above, assume the security plan attempts to mitigate the threat of fire by installing a sprinkler system in the terminal. Objectively, the vulnerability to fire will be reduced because the internal resources are now stronger. The recalculated risk factor would also be reduced. The values become meaningful when they are used as a framework for comparing and prioritizing assets with respect to identified threat scenarios, considering each asset's criticality and vulnerability, and the probability of occurrence.

The risk quantification, of course, can be done using a variety of methodologies as well as sophisticated algorithms and software tools available in the marketplace to the security manager. The above example is intended to illustrate how one can rationally quantify risk and compare alterative security solutions to specific threat environments.

It demonstrates that the port security manger can weigh the pros and cons of alternative security solutions relative to perceived threats, and justify security expenditures to port management, users, and government officials regulating Port FSPs.

4.7 Recommended Resources for Conducting Port Facility Risk/Vulnerability Analyses

4.7.1 FEMA

In providing risk management guidance for building design, FEMA (2003) provides risk managers, facility security managers, architects, and engineers with a practical manual for mitigating terrorist attacks against buildings. Port FSOs can access these and other resources in understanding risk assessment applications for a variety of physical plant configurations.

4.7.2 United States Coast Guard

Part of the compliance activities associated with the MTSA of 2002 requires Port FSOs to complete the Facility Vulnerability and Security Measures Summary, Form CG-6025. This form and the instructions for completion can be found in the unsecured portion of *Homeport*, the U.S. Coast Guard's (2007) Web portal for maritime security, located on the World Wide Web at http://homeport.uscg.mil. In completing this form, the FSO identifies the facility or facilities of responsibility and provides a report of the facility's vulnerabilities and security measures being taken. The U.S. Coast Guard categorizes port facility vulnerabilities into nine basic categories:

1. Physical Security: Physical measures designed to protect people, equipment, installations, and documents against threats associated with terrorism, espionage, sabotage, damage, and theft.
2. Structural Integrity: Design and material characteristics of piers, facilities, and associated structures.
3. Transportation Infrastructure: Other than utilities, infrastructure that may be exploited during an attack scenario.
4. Utilities: Essential equipment and services necessary for port facility operation.
5. Radio and Telecommunications: Measures to protect radio and telecommunication equipment, including computer systems and networks.
6. Personnel Protection Systems: Equipment, gear, or systems designed to protect facility personnel (i.e., weapons, body armor).
7. Procedural Policies: The plans, policies, and procedures for specific port facility operations.
8. Coordination and Information Sharing: The ability of the port to coordinate, receive, and share information with local, state, and federal agencies and commercial organizations.

9. Preparedness: Plans, policies, procedures, training, drills, and exercises conducted to improve security awareness, prevention, and response.

Form CG-6025 also requires the FSO to identify appropriate security measures to be implemented in response to each identified vulnerability. These measures are categorized into twenty-one specific areas: access control, barriers, cargo control, communications, coordination, credentialing, detection, guard force, information technology security, inspections, intelligence, lighting, patrols, planning/policies/procedures, redundancy, response, stand-off distance, structural hardening, surveillance, training, and vessels/vehicles. While completion of Form CG-6025 is a federal statutory requirement, the FSO must broadly consider the concept of vulnerability when assessing risk in preparation for the development of the FSP.

4.7.3 Vulnerability Assessment Methodologies Report

Published in July 2003 by the U.S. DHS are the results of a study that examined and classified various types of vulnerability assessment methodologies that could be used by state and local governments to assess the risk associated with various assets within their areas of responsibility. This document is available on the World Wide Web at http://www.ojp.usdoj.gov/odp/docs/vamreport.pdf.

References

Booz Allen Hamilton. 2005. Convergence of enterprise security organizations. http://www.boozallen.com/media/file/Convergence_of_Enterprise_Security_Organizations_v2.pdf (accessed June 15, 2007).

Broder, James F. 2006. *Risk analysis and the security survey*. Elsevier: London.

Energy Reorganization Act. U.S. Code 10 (1974) 73.1(a).

Federal Emergency Management Agency. 2003. Risk management series, reference manual to mitigate potential terrorist attacks against buildings: Providing protection to people and buildings. FEMA Publication No. 426. Washington, DC: Department of Homeland Security.

Florida Statutes. 2006. Seaport security standards. Section 311.12(2)(a). http://www.leg.state.fl.us/statutes/index.cfm?App_mode=Display_Statute&Search_String=&URL=Ch0311/SEC12.HTM&Title=-%3E2006-%3ECh0311-%3ESection%2012#0311.12 (accessed June 5, 2007).

Fryer, A. 2003, August 5. Terror experts doing the math to assess risks. *Seattle Times*. International Security and Counter Terrorism Reference Center Database (accessed January 5, 2007).

Government Accountability Office. 2007. Port risk management: Additional federal guidance would aid ports in disaster planning and recovery. http://www.gao.gov/new.items/d07412.pdf (accessed July 6, 2007).

Government Accountability Office. 2008. Highlights of a GAO forum: Strengthening the use of risk management principles in homeland security. http://www.gao.gov/highlights/d08627sphigh.pdf (accessed April 24, 2008).

Haimes, Y.Y., and Barry M. Horowitz. 2004. Adaptive two-player hierarchical holographic modeling game for counterterrorism intelligence analysis. *Journal of Homeland Security and Emergency Management* 1(3): Article 302. http://www.bepress.com/jhsem/vol1/iss3/302 (accessed July 14, 2007).

Haimes, Y.Y., and T. Longstaff. 2002. The role of risk analysis in the protection of critical infrastructures against terrorism. *Risk Analysis: An International Journal* 22: 439–444.

Insurance Information Institute. 2007. Catastrophe modeling. http://www.iii.org/media/hottopics/additional/catmodeling/ (accessed June 20, 2007).

International Maritime Organization. 2004. International ship and port facility security code. http://www.imo.org/TCD/mainframe.asp?topic_id=897 (accessed May 7, 2008).

Maritime Transportation Security Act. 2002. Public Law 107–295. http://www.tsa.gov/assets/pdf/MTSA.pdf (accessed May 7, 2008).

McEntire, David A. 2009. *Introduction to homeland security: Understanding terrorism with an emergency management perspective.* New York: John Wiley & Sons, Inc.

Mintzberg, Henry, and James Bryan Quinn. 1992. *The strategy process: Concepts and contexts.* Englewood Cliffs, NJ: Prentice Hall.

Moteff, J. 2004. Risk management and critical infrastructure protection: Assessing, integrating, and managing threats, vulnerabilities and consequences. *Congressional Research Service.* Report No. RL32561. International Security and Counter Terrorism Reference Center Database (accessed January 8, 2007).

Tuckey, S. 2005. Terrorism models help, but only go so far: Underwriters eager to avoid large concentrations of risk in case a terrorist strikes. *National Underwriter Property and Casualty* 109:17.

U.S. Coast Guard. 2007. Facility vulnerabilities and security measures summary form CG-6025 and form CG-6025 instructions. http://homeport.uscg.mil/mycg/portal/ep/contentView.do?contentTypeId=2&channelId=-18386&contentId=16686&programId=13136&programPage=%2Fep%2Fprogram%2Feditorial.jsp&pageTypeId=13489&BV_SessionID=@@@@1078315427.1182372934@@@@&BV_EngineID=cccfaddkmhlflikcfjgcfgfdffhdghl.0 (accessed June 20, 2007).

U.S. Department of Transportation, Maritime Administration. 2008, May. U.S. water transportation statistical snapshot. http://www.marad.dot.gov/documents/US_Water_Transportation_Statistical_snapshot.pdf (accessed January 4, 2009).

U.S. Nuclear Regulatory Commission. 2007. Design-basis threat. http://www.nrc.gov/reading-rm/basic-ref/glossary/design-basis-threat.html (accessed June 20, 2007).

White House. 2005. National strategy for maritime security. http://www.whitehouse.gov/homeland/maritime-security.html (accessed January 5, 2007).

5

PORT FACILITY SECURITY AS A MANAGEMENT FUNCTION

As illustrated in Figure 5.1, port operations may present complex questions and concerns for security planners and managers. In this instance, shrink-wrapped, break-bulk cargo is being staged on this port's wharf prior to vessel loading. In many ports, cargo terminal operators lease facilities and/or equipment from the port administration. Has the terminal operator implemented the recommended and required security precautions with respect to the staging of this cargo? What is under the shrink-wrap? Is the port's FSO working with cargo terminal managers to ensure that all government regulations related to securing this cargo are being followed? Have the security risks to the port been assessed with respect to the staging of this cargo? Developing an understanding of the risks and planning security in a port facility entails consideration of three essential management issues:

1. How can the security organization engage the cooperation of the port's internal and external clients and stakeholders to effect protection of the port facility?
2. How can port security management identify and develop problem-solving strategies and plans to address the risks of terrorism, general criminal activity, and threats to safety in the port?
3. What management approaches can be developed or adapted in structuring security plans and mitigating these threats?

5.1 The Acts and Functions of Management

5.1.1 Organizational Behavior and Organizational Theory

Understanding the acts and functions of port security management begins with understanding what people actually do in organizations. This can be approached in two ways. First, we can understand organizational life from the perspective of the behavior of the people who comprise its essential elements. In this microanalaytic view, we are interested in the behavior of people as they interact in organizations. Hence, the term *organizational behavior* refers to the study of how people, individuals, and groups perform essential tasks in organizations. This sort of study uses a systems approach in understanding the relationships between people and organizations by focusing on essential behaviors, attitudes, and performances (Vasu, Stewart, and Garson 1998). For example, a humanistic approach to leadership proposes that workers in structured

Figure 5.1 Break-bulk cargo staged for vessel loading.

organizations can be enabled to fulfill their own needs in furtherance of the organizational mission. Security departments, like law enforcement agencies, are often patterned after military organizations. Quasi-military organizations traditionally have been highly structured and controlled but usually employ people with an intrinsic motivation toward service. Leaders in service-providing organizations can be either catalysts for success or obstacles to effectiveness. A crucial responsibility for security agencies is the identification and development of leadership and management behaviors such that subordinates in the organization can be included in decision-making processes in the accomplishment of organizational goals and objectives. Thus, studying interactions in security organizations between managers and employees that lead to productive outcomes helps in understanding different approaches to similar tasks.

Because ports must remain responsive to the changing complexion of the maritime industry, there is always a need for port leadership to identify and manage constraints impeding productivity. Often times, port management and staff may have become complacent with doing things the way they have always been done. With an enhanced homeland security emphasis on securing maritime assets and infrastructure, port leadership may have to reject old conventions for security management and embrace new ideas and technologies to enable convergent practices to surface in mitigating risk. Thus, the first way to approach port security management is by understanding the components of productive organizational behavior, which necessarily proceeds from the human resource management function.

A second way of understanding port security management is by studying *organizational theory*. In this macroanaylytical approach, we are interested in describing, comparing, and evaluating organizations at the macro level of analysis. A theory is a coherent set of interrelated definitions or propositions, presenting a systematic view of an event or phenomenon with the objective of explaining and predicting that event or phenomenon. Organizational theory is a field of study that seeks to provide a framework for understanding and predicting organizational outcomes. So, we can examine the Theory of Scientific Management, or Human Relations Theory, and so forth as ways of applying management practices in different settings to positively affect the productivity equation. We study organizational outcomes in terms of the application of different management theories to see which one, or which combination, produces the desired outcomes.

The modern movement toward scientific management principles and assertive control over worker behavior was preceded by nineteenth century craftsmen who exerted control and influence over their own operations due to their unique knowledge and skills. The basis of this approach is that management introduces catalysts into the organization, such as specific training or directives, to obtain the highest productivity from the employee. The theory asserts that the combination of worker initiative and management activity, such as directing employee tasks, results in maximum output and prosperity for both the organization and the worker. Scientific management approaches contributed to organizational efficiency by maintaining wages at proper levels, screening job applicants, handling grievances, dealing with unions, and meeting employees' needs. This was the foundation that led to the development of bureaucracies and administrative processes that we understand as machine models of organizations. In the first quarter of the twentieth century, however, the movement toward more worker participation in decision making began to develop as an organizational construct. Human relations management theories advance the notion that individual motives, goals, and aspirations, which have no role in traditional bureaucratic or scientific management models, are placed at the center of the organization. Organizational success is conditioned upon individual motivation and interpersonal relationships, especially the relationship between supervisor and subordinate. Employee participation was one device which came to be seen as a method of motivating workers and developing their sense of purpose in organizations. The spread of human relations approaches to management called for a mix of diagnostic and interpersonal skills for managers to deal with human conflict. Likert (1967) described three basic concepts underlying a theory of participation in management that illustrates a macroanalytical, theoretical approach that can be used in understanding port security management:

> *Principle of supportive relationships.* The relationship between the supervisor and the subordinate is supportive in that the supervisor considers the background,

values, and expectations of the subordinate. By doing so, leaders develop organizational processes that build on individuals' sense of personal worth and importance. A security manager's ability to engage his/her employees in identifying security risks and contributing to security planning is founded upon relationships with employees who value their participation and engagement.

Group decision making and group methods of supervision. Interaction among organizational members is overlapping. In a participative management approach, all subordinates who are affected by a decision's outcome are involved in it. There is substantial confidence and trust, with clear communications and an emphasis on high productivity. "The group's capacity for effective problem solving is maintained by examining and dealing with group processes when necessary. The superior is accountable for all decisions, for their execution, and for the results" (Likert 1967, p. 51). Similarly in port security organizations, the ability to engage the workforce collectively in problem solving will be a significant asset to an organization focused on responding holistically to evolving security problems. It is not unusual in twenty-four-hour security operations for various employees and units to experience problems in one area that are also being felt in other areas. Management's development of processes, such as regular staff meetings and communications vehicles, will advance group processes for problem solving.

High-performance goals for the organization. Participative approaches to management are a means for organization members to set high-performance goals that satisfy their own motivational needs. This represents an optimization of the integration of organizational goals and individual needs and desires. By providing employees with pride in their own work, job security, adequate compensation, and promotional opportunities, organizations can succeed and grow. High-performance goals must not be imposed but must be desired by both supervisors and subordinates. Participative and group decision making is the structure that allows for this growth. In law enforcement, research has shown that police chiefs support shared decision making and greater involvement of line officers in decision making (Hoover and Mader 1990). As many security structures follow law enforcement administration models, the capacity for developing high-performance goals in security organizations is thus viewed as logical and desirable.

5.1.2 A Problem-Solving Approach to Port Security Management:
Lessons from the Police Experience

In an evolving security and risk environment, security administrators and managers cannot simply rely on traditional incident-driven approaches to threat mitigation. As we have observed, concerns about threats to the maritime and port sectors of transportation have risen considerably within the past several years. The threat environment is such that it would border on negligence for port security officials to rely on management practices that trend toward response and reaction as opposed to aggressive planning for problem identification and resolution before events occur. In law enforcement, police agencies have traditionally used an incident-driven approach in which contact with the public is primarily reactive in response to observed criminal behavior and calls for service. In this mode, organizational management and decision-making are typically conducted from the top down, with leadership being provided in a traditionally autocratic style. A movement toward problem-oriented policing, a strategy in which police officers are involved more proactively in problem identification, solutions, and organizational decision mak-ing, has challenged police administrators to trade the autocratic approach to leader-ship for a more participative style, which encourages shared decision making at all organizational levels.

Between 1931 and 1973, five national commissions identified the lack of leader-ship as a central problem facing police departments (Pursley 1974). The autocratic leadership styles of many police leaders do not fit the problem-solving role needed to deal with crime trends (Enter 1991). Today's police chiefs have demonstrated support for shared decision making and greater involvement of line officers in organizational processes (Hoover and Mader 1990). In one specific case, Gray, Stohr-Gillmore, and Lovrich (1991) documented the Washington State Patrol's efforts to modify its tradi-tional control-oriented organizational structure by implementing a participative man-agement program called TEAMS.

> TEAMS evolved from a traffic management productivity model to a comprehensive man-agement philosophy, one in which decision-making authority is delegated to lower-level units closest to the problems to be faced, and in which those units are employing an interac-tive group problem-solving approach to organizational and operational problems all the way from the work unit level up through the entire chain of command (Gray, Stohr-Gillmore, and Lovrich 1991, p. 29).

The authors traced the development of this participative management philosophy from the historical perspective that most formal police organizational structures have developed along paramilitary lines. They documented the history of the Washington State Patrol, noting how the agency has been challenged to provide higher levels of service to a growing population. Concurrent with this growth, its police officers matured organizationally, with higher levels of education and a need for greater input into the department's operations. The participative management model adopted by the Washington State Patrol was developed to give officers more operational autonomy. "Emphasis was placed on the personal and team responsibility for the implementation of the problem solutions devised. . ." (Gray, Stohr-Gillmore, and Lovrich 1991, p. 41).

Given the challenges faced by security organizations charged with developing new organizational processes to function in a terrorism-driven risk environment, perhaps a similar participative leadership modality and problem-oriented approaches to security planning can be adapted in ports from the experiences of law enforcement. The identification and development of leaders able to operate confidently in a dynamic, problem-solving management environment require an understanding of antecedents that relate to a leader's disposition toward participative leadership behavior. Participative leadership is a humanistic approach to organizational control and direction that theorizes that leaders are change agents who have the ability to motivate subordinates to perform well by helping them to satisfy their own psychological needs. By enabling organizational members to fulfill their own needs, participative leaders can provide an environment in which followers have the freedom to make decisions.

5.1.3 What Managers Do in Organizations

Problem-solving strategies are required to respond to constraints that develop in security management. Managers in organizations tasked with developing response mechanisms to homeland security and terrorism preparedness policies must draw from resources, often limited, in crafting plans and solutions. These must both make sense from a risk management perspective and be cost-efficient as a business management function. Port security managers must focus on the essential acts and functions that collectively operate to develop the problem-solving capabilities of the staff. One useful construct, which has a long history in the management literature, is POSDCORB (Gulick and Urwick 1937). POSDCORB is an acronym that calls attention to the various functional elements of the work of a supervisor or manager. It stands for the following activities:

- Planning: Working out in broad outline the things that need to be done and the methods for doing them to accomplish the purpose of the organization. Fundamentally, in the port environment, the planning function will be considerable as the development and maintenance of a Port FSP will be a predominant activity. The FSP both addresses the port's general and specific risks and complies with prevailing governmental regulations. Beyond this, security managers must develop both long-range strategic plans that consider the port's current and future business goals and short-term tactical plans to manage special events, staff limitations, and daily operations in the port.
- Organizing: The establishment of the formal structure of authority through which work subdivisions are arranged, defined, and coordinated for the specified objective. Port security managers have the challenge of making decisions as to how the security organization itself will be structured and how that structure will integrate with the larger port management system. Organizational structure, operations and training schedules, cash management activities, credentialing processes, and office administration are examples of some of the activities that require organizational skills in port security.

- Staffing: The personnel function of bringing in and training the staff and maintaining favorable conditions of work. Major decisions in security staffing will consider whether port security will be proprietary, contracted, or a hybrid of both; what roles law enforcement agencies will play in the port's security functions; what job tasks, job specifications, and job classifications will be required to implement security plans; and what combinations of management education and experience will best serve the needs of the port community.
- Directing: The task of making decisions and embodying them in specific and general orders and instructions. This includes the development of standard operating procedures necessary to implement the Port FSP, as well as specific post orders, supervisory guidelines, administrative orders, and directives that are necessary to guide staff in the performance of their functions.
- Coordinating: Interrelating the various parts of the work. Identifying and maintaining effective coordinating roles in port security will be essential in strengthening partnerships and relationships to ensure the agreement of operating plans and security procedures of the various port entities. Processes such as communications and systems development will be driven by the port security manager's ability to coordinate among the diverse functions of port operations.
- Reporting: Keeping informed as to what is going on through reports, records, research, and inspections. Many managers fail to appreciate the value of reporting mechanisms that provide the data and information necessary for effective decision making. Incident reports, daily activity reports, statistical compilations, and a host of operational and systems data-gathering instruments provide the basic tools for management's understanding of the variances within organizations. Managers who are attuned to changes in variance, for example a spike in the number of security breaches or an increase in employee-involved traffic crashes, prepare themselves for responding to operational issues requiring intervention and assertive strategies that work to reduce the chances of future problems.
- Budgeting: Fiscal planning, accounting, and control. A budget is essentially a work plan with money attached to it. It is the mechanism by which organizations identify what will be needed to implement its plans and achieve its missions. The ability to plan efficiently for the human and physical resources that will be needed to implement Port FSPs will reflect a manager's business acumen and organizational abilities.

These management functions must be brought to bear in conducting a needs assessment of organizational changes required to meet goals and objectives in the port security environment. As public policy is developed to prioritize homeland security issues, port security administrators must be cognizant of developing staff and organizational capabilities for compliance, not to mention addressing the security risks in the port. In a recent Police Executive Research Forum study of best practices in port security, Pate, Taylor, and Kubu (2007) keyed in on the crucial role managers play in the effective development of port security protocols and programs.

Key ingredients for successful security operations relate to port leadership, funding/resources, organizational structures that integrate security into key operational aspects of the port, communication systems and information sharing, qualified professional staff, training, teamwork, and clarity of mission. Other important features of port security operations include the use of incident management systems, attention to communications interoperability, public/media relations, written policies, plans and procedures, and mutual aid agreements (Pate, Taylor, and Kubu 2007, p. 18).

Clearly, port security managers must be cognizant of determining how they can best meet the operational and security needs of the port's clients. In this regard, the role of leaders in establishing the culture and framework for security is essential. In a recent interview, Natalie Givens, a vice president with the global security consulting firm Booz Allen Hamilton, suggested that organizational leadership is essential in ensuring that security policies support a culture of security. "The first thing the senior leaders of any organization should do is publicly embrace and advocate security. . . An organization's leaders need to ensure that there is accountability, a way to link stakeholders' incentives to the desired level of security maturity" (Jackson 2008, p. 3). The development of a problem-solving security organization, using strategies designed to engage port staff, necessary external specialists, and participating government agencies, will work positively to mitigate new risks facing ports in the homeland security environment.

5.2 Port Security Planning

Security planning in port organizations must proceed from the three following fundamental perspectives.

5.2.1 Design and Architecture Stage

While it may not be possible for many port organizations to initiate a security program from scratch, a best-practice approach to security truly suggests that security planning for facilities should occur during the initial stages of design. A port is a dynamic environment of development. The maritime industry is driven by new ship designs, capacities, and responsiveness to markets. For example, passenger cruise lines, which have seen unprecedented growth within the past twenty years, are building larger, faster ships, which will require more dock space, deeper channels, and larger terminals. Some cruise lines are operating in ports that have not previously served the passenger cruise market. Port infrastructures will have to accommodate cruise lines' needs with increases in road capacity, provisions deliveries, utilities availability, customs inspection stations, and so forth. As ports work to redevelop their

Figure 5.2   Truck and cargo inspection facility. Will this provide effective port security and capacity in three, five, or ten years?

capacities, new and redesigned facilities will require important security provisions, such as closed-circuit television, access control systems, secure buffer zones, and alarm monitoring capabilities. Figure 5.2 illustrates a port's truck and cargo inspection station that may be barely adequate to handle the volume and type of cargo coming into the port. How will it adapt to changing market conditions, higher threat levels, and increased traffic volumes? As security technology becomes more available and adaptable in diverse operating environments, will security considerations be included in plans for the expansion of this inspection function? Network architecture—incorporating state-of-the-art technology, such as fiber optics, is best built-in to facilities as they are developed rather than after construction is completed. To the extent that security infrastructure needs are planned for and accommodated during the design and architecture stages, it will be less likely that security managers will have to advocate for changes that may require costly retrofitting in the future.

5.2.2 Focus on Integration and Cooperation

When all interested parties to an organizational system can both understand and concur in the mission and strategy for accomplishment, there is less likelihood that conflicts will surface to obstruct progress. This is not to suggest that there will not be disagreements and suggestions for change. In fact, most leaders in organizations will welcome and invite discourse that surfaces to identify competing agendas and reservations that, if hidden, work behind the scenes to the detriment of the organization. Another best practice for security planning is to focus on methods and tactics wherein all parties in the process perceive their input as valued and desired. Both individually and in groups, security managers should be assertively working to obtain users' concerns, answer their questions, and solicit their suggestions as plans are developed and refined to address specific and general security risks in the port. Basic aspects of physical security planning, such as the placement of fences, gates, and access controls, should be occasions for consulting with end users as to the efficacy of the mitigation and understanding to what extent it might adversely affect user operations within the port. Even basic facility considerations, such as restrictions on parking and vehicle movement (see Figure 5.3), deserve resolution as part of collaborative activities versus administrative fiat. By working to resolve conflicting interests and engaging the cooperation of port users in planning activities, the port security manager will make strides in achieving efficiencies in security planning management.

5.2.3 Minimize "Fortress Mentality"

A fortress, using a military understanding of the term, is a facility specially designed to protect the inhabitants from attack. Historically, fortresses were built using specific

Figure 5.3 Parking restrictions may be a source of conflict for port users competing for space in the limited geographical confines of some port facilities.

defenses, such as high walls and moats, to deter an attacking army from invading the safety of the protected space. As weapons and armies became more sophisticated, the ability of a nation's fortresses to withstand invasion diminished. The term *fortress mentality*, from a security planning perspective, refers to an approach that tries to effect security precautions without considering their costs or effects on organizational productivity (Schultz and Shumway 2001, p. 14). Consider the challenges facing an urban police chief. Crime may go up in certain neighborhoods but remain static in others. The citizens in the neighborhoods where more crime is occurring may clamor for more police officers. Should the chief shift officers from the more stable neighborhoods to the high-crime areas? Perhaps a police officer on every block in the high-crime neighborhood will have a positive effect. But what would be the effect of removing officers from the others? Is it a realistic solution to build the "police fortress" in the high-crime areas at the expense of other citizens and residents of the city? Similarly, in port security planning, managers must weigh the effective costs of security on the entire organization. It may be a simple solution to respond to a growing threat that a terrorist group might deploy a chemical weapon of mass destruction in an attack on a port. Does this mean that the port should search every person, every vehicle, and every container that comes into the port? What impact will this have on operations? The challenge for managers in port security planning will be to trade the fortress mentality for one that balances security with commerce. There is no suggestion here that security risks should be ignored in favor of a "business at all costs" mentality. Rather, the balancing of commercial activities with sensible security precautions demands that security managers remain highly attuned and responsive to the security risk environment and work to implement mitigation efforts that can be quickly implemented or scaled back in direct response to the nature and levels of the threats being faced by the port.

5.3 Developing a Port FSP

A port facility is required to plan and effect security at the levels identified in the risk assessment process and as established by the governmental entities with statutory responsibilities for port security oversight. Security measures and procedures should be developed and applied in a way that minimizes inconvenience with or delay to passengers, ships, goods, and services. Ports operate within a complex intermodal transport system, and weak linkages between components equates to higher vulnerability. Port security is impacted by the actions of many organizations. If intelligence sharing is inadequate, port security may not be well informed about the threats they face. As the term *security* means different things to different people in different environments, it is important for those responsible for port security planning to work constructively within the organization to develop a Port FSP upon which all stakeholders have buy-in and concurrence.

Prior to the implementation of the globe-spanning International Ship and Port Facility Security Code, and the enactment of the MTSA in the United States, recognized standards for port facility security did not have a defined scope. For the purposes of creating a security plan at the port facility, a working understanding of security should consist of measures aimed at the following:

- Neutralizing vulnerabilities for criminal activity within the port
- Identifying and responding to safety issues
- Minimizing the threat of terrorism
- Reducing opportunities for internal criminal conspiracies
- Disrupting links between corruption, terrorism, and organized crime
- Sharing intelligence and investigative information with appropriate law enforcement agencies
- Promoting opportunities for the exchange of best practices in port security

The impetus for this framework has been the considerable public policy and industry response to enhance port facility security across the diverse sectors of the maritime domain.

5.3.1 Planning a Layered Approach to Security

Developing a layered approach to security means using a variety of tools that, when combined, provide a strong defense against terrorism, crime, and other identified risks. The concept of a *force multiplier* is useful for port security managers in planning a layered approach to security. Force multipliers are added organizational devices or capabilities that improve the chances of mission success. In and of themselves, diverse security activities, such as checking identification credentials or patrolling the navigational channels of a port, may not be effective mitigation strategies for particular security risks. But, when the managers plans activities in concert with one another, as a strategy in managing specific risks, these seemingly diverse activities may significantly increase the threat-reduction potential of the strategy and enhance the safety and security of the environment. Port security is therefore enhanced through the development of multiple security systems and processes. A layered approach to security refers to the implementation of a variety of security tools to build an interconnected security program. As organizations change, the development of a security network, one in which the security and enforcement activities of internal and external agencies are planned and coordinated, provides strength. Physical security measures, combined with access controls, present a multidimensional security barrier. The intention is that if one layer of security fails to detect an unwanted threat, another layer will work to identify and neutralize the threat. Consider the following security and law enforcement activities and scenarios likely occurring in any one major seaport. What is the potential for layering and overlapping port security responsibilities?

- The port authority employs a proprietary security guard force responsible for port access control, identification and credentialing, and the screening of vehicles and personnel entering port restricted access areas. Security officers are assigned to protect port property and ensure the safety of people at the port. Duties include patrolling port property on foot and by vehicle to prevent theft, pilferage, vandalism, fire, trespassing, accidents, property damage, and misuse and abuse of equipment, and to ensure the safety of patrons and employees.

- The local police department is responsible for providing police patrol, law enforcement, and criminal investigations of state and local crimes occurring within the port's jurisdiction. It delivers line and staff police services to the port community, including patrol and observation; enforcement of criminal, traffic, and parking laws; response to calls for service; investigation of observed and reported criminal activity; and traffic crash investigation.

- The primary port users (passenger cruise lines, cargo terminals, ferry operators, miscellaneous port tenants, etc.) employ their own contracted or proprietary security services to provide leasehold, terminal, and/or vessel security in compliance with government regulations and/or internal business operating procedures. These security services also provide security patrols, access controls, and protective services for the property and personnel transiting their facilities.

- The U.S. DHS has agencies within its organization responsible for diverse activities that occur in the port. The U.S. Coast Guard, in addition to its traditional mission of providing for maritime safety, has renewed and enhanced responsibilities for maritime security and national defense, which include a comprehensive role in assessing security risks to ports and ensuring they have adequate and reliable Port FSPs as part of the NSMS. The U.S. Customs and Border Protection has a significant presence in the port and a mission to keep terrorists and weapons of mass destruction out of the United States. It is also primarily responsible for securing and facilitating trade and travel while enforcing U.S. laws related to immigration and narcotics.

- In addition, there are any number of local, state, and federal government agencies with diverse responsibilities in many economic areas, such as the safety of commercial transportation, law enforcement, and industrial safety, that may have a presence on the port in performing their various missions.

- Private organizations operating within port facilities have personnel and assets deployed in carrying out a variety of missions and activities. Harbor and waterway pilot boats, such as the one in Figure 5.4, regularly transit port waters. Assets such as these are in an ideal position to observe and report suspicious people, vessels, and activity.

Considering the number and variety of public and private agency resources available, the port security manager may be able to identify many opportunities for developing

Figure 5.4   Harbor and waterway pilots have a unique observational perspective on port activities and can be a component of a port facility's layered security strategy.

layered security applications and partnerships. While this ability to bridge overlapping security missions may be limited by statutory provisions, political concerns, business operations, and funding issues, the truth is that effective management proceeds from coordinating available resources to best achieve mission success.

5.4 Port Management in a Homeland Security Environment

The enhanced emphasis on critical infrastructure security that has developed in the post-September 11 homeland security environment will continue to affect all aspects of port security management and planning. While working toward achieving full compliance with all government-mandated security regulations, the security manager must continue to integrate security planning with port operations, which may require significant investment and expansion of capital infrastructure to facilitate. Port interfaces with national and international port facility security requirements may be heavily driven by compliance with regulations and require significant expenses for resources in terms of documentation, correspondence, personnel, and training. Many operational needs of the port may be driven by concerns over security. For example, a cargo terminal operator may need to shift cargo operations from one wharf to another to accommodate various sizes of vessels or to access specialized loading or moving equipment. These shifts may not be possible until the regulatory and enforcement agencies with responsibilities for oversight of port security are convinced that security in the shifted operations is compliant with existing laws and regulations and can effectively mitigate any risks to the port, vessels, and crews. The writing and submittal of Port FSPs and amendments, which may be heavily bureaucratic in some jurisdictions, with threats of penalties for noncompliance, places burdens on port facilities to coordinate all of the tenants' activities. In some cases, obtaining tenant compliance with security plans and procedures may require changes to local ordinances, tariffs, and leases. This may not be a simple process.

Port management in a homeland security environment should have one constant: uncertainty is the norm. In this respect, strategic foresight and planning are key in achievement of objectives. Security infrastructure improvements for homeland security may include portwide access controls, development of protected buffer zones to protect terminals and other public facilities, designation of restricted access areas, complex surveillance and detection capabilities, as well as other safety and deterrent measures and enhancements. These changes and improvements may require significant increases in security costs, which may be a difficult pill for port management to swallow. In the United States, the public policy driving port-related homeland security enhancements has been quite comprehensive. Port leadership has had to develop fundamental understandings of a number of major pieces of legislation at the federal level.

5.4.1 Homeland Security Act of 2002

In the aftermath of September 11, the DHS was established as a cabinet-level agency of the U.S. government with primary responsibility for protecting against terrorist attacks and responding to natural disasters. With two hundred thousand employees, DHS is not as large as the Department of Defense, but in terms of its scope of operations and responsibilities, it represents the most complex government agency created in the United States within the past fifty years or so. DHS consolidated the operations of twenty-two federal agencies under one comprehensive organizational structure. Agencies as diverse as the U.S. Coast Guard (from the Department of Transportation), the U.S. Customs Service (from the Department of Treasury), and the Immigration and Naturalization Service (from the Department of Justice) were reorganized and realigned into a single department as part of the national strategy for homeland security. Evidence of how much the security field has changed can be seen from the Homeland Security Advisory System, a color-coded terrorism threat advisory scale developed by DHS soon after September 11, 2001, as a means of alerting the public to changes in the terrorism threat level. Each level is represented by a different color. The different levels trigger specific actions by federal agencies and state and local governments, and they affect the level of security in any number of public facilities and industrial sectors. Interestingly, the threat level may be different for different sectors. The government realized there was a need to develop specificity with respect to applications of threat levels, because raising the threat level from, say, elevated to high in all sectors may trigger security plans that are very costly and perhaps unnecessary (i.e., deployment of more police officers may incur extreme amounts of overtime pay).

5.4.2 Homeland Security Presidential Directives

In 2003, President George W. Bush issued two significant Homeland Security Presidential Directives (HSPDs), which provided strategic direction for U.S. government agencies coping with renewed emphases on the protection of infrastructure and security planning in a terrorism-risk environment. HSPD-7, *Critical Infrastructure Identification, Prioritization, and Protection*, established a national policy requiring agencies of the federal government to identify and prioritize critical infrastructure and resources for protection from terrorist attacks. The foundation for this policy direction is defining critical infrastructure as that being "so vital that its incapacitation, exploitation, or destruction, through terrorist attack, could have a debilitating effect on security and economic well-being." Certainly this includes ports and related maritime transportation assets, which are vital to national security and the national economy. In implementing this policy, federal agencies are required to work with state and local governments and the private sector (White House 2003a). The second directive, HSPD-8, *National Preparedness*, addressed policies designed to strengthen U.S. preparedness in preventing and responding to domestic terrorist attacks, major disasters, and other emergencies. The foundation for this policy is an all-hazards preparedness mentality, which establishes mechanisms and action plans for assistance to state and local governments (White House 2003b).

5.4.3 MTSA of 2002

Signed on November 25, 2002, the Maritime Transportation Security Act (MTSA) is designed to protect the nation's ports and waterways from a terrorist attack. The MTSA elements of fundamental concern to port security managers are embodied in Title 33, Code of Federal Regulations, Part 105 (33 CFR 105). It is the U.S. equivalent of the ISPS Code and requires vessels and port facilities to conduct vulnerability assessments and develop security plans that may include passenger, vehicle, and baggage screening procedures; security patrols; establishing restricted areas; personnel identification procedures; access control measures; and/or installation of surveillance equipment. The U.S. Coast Guard, the responsible federal agency for verifying that port facilities comply with regulations issued under MTSA, publishes a development guide for owners or operators of port facilities. Port owners and operators in the United States are required to develop and submit a Port FSP to the U.S. Coast Guard Captain of the Port (COTP) for the area in which the port is located.

5.4.4 Navigation and Vessel Inspection Circulars

The U.S. Coast Guard publishes Navigation and Vessel Inspection Circulars, otherwise known as NVICs, which provide detailed guidance about enforcement of or compliance with certain federal marine safety regulations and U.S. Coast Guard marine safety programs. NVICs do not have the force of law but do assist organizations in complying with laws under the Coast Guard's jurisdiction. Noncompliance with an NVIC is not a violation of law but may be interpreted as an indication of noncompliance with a law, regulation, or policy. In developing the Port FSP required by MTSA, NVIC 03-03, entitled *Implementation Guidance for the Regulations Mandated by the Maritime Transportation Security Act of 2002 for Facilities*, is especially useful in identifying those portions of the plan that the U.S. Coast Guard will be particularly concerned about. NVIC 03-03 contains a review checklist for the Port FSP. This is the same checklist that will be utilized by Coast Guard personnel when conducting reviews and inspections of the port facility for compliance with Code of Federal Regulations, Title 33, Part 105 (33 CFR 105). The checklist items are summarized in Figure 5.5.

5.4.5 SAFE Port Act

Signed into law in 2006, the Security and Accountability for Every Port Act of 2006 (SAFE Port Act) enacted requirements relating to maritime FSPs. Of significance to port facility security planning, the legislation requires the following:

- One hundred percent scanning of imported containers for radiation
- Allocation of risk-based funding through grants to help U.S. ports secure against terrorist attacks
- Establishment of joint operations centers at ports to integrate local, private-sector companies and state and federal partners for a unified event response
- DHS to create protocols for operations after a transportation incident
- DHS to conduct and assess security measures in foreign ports
- Unannounced inspections of maritime facilities
- Verification of the effectiveness of FSPs at least twice a year
- Transportation security cards not issued to people convicted of certain felonies (U.S. Congress 2006)

5.5 Developing Security Partnerships

Port security is not the responsibility of any one person, agency, or entity. The responsibility must be shared among all port stakeholders. Each individual's participation in the security program is important, but most critically, port administration must look for ways to educate and inform stakeholders of the importance of their respective roles. Responsibility must be shared among those having an interest in efficient

Facility Security Plan Content Requirements

- Does the plan follow the order as it appears below?
- If no, does the plan contain an index identifying the required elements and their location?

1. Security administration and organization of the facility
   - Does the plan contain a security organization?

2. Personnel training
   - Does the plan contain personnel training procedures?

3. Drills and exercises
   - Does the plan contain drill and exercise procedures?

4. Records and documentation
   - Does the plan contain facility recordkeeping and documentation procedures?

5. Response to change in MARSEC (Maritime Security) Level
   - Does the plan contain procedures for responding to MARSEC Level changes?

6. Procedures for interfacing with vessels
   - Does the plan contain procedures for interfacing with vessels?

7. Declaration of Security (DoS)
   - Does the plan identify DoS procedures?

8. Communications
   - Does the plan contain communication procedures?

9. Security systems and equipment maintenance
   - Does the plan contain security systems and equipment maintenance procedures?

10. Security measures for access control, including designated public access areas
    - Does the plan contain security measures for access control?

11. Security measures for restricted areas
    - Does the plan contain security measures for restricted areas?

12. Security measures for handling cargo
    - Does the plan identify security measures for handling cargo?

Figure 5.5   Port Facility Security Plan Checklist.

Facility Security Plan Content Requirements

13. Security measures for delivery of vessel stores and bunkers
   - Does the plan address the security procedures for delivery of vessel stores and bunkers?

14. Security measures for monitoring
   - Does the plan identify security measures for monitoring?

15. Security incident procedures
   - Does the plan contain security incident procedures?

16. Audits and security plan amendments
   - Does the plan contain procedures for auditing and updating the plan?

17. Facility Security Assessment (FSA) report
   - Does the plan contain an FSA report?

18. Facility Vulnerability and Security Measures Summary (Form CG-6025)
   - Does the plan contain a completed CG-6025 form?

Source: U.S. Coast Guard. Navigation and Vessel Inspection Circular No. 03-03, Implementation Guidance for the Regulations Mandated by the Maritime Transportation Security Act of 2002 (MTSA) for Facilities.

Figure 5.5   (continued)

and effective port operations. The cruise and cargo ship industries, maritime energy distribution systems, and entities with a role in ship and port operations represent significant stakeholders with a valuable role to play in port security. Seaports must coordinate and integrate each stakeholder's role to optimize the port's security posture. Without systemic efforts to coordinate and integrate each stakeholder's role, the port's security posture will not be optimized.

Ports must develop partnerships to protect against security threats. Working cooperatively with stakeholders and appropriate governments and governmental agencies, seaports can tap into and use the combined resources of many organizations to improve intelligence gathering, threat assessments, risk-based decision making, and response planning.

Some of the stakeholders and agencies that can be part of this partnership include the following:

- Federal Government: This includes DHS, Coast Guard, Customs and Border Protection, Immigration, and Customs Enforcement.

- State and Local Police: Law enforcement agencies play a critical role in seaport security by providing an enforcement component for state and local laws and by providing a criminal intelligence gathering capability.
- Transportation Regulatory Agencies: Seaports work within multiple intermodal transportation networks. Government agencies regulate many sectors of this industry, such as railroads, highways, bridges, locks, dams, and trucking. All of these elements have an important role in working with seaports with their security plans and strategies.
- Harbor and Waterway Pilots: Harbor pilots are responsible for guiding large ocean-going vessels in and out of seaport waters. They play an important role in the operations of seaports and must be a partner in the overall seaport security program.
- Terminal Operators: Cargo terminal operators are one of the key reasons that a port can exist. Terminal operators manage the port facilities responsible for receiving, delivering, and transferring cargo coming into and going out of seaports. Their cooperation and participation in security management is crucial to ensuring that a cooperative strategy is implemented.
- Stevedores: A stevedore is the organization used by a vessel operator to determine the method cargo is to be loaded/discharged and to provide the necessary equipment and labor to execute the handling and supervise the actual handling process. Stevedores' participation in port security is necessary to a successful port security program.
- Labor: The people who work regularly at seaports are logically the ones who have the most familiarity with normal port operations. Things that seem out of place, unusual, or suspicious will be apparent first to those who work at the port every day.
- Transportation Workers: People who work in the transportation industries that interface with the port also have a familiarity with normal operations and with people who access the port. Truck, bus, limousine, and taxi drivers are in the business of transporting passengers to and from seaports. Unusual or inappropriately dressed people or those carrying unusual packages or containers would be apparent to transportation workers.
- Construction Workers: Seaports may be engaged in construction projects, building new roads, bridges, terminals, ship berths, and so forth. Construction workers who access the port frequently on these projects become a component of port operations. Their awareness of security concerns and participation in partnerships with the port may also be recommended.
- General Public: There may be a role for the general public to play in participating in forums and community meetings, especially as it relates to security development and operational issues that impact the external community.

5.5.1 Port Security Steering Committee

The responsibility for port security must be shared by all who have an interest in efficient and effective seaport operations: cruise lines, cargo operators, shipping lines, stevedores, employees, labor groups, vendors, port management, and the transportation industry. Seaports must develop complementary relationships among users and stakeholders. Cooperation among port users is essential in identifying and mitigating threats to the security of seaports. It is also essential that all employees of stakeholder groups have a basic understanding and buy into the port security program.

One method that seaports use to develop and strengthen these relationships is the establishment of a Port Security Steering Committee. These committees, required by both the ISPS Code and the MTSA, are comprised of appropriate federal, state, and local agencies, as well as representatives from port stakeholders. The benefit of a Port Security Steering Committee to enhancing seaport security is that the committee receives information relevant to port security resulting from threat assessments conducted by law enforcement agencies. By sharing this information with port users and stakeholders, ports are able to work in a coordinated fashion to develop plans and strategies to address and neutralize identified threats and vulnerabilities.

References

Enter, J. E. 1991. Police administration in the future: Demographic influences as they relate to management of the internal and external environment. *American Journal of Police* 10(4): 65–81.

Gray, K., M.K. Stohr-Gillmore, and M.P. Lovrich. 1991. Adapting participatory management for a paramilitary organization: The implementation of teams in the Washington State Patrol. *American Journal of Police*, 10(4): 27–47.

Gulick, Luther, and Lyndall Urwick (Eds.). 1937. *Papers on the science of administration.* New York: Institute of Public Administration.

Hoover, L. T., and E. T. Mader. 1990. Attitudes of police chiefs toward private sector management principles. *American Journal of Police* 19(4): 27–47.

Jackson, William. 2008, April 28. Natalie Givans: Security gets into the mix: GCN interview. Government Computer News. http://www.gcn.com/print/27_9/46166-1.html?page=3 (accessed July 6, 2008).

Likert, Rensis. 1967. *The human organization.* New York: McGraw-Hill.

Pate, Anthony, Bruce Taylor, and Bruce Kubu. 2007. Protecting America's ports: Promising practices: A final report submitted by the Police Executive Research Forum to the National Institute of Justice. http://www.ncjrs.gov/pdffiles1/nij/grants/221075.pdf (accessed July 4, 2008).

Pursley, R. D. 1974. Leadership and community identification: Attitudes among two categories of police chiefs. *Journal of Police Science and Administration* 2: 414–422.

Schultz, E. Eugene and Russell Shumway. 2001. *Incident response: A strategic guide to handling system and network security breaches.* Indianapolis, IN: Sams Publishing.

U.S. Coast Guard. 2003a. Facility security plan development guide. http://www.rmaworld.com/ USCG%20FSP%20Pamphlet.pdf (accessed May 20, 2008).

U.S. Coast Guard. 2003b. Navigation and vessel inspection circular No. 03-03: Implementation guidance for the regulations mandated by the Maritime Transportation Security Act of 2002 (MTSA) for facilities. http://www.uscg.mil/hq/g-m/mp/pdf/NVIC_03-03.pdf (accessed May 20, 2008).

U.S. Congress. 2006. Security and Accountability for Every Port Act of 2006. http://frwebgate. access.gpo.gov/cgi-bin/getdoc.cgi?dbname=109_cong_bills&docid=f:h4954enr.txt.pdf (accessed July 4, 2008).

Vasu, Michael, Debra W. Stewart, and G. David Garson. 1998. *Organizational behavior and public management*. 3rd Ed. New York: Marcel Dekker, Inc.

White House. 2003a. Homeland security presidential directive/HSPD-7: Critical infrastructure identification, prioritization, and protection. http://www.whitehouse.gov/news/releases/2003/12/20031217-5.html (accessed August 17, 2008).

White House. 2003b. Homeland security presidential directive/HSPD-8: National preparedness. http://www.whitehouse.gov/news/releases/2003/12/20031217-6.html (accessed August 17, 2008).

PART III

IMPLEMENTING A PLAN FOR PORT SECURITY: MANAGEMENT TASKS AND RESPONSIBILITIES

6

FACILITY AND PERSONNEL SECURITY

6.1 Port Facility Security Officer

The Port FSO is the point person for planning and managing the security function. Although the Port FSO can be the port's chief security officer, it may be wise for port management to consider these as two separate positions. The reason is that the Port FSO will be required to have a ground-level view of the daily operations of the port, but the security chief's time may be constrained with administrative tasks not necessarily related to security planning and implementation. In multiuse ports, such as those that have both cargo and passenger operations and mixed-use complexes with significant nonmaritime, public, or commercial activities, government authorities with security oversight responsibilities will seek regular access to the Port FSO to mitigate conflicts and address security concerns. The U.S. Coast Guard, and similar agencies in other countries, may review the Port FSP to ensure that the Port FSO has a close enough relationship with port operations and decision-making abilities to address concerns on a continuing basis.

The IMO's (2004) ISPS Code defines the Port FSO as "the person designated as responsible for the development, implementation, revision and maintenance of the Port FSP and for liaison with the Ship Security Officer(s) (SSO) and Company Security Officer(s) (CSO)." The ISPS Code also provides guidelines for developing the Port FSO job description. In the United States, the MTSA of 2002, as codified in the Code of Federal Regulations (CFR 2003a, p. 320), designates the FSO as the person "responsible for the development, implementation, revision and maintenance of the FSP and for liaison with the COTP (Captain of the Port) and Company and Vessel Security Officers." The MTSA also details the qualifications and responsibilities of the Port FSO. The following summarizes pertinent aspects of these provisions, but Port FSOs and managers are cautioned to review the full text of the CFR (2003b) provisions applicable to Port FSOs when developing their port security regimes.

6.1.1 General Provisions

As suggested above, the FSO may perform other duties within the port organization. For example, the FSO could be the head of the security department or be delegated the position by the chief security officer. The decision is up to each port and security manager, but it would be advantageous for the Port FSO to be the person with the ability to work closely with the users and the relevant enforcement agencies in managing the FSP versus an administrator or higher-level executive who might not always be available to mitigate ground-level security issues. With some exceptions under U.S. federal law, the same person may serve as the FSO for more than one port facility. The FSO may assign security duties to other facility personnel; however, the FSO retains the responsibility for these duties.

6.1.2 Qualifications

Pursuant to MTSA requirements, the Port FSO must have general knowledge, thorough training, or equivalent job experience in the following areas:

- Security organization of the facility
- General vessel and facility operations and conditions
- Vessel and facility security measures, including the meaning and the requirements of the different MARSEC levels
- Emergency preparedness, response, and contingency planning
- Security equipment and systems and their operational limitations and methods of conducting audits, inspections, control, and monitoring techniques

The Port FSO must also have knowledge of *and* receive training in the following areas:

- Relevant international laws, codes, and recommendations
- Relevant government legislation and regulations
- Responsibilities and functions of local, state, and federal law enforcement agencies
- Risk assessment methodology
- Methods of facility security surveys and inspections
- Instruction techniques for security training and education, including security measures and procedures
- Handling sensitive security information and security-related communications
- Current security threats and patterns
- Recognizing and detecting dangerous substances and devices
- Recognizing characteristics and behavioral patterns of people who are likely to threaten security
- Techniques used to circumvent security measures
- Conducting physical searches and nonintrusive inspections
- Conducting security drills and exercises, including exercises with vessels, and assessing security drills and exercises

6.1.3 Responsibilities

Under MTSA, the Port FSO is responsible for ensuring the following:

- The Facility Security Assessment (FSA) is conducted
- The FSP is developed and implemented
- An annual audit is conducted, and if necessary, that the FSA and FSP are updated
- The FSP is exercised
- Regular security inspections of the facility are conducted
- The security awareness and vigilance of the facility personnel
- Adequate training to personnel performing facility security duties
- Occurrences that threaten the security of the facility are recorded and reported to the owner or operator
- Required records are maintained
- Any required reports are prepared and submitted
- Any required Declarations of Security with Vessel Security Officers are executed
- Security services are coordinated in accordance with the approved FSP
- Security equipment is properly operated, tested, calibrated, and maintained
- Attainment changes in MARSEC levels are recorded and reported to the owner or operator and the cognizant U.S. Coast Guard COTP
- The Vessel Security Officers, when requested, receive assistance in confirming the identity of visitors and service providers seeking to board the vessel through the facility
- Law enforcement personnel and other emergency responders are notified of any transportation security incident as soon as possible to permit a timely response
- The FSP is submitted to the cognizant U.S. Coast Guard COTP for approval, as well as any plans to change the facility or facility infrastructure prior to amending the FSP
- All facility personnel are briefed of changes in security conditions at the facility

6.2 Port Facility Security Plan

The Port FSP is the document developed to ensure the application of security measures designed to protect the port facility and its servicing vessels or those vessels interfacing with the facility, their cargo, and people onboard at the respective MARSEC levels. In the legislation and regulations that have been developed to address port security in the past several years, much attention is directed to the development of this document. Organizations of many types and structures develop plans and procedures to affect activities associated with carrying out agency missions. Unfortunately, sometimes these plans fail to fully address critical issues affecting organizational success. They may exist in paper form but are rarely pulled off the shelf to test their effectiveness. The key to successful port security management in terms of the FSP is to understand it as a *living document*. The FSP should not be viewed as a tedious regulatory compliance activity, but as a necessary ingredient to the effective security of the port facility. The FSP should not be written as a one-time effort, but should truly be a working document that addresses the security threats facing the port facility twenty-four hours a day, seven days a week. This means that the FSP, like the security function itself, must be continually updated and tested to be certain that it mitigates the threats identified in risk assessment. By treating the FSP as an essential component of the overall structure of port operations, the Port FSO contributes not only to the safety and security of the port and its patrons, but to the local, regional, national, and/or international maritime security strategies, which is what much of U.S. port security legislation has had as a driving feature.

6.2.1 Organization of the Port FSP

In 2003, the U.S. Coast Guard specified that port facility owners and operators subject to MTSA requirements (Code of Federal Regulations 2003c) must develop and submit a Port FSP for Coast Guard review and approval. The U.S. Coast Guard (2003) has recommended that port facility owners and operators ensure that the FSP includes the following individual sections:

- Section 1, Security administration and organization of the facility
- Section 2, Personnel training
- Section 3, Drills and exercises
- Section 4, Records and documentation
- Section 5, Response to change in MARSEC level
- Section 6, Procedures for interfacing with vessels
- Section 7, Declaration of Security
- Section 8, Communications
- Section 9, Security systems and equipment maintenance
- Section 10, Security measures for access control
- Section 11, Security measures for restricted access
- Section 12, Security measures for handling cargo
- Section 13, Security measures for delivery of vessel stores and bunkers
- Section 14, Security measures for monitoring
- Section 15, Security incident procedures
- Section 16, Audits and security plan amendments
- Section 17, FSA Report

- Section 18, Vulnerability and Security Measures Summary (Form CG-6025) Appendix A to Part 105-Facility Vulnerability and Security Measures Summary (Form CG-6028)

In providing guidance for FSP developers, the U.S. Coast Guard (2004) has addressed some problematic areas the agency has seen while reviewing plans and amendments in development. The agency suggests that, while not required, the Port FSP should describe the port facility, including the number of employees, physical dimensions, and descriptions of the types of operations and cargo handled, as well as the types of vessels it handles. The Coast Guard also specifies that the Port FSP provide enough detail and organization to enable present and future security personnel to use the FSP as a comprehensive reference guide. One major area of concern is the use of noncommitment verbiage, such as "should," "may," "as appropriate," and "as deemed necessary by the FSO" in developing security operational guidelines and procedures. The FSP must provide details as to who conducts training, a schedule of training, and how knowledge from training is evaluated with respect to both security and nonsecurity personnel. The FSP must also describe, and not merely name, the drills and exercises that will be conducted. Further, the FSP must list facility security and communications systems and equipment, and provide a schedule for inspection, testing, calibration, and maintenance.

6.3 MARSEC Levels

At the international level, the ISPS Code (IMO 2002) specifies three distinct levels of security for vessels and ports. Security level 1, or normal, is the level at which ship or port security normally operates. It refers to the minimum appropriate protective security measures which must exist at all times. Security level 2, or heightened, will apply when there is a heightened risk of a security incident and additional protective security measures must be implemented. Security level 3, or exceptional, applies when there is the probable or imminent risk of a security incident. Further specific protective security measures must be implemented. In the United States, MARSEC refers to the three security levels used by the U.S. Coast Guard (2008) consistent with the DHS's Homeland Security Advisory System. MARSEC levels are set by the Commandant of the U.S. Coast Guard to reflect the prevailing threat environment to the marine elements of U.S. transportation systems, including ports, vessels, facilities, and infrastructure. Changes in the Homeland Security Advisory System will not necessarily involve changes in MARSEC levels because these are designed to be changed in response to an evaluation of local conditions by the U.S. Coast Guard COTP. Changes in MARSEC levels will initiate preplanned scalable responses, which should be included in a Port FSP, to increased threat levels. MARSEC levels provide increasing levels of security based on threat assessment and communicate actions to be taken by vessels and port facilities in response.

6.3.1 MARSEC Level 1

The level for which minimum appropriate security measures shall be maintained at all times, MARSEC 1 generally applies when Homeland Security Advisory System threat levels green (low), blue (guarded), or yellow (elevated) are set.

6.3.2 MARSEC Level 2

The level for which appropriate additional protective security measures shall be maintained for a period of time as a result of heightened risk of a transportation security incident, MARSEC 2 generally corresponds to Homeland Security Advisory System threat level orange (high).

6.3.3 MARSEC Level 3

The level for which further specific protective security measures shall be maintained for a limited period of time when a transportation security incident is probable, imminent, or has occurred, although it may not be possible to identify the specific target, MARSEC 3 generally corresponds to Homeland Security Advisory System threat level red (severe).

6.3.4 MARSEC Level Change Action List

FSOs can develop port-specific task lists to identify actions that must be taken pursuant to changes in MARSEC levels. Many of the changes that will be required as part of a change in MARSEC will affect port operations. For example, there will likely be a need to increase the rates of vehicle, passenger, and pedestrian screening, or restrictions on the ingress of vehicles containing hazardous materials into the port. Naturally, each Port FSO will have to ensure the Port FSP takes account of unique environmental and organizational conditions that impact increased security conditions. For this reason, the development of specific task lists should be included in the Port FSP and as part of security staff operating procedures and training curricula.

The following are examples of the types of tasks that can be included in a MARSEC Level Change Action List. They are not meant to address every conceivable operation, MTSA provision, or component of an FSP, but they illustrate how a foundation can be built for developing similar lists in different port facilities. As always, the Port FSO should carefully review the relevant federal, state, and local laws affecting port security in the jurisdiction and fine-tune the list to be as comprehensive as possible.

- Within twelve hours, implement additional security measures.
- All communications and interactions are logged with date and time.
- Contact port users with information about changes in MARSEC levels.
- Coordinate and provide prevailing threat and response information.
- Coordinate with U.S. Coast Guard, U.S. Customs and Border Protection, state and local police, emergency management, fire department, and so forth as appropriate.
- Vessels moored and scheduled to arrive within ninety-six hours are notified, and Declarations of Security are revised.
- Report compliance to U.S. Coast Guard COTP within twelve hours.
- Ensure recording and reporting of attainment changes in MARSEC Levels Log to the port tenants, facility FSOs, and COTP.
- Coordinate with law enforcement and/or contract security to ensure additional land-based and/or waterside patrols to address security needs and requirements at MARSEC 2 and 3.
- During MARSEC 2 and 3, additional armed personnel are assigned to provide reinforced staffing around the clock.
- Coordinate with law enforcement and/or contract security to optimize multi-agency efforts to conduct security checkpoint inspections.
- Increases in MARSEC level require communications to security and facility personnel.
- Conduct random inspections to ensure compliance with security requirements.
- Distribute appropriate information to law enforcement commands.
- Convene meeting of port users' security committees.
- Implement additional inspections of piers and wharves, including underwater inspections.
- Inform tenants and all facility personnel about identified threats, reporting procedures for potential threats, suspicious people and conveyances (vehicles and waterside crafts), and reinforcing need for personal vigilance.
- Communicate changes in MARSEC levels to vessels enroute to port via harbormaster, harbor pilots, and/or berthing operations.
- FSO ensures Declaration of Security is signed and implemented prior to moving passengers, cargo, and ships' stores to and from common-use vessels.

6.4 Facility Security Assessment

Security assessments, including on-scene surveys, are essentially physical examinations of facilities, operations, systems, and procedures to determine the existing state of a target environment's security (Fischer, Halibozek, and Green 2008, pp. 149–150). Under MTSA provisions (CFR 2003a), the FSA refers specifically to "an analysis that examines and evaluates the infrastructure and operations of the facility taking into account possible threats, vulnerabilities, consequences, and existing protective measures, procedures and operations" (p. 320). In the port security environment, the FSA is a written document developed pursuant to the assembly of background information, an on-scene survey, and analysis of that information. The FSA should address several primary components, including port assets and infrastructure, threats, countermeasures and procedures, and vulnerabilities. Consultants or knowledgeable third parties may be used to assist the Port FSO in conducting the FSA, and in some cases, this may be advisable to ensure unbiased security assessments. Given that the owners and operators of port facilities may be concerned about the costs associated with mitigation of security risks, it may be practical for the Port FSO to delegate the FSA task to a neutral expert to eliminate this dynamic. Individuals who conduct an MTSA-required FSA for the port must be able to draw upon expert assistance in the following areas:

- Knowledge of current security threats and patterns
- Recognition and detection of dangerous substances and devices
- Recognition of characteristics and behavioral patterns of people who are likely to threaten security
- Techniques used to circumvent security measures
- Methods used to cause a security incident
- Effects of dangerous substances and devices on structures and facility services
- Facility security requirements
- Facility and vessel interface business practices
- Contingency planning, emergency preparedness, and response
- Physical security requirements
- Radio and telecommunications systems, including computer systems and networks
- Marine or civil engineering
- Facility and vessel operations

The FSA, the FSA report, and the FSP must be protected from unauthorized access or disclosure. Specific requirements of an MTSA FSA are outlined below and further detailed in Title 33 of the CFR (2003d), Part 105. As always, the Port FSO should closely review the regulations themselves to fully understand and appreciate the requirements.

6.4.1 Background Information

The Port FSA includes background information as follows:

- The general layout of the facility, including location of each active and inactive access point to the facility; number, reliability, and security duties of facility personnel; security doors, barriers, and lighting; location of restricted areas; emergency and standby equipment available to maintain essential services; maintenance equipment, cargo spaces, storage areas, and unaccompanied baggage storage; location of escape and evacuation routes and assembly stations; and existing security and safety equipment for protection of personnel and visitors
- Response procedures for fire or other emergency conditions
- Procedures for monitoring facility and vessel personnel, vendors, repair technicians, and dockworkers
- Existing contracts with private security companies and existing agreements with local or municipal agencies
- Procedures for controlling keys and other access prevention systems
- Procedures for cargo and vessel stores' operations
- Response capability to security incidents
- Threat assessments, including the purpose and methodology of the assessment, for the port in which the facility is located or at which passengers embark or disembark
- Previous reports on security needs
- Any other existing security procedures and systems, equipment, communications, and facility personnel

6.4.2 On-Scene Survey

The survey is an examination and evaluation of existing facility protective measures, procedures, and operations to verify or collect the required background information.

6.4.3 Analysis and Recommendations

The Port FSO must analyze the background information and the on-scene survey and provide recommendations to establish and prioritize the security measures that should be included in the Port FSP. The analysis must consider each vulnerability found during the on-scene survey as follows:

- Waterside and shoreside access to the facility and vessel berthing at the facility
- Structural integrity of the piers, facilities, and associated structures
- Existing security measures and procedures, including identification systems
- Existing security measures and procedures relating to services and utilities
- Measures to protect radio and telecommunication equipment, including computer systems and networks

- Adjacent areas that may be exploited during or before an attack
- Areas that may, if damaged or used for illicit observation, pose a risk to people, property, or operations within the facility
- Existing agreements with private security companies providing waterside and shoreside security services
- Any conflicting policies between safety and security measures and procedures
- Any conflicting facility operations and security duty assignments
- Any enforcement and personnel constraints
- Any deficiencies identified during daily operations or training and drills
- Any deficiencies identified following security incidents or alerts, the report of security concerns, the exercise of control measures, or audits

The analysis must also consider possible security threats, including the following:

- Damage to or destruction of the facility or a vessel moored at the facility
- Hijacking or seizure of a vessel moored at the facility or of people on board
- Tampering with cargo, essential equipment or systems, or stores of a vessel moored at the facility
- Unauthorized access or use, including the presence of stowaways
- Smuggling dangerous substances and devices to the facility
- Use of a vessel moored at the facility to carry those intending to cause a security incident and their equipment
- Use of a vessel moored at the facility as a weapon or as a means to cause damage or destruction
- Impact on the facility and its operations due to a blockage of entrances, locks, and approaches
- Use of the facility as a transfer point for nuclear, biological, radiological, explosive, or chemical weapons

The analysis must also consider the following:

- Threat assessments by government agencies
- Vulnerabilities, including human factors, in the facility's infrastructure, policies, and procedures
- Any particular aspects of the facility that make it likely to be the target of an attack, including the vessels using the facility
- Likely consequences of an attack on or at the facility in terms of loss of life, damage to property, and economic disruption, including disruption to transportation systems
- Locations where access restrictions or prohibitions will be applied for each MARSEC level

6.4.4 FSA Report

A completed, written FSA report must be submitted and included with the FSP each time the FSP is submitted to the U.S. Coast Guard for reapproval or revisions. The following is a listing of the elements required in the written FSA report for port facilities required to comply with MTSA, as specified in Title 33 of the CFR, Part 105, Subpart C, Section 300, *Facility Security Assessment*:

- A summary of how the on-scene survey was conducted
- A description of existing security measures, including inspection, control, and monitoring equipment; personnel identification documents and communication; alarm, lighting, access control, and similar systems
- A description of each vulnerability found during the on-scene survey
- A description of security measures that could be used to address each vulnerability
- A list of the key facility operations that are important to protect
- A list of identified weaknesses, including human factors in the infrastructure, policies, and procedures of the facility
- A description of the following elements within the facility: physical security; structural integrity; personnel protection systems; procedural policies; radio and telecommunication systems, including computer systems and networks; relevant transportation infrastructure; and utilities
- A list of the people, activities, services, and operations that are important to protect, in each of the following categories: facility personnel; passengers, visitors, vendors, repair technicians, vessel personnel, and so forth; capacity to maintain emergency response; cargo, particularly dangerous goods and hazardous substances; delivery of vessel stores; any facility security communication and surveillance systems; and any other facility security systems
- An accounting for any vulnerabilities in the following areas: conflicts between safety and security measures; conflicts between duties and security assignments; the impact of watch-keeping duties and risk of fatigue on facility personnel alertness and performance; security training deficiencies; and security equipment and systems, including communication systems
- A discussion and evaluation of key facility measures and operations, including: ensuring performance of all security duties; controlling access to the facility, through the use of identification systems or otherwise; controlling the embarkation of vessel personnel and other people and their effects (including personal effects and baggage, whether accompanied or unaccompanied); procedures for the handling of cargo and the delivery of vessel stores; monitoring restricted areas to ensure that only authorized personnel have access; monitoring the facility and areas adjacent to the pier; and the ready availability of security communications, information, and equipment

6.5 FSP Audit

Under MTSA, an audit is an "evaluation of a security assessment or security plan performed by an owner or operator, the owner or operator's designee, or an approved third-party, intended to identify deficiencies, non-conformities and/or inadequacies that would render the assessment or plan insufficient" (CFR 2003a, p. 319). An MTSA-regulated port facility is required to conduct an annual audit of its Port FSP. The audit must be conducted by personnel who do not have regularly assigned security duties at the port facility, and it must be independent of any security measures being audited. The Port FSO should first determine if there is any organizational staff, or staff in collateral functions and elements not involved with port security, who are capable of assisting with this audit. If the port facility is part of a government organization, there may be external agencies or resources (e.g., a city or county's audit management or staff inspections element) that could be tapped into. There might also be private elements or contractors available on a current government contract that could be requested to assist with the audit.

If the port elects to contract with an external consultant to perform the audit, then a contract or bid for port security audit-related services will need to be submitted. Appendix A provides suggested language for a *scope of services* document, which could be adapted for outsourcing audit-related services. In all respects, the Port FSO should review the relevant portions of the MTSA to ensure compliance with federal law in this area.

6.6 Port Personnel Security Awareness

One of the Port FSO's most important responsibilities will be to instill an awareness of port security for all facility employees and visitors. An awareness philosophy will provide port employees, users, and stakeholders with a basic appreciation and understanding of security at the port, thereby strengthening the port's security posture. The adoption of an all-inclusive approach to security awareness will help to enable the facility to comply with MTSA, which requires a general level of security awareness training for port personnel. This approach enables the general port user or employee to become cognizant of the enhanced emphasis on security at ports due to the threat of acts of global terrorism. A comprehensive security awareness program should:

- provide port users with a basic introduction to port security,
- illustrate why it is important for port users to understand the need for a culture of security in the port facility,
- outline a basic framework for understanding the relationship between risk and vulnerabilities at seaports, and

- show specific ways in which port users can help to reduce the risks associated with those vulnerabilities as part of the port's overall security infrastructure.

By providing port users with this basic level of security awareness, the seaport adds another layer to its security program, which enhances its ability to identify and respond to potential threats to the security of the port. Training for general employees assists port security with detecting criminal activity and suspicious people, vehicles, and activities and with identifying security and safety concerns. In doing so, port administrators systematically add another dimension to the variety of processes and systems that build an interconnected security program. By making port users aware of the threats to seaports and the importance of security through this initiative, they become a valuable component of the layered approach. Port users are stakeholders: people and groups who have an interest in the continued successful operation of the port. As such, port users have vested interests in ensuring that the seaport remains safe, secure, and able to operate effectively to achieve its goals and objectives. Security and safety at seaports is a responsibility of all people with a vested interest in ensuring a port's continued viability and development.

6.6.1 *Objectives for a Port Security Awareness Program*

Port FSOs should take the position that security is everyone's business at the port and that employee, staff, and visitor awareness and vigilance is important to detect and deter criminal activity. The following are suggested components of a security awareness orientation or training program that can be developed as part of the port's human resources management function:

- Promote a Culture of Security. A culture of security is needed to encourage port users to be more aware of the activities and people that could damage or injure seaport property and personnel. By encouraging all port users to be more aware and more vigilant, maritime security is strengthened for both the vessels using the port and the operating conditions in port facilities. A security culture will aid seaports in identifying people and situations that might be a threat to public safety.
- Ensure the Unimpeded Flow of Commerce. International commerce depends on the free flow of vessels and cargo to and from the world's seaports. Security awareness among port users enables the flow of commerce to continue as the port interfaces with the wider transportation network.
- Deter the Possibility of Terrorist Attacks. A terrorist incident in even one seaport will likely severely impact commerce and business at many seaports. For example, a terrorist event involving a passenger cruise ship in one regional port will affect cruise industry operations throughout the region, or even around the world. It is important for port and maritime interests to work cooperatively to deter incidents of terrorism, which could severely disrupt shipping, trade, and commerce.

- Prevent and Detect Criminal Activity. One of the biggest challenges to security at seaports is identifying and neutralizing internal criminal conspiracies. Criminal activities committed by smugglers or other organized criminal groups may be aided by corrupt individuals working in seaports or within the transportation industry. This is why it is essential that all port users become a component of the layered security program at seaports. Port staff can work cooperatively to identify and reduce opportunities for the establishment of internal criminal conspiracies at seaports.
- Prevent Unauthorized Access to Vessels and Port Facilities. All port users must take responsibility for preventing unauthorized people from access to the restricted areas of seaports.
- Provide a Means for Raising the Alarm in Reaction to Security Threats or Incidents. Port users with enhanced awareness of security provide another set of "eyes and ears." It should not be the responsibility of only police and security officers. All port users have a vested interest in ensuring a safe and secure port. Alerting authorities to unusual situations or suspicious people, vehicles, and cargo is one of the primary reasons for educating users about seaport security.

6.6.2   *Port Security Awareness Components: What Personnel Need to Know*

General awareness. All employees and regular port users must be knowledgeable of their role in helping to prevent terrorist and criminal acts. Port administrators have a responsibility to help employees understand why security is important and what role they play in the process. Employees and port users become a vital component of the overall security program when they can assist the port in the following areas.

Crime threats. Regular port employees and users should notify supervisors, law enforcement, security, and/or port officials about any behavior or activity that is suspicious or criminal in nature. Port users should develop a *security perspective* when engaged in activities on the port. If a person, vehicle, or condition seems out of place or unusual (e.g., a person taking photographs of machinery or guard posts, a vehicle parked in an unusual location, oddly dressed people), notify the police or security staff to investigate.

Terrorism threats. Be aware of and keep informed about incidents and threats of terrorist activities. Know and understand the U.S. DHS's color-coded Homeland Security Advisory System and the significance of the alert levels. Be aware of the current MARSEC level at the port facility and what changes in MARSEC level may mean and require. If employees don't understand these advisories, they should be instructed to obtain guidance from a supervisor or security official.

Security procedures and emergency response plans. Employees should know and understand the necessary procedures and requirements for security at their port facility. If the facility requires the issuance of a credential for access, employees should know what is required to obtain one, for how long it is valid, and for what areas it provides access. Employees should become familiar with their organization's emergency and contingency procedures.

Communications. It is especially important to establish open and unimpeded communications among employees, employers, tenants, and port facility administrators. All port users should be apprised of information affecting port operations and security. Use all available technologies (radio, telephones, cell phones, e-mail) to transmit vital communications between and among port users.

Restricted access areas. Ports designate which areas of the facility are restricted to only authorized personnel and vehicles. Restricting access is a key component of the port's overall security strategy. As illustrated in Figure 6.1, ports must designate and identify restricted access areas and develop security checkpoints. Pedestrians and vehicles must present required access credentials to obtain access. All port users should respect and adhere to the restrictions concerning access. Enabling unauthorized people to enter the seaport or failing to report the presence of unauthorized people to appropriate personnel compromises the safety and security of the port and its users.

Figure 6.1　Restricted access area security checkpoint.

Port visitors. Ports must develop specific procedures and systems for admitting visitors and nonregular or itinerant workers. Typically, ports utilize some type of visitor pass or identification badge system to identify those who have been authorized entry to particular port areas. Port users expecting visitors should inform them of the necessary procedures and work cooperatively with port authorities to ensure that proper authorizations for visitors are issued and that any and all visitor escort procedures are followed.

Computer and information security. Seaports are required to maintain procedures to protect computerized information from unauthorized disclosure. Port users with access to computerized information must be aware of procedures to prevent unauthorized disclosure and have processes and procedures in place to protect against the release of information to unauthorized individuals.

Firearms and weapons restrictions. Employees and port users should be aware of the restrictions against bringing firearms and weapons onto the seaport. Many local and state jurisdictions have laws restricting the transportation or possession of firearms and weapons. There may be more specific regulations and administrative orders concerning the carriage of weapons into a seaport's restricted access areas, such as passenger terminals and areas of cargo operations. The effect of any state or local concealed weapons permits on port property should be explained so that all employees and visitors understand the regulations. Signage should be developed that clearly educates the public about the rules and restrictions of these weapons.

Bomb threat plans. All employees and port users should become familiar with the procedures in place concerning bomb threats made to port facilities. Do all those responsible for answering telephones understand how to react in the event a bomb threat is made by telephone? All staff should know how to report bomb threats to the designated law enforcement agency.

Emergency evacuation plans. Seaports must develop and maintain current plans in the event of emergencies requiring the evacuation of large numbers of people from port facilities. Bomb threats, fires, unsafe conditions, and hazardous materials incidents may necessitate total or partial evacuations. Port users and employees should be familiar with evacuation plans and routes of escape.

Natural disaster response plans. Seaports may be susceptible to fires, hurricanes, tornadoes, earthquakes, and other naturally occurring phenomena. Disaster response plans are developed to enable users and employees to be able to prepare for and respond to natural disasters in a coordinated manner. Plans should be exercised and updated, and all staff should be familiar with their role in the plan.

Contingency plans. Contingency plans explain procedures that port users can follow in the event normal operations of the seaport are suspended or impeded in some way. Examples include such things as shifting berthings of vessels and opening/closing access gates to accommodate port operations. Port users should maintain communications with port administrators to ensure that changes to operational and security procedures are communicated to all appropriate individuals.

Follow the rules. Rules pertaining to credentials, access to certain areas, hours of operation, documents required, and so forth are an important element of the security of the port. By following the rules and taking note of and reporting individuals in violation, all port users work together to create a strong security presence.

Report unidentified people and vehicles. People and vehicles who cannot be identified may pose a threat to the port facility. Employees should be instructed to immediately notify port security or law enforcement personnel if they suspect there has been an intrusion by individuals who have no permission to be in a particular location or facility.

Report unusually dressed people or atypical behavior. Individuals with unusual or inappropriate clothing (e.g., wearing a large coat in summer months) may be concealing contraband, weapons, or items that may pose a threat to the port facility and public safety. Individuals acting erratically or unable to communicate appropriately should similarly be reported to security and/or law enforcement officials for investigation.

Report people taking photographs in unusual locations. It is not unusual to find tourists or cruise passengers taking photographs in the port facility, but it may be unusual for people to be taking photographs of critical infrastructure or port operations. Ports may restrict the locations and times photos may be taken. Report any questionable photography activities to security/law enforcement.

Know port layout and facility operations. All port users, employees, and regular staff should be familiar with the geographical layout of the seaport. They should be prepared to provide locations, routes of travel, and landmarks to officials when reporting suspicious or illegal behavior, people, and vehicles.

Report unexpected cargo and visitors. Port users, terminal operators, and cargo facilities should be aware of the vehicles, people, and cargo anticipated in their respective facilities. Unexpected people and cargo should be thoroughly scrutinized to ensure the safety and security of the port is not compromised.

Report unexpected ship crew members and vendors. Ensure ship crew members, visitors, vendors, and so forth are expected, properly documented, and possess valid, displayable identification credentials.

Know the MARSEC level. Changes in MARSEC levels affect port operations in significant ways, particularly with the amount of screening and security precautions that must be taken. Increasing the level of security as the MARSEC level rises is essential to protecting and safeguarding seaport operations. Port employees must understand the impact of this on their activities, their employer's operations, and overall port security.

Keep emergency contact records updated. Maintain current, updated emergency contact information for all port users, employees, and staff. This is essential in the event emergency conditions require contacting staff for assignments, advisories, and coordination of operations.

Drills and exercises. Employees should participate in training drills and exercises to ensure familiarity with security plans and procedures. Seaports are required to conduct regular drills and exercises of their Port FSP. Plans must be exercised to ensure they are current, viable, and provide for effective deployment of resources to meet the security needs. Employee participation in these exercises and drills is critical to ensuring the continuity of operations required in emergencies and unusual situations.

Keeping individuals secure and safe on the port and maintaining a general climate of public safety in order to conduct business is a paramount function for the Port FSO. The safety and security of people working at and visiting the seaport must be a critical activity for all port operators. Many seaports are complex facilities that may include combinations of cargo and passenger operations. Maintaining a safe and secure seaport environment for people to work and visit requires a dedication to providing the best-trained employees and best-managed resources possible. These include well-trained security guard and police forces, as well as a knowledgeable and security-conscious port operational staff.

References

Code of Federal Regulations. 2003a. Title 33, Navigation and Navigable Waters, Chapter I, Coast Guard, Department of Homeland Security, Part 101, General Provisions, Section 101.105, Definitions. http://edocket.access.gpo.gov/cfr_2003/julqtr/33cfr101.105.htm (accessed July 8, 2008).

Code of Federal Regulations. 2003b. Title 33, Navigation and Navigable Waters, Chapter I, Coast Guard, Department of Homeland Security, Part 105, Facility Security, Section 105.205, Facility security officer. http://edocket.access.gpo.gov/cfr_2003/julqtr/33cfr105.205.htm (accessed July 9, 2008).

Code of Federal Regulations. 2003c. Title 33, Navigation and Navigable Waters, Chapter I, Coast Guard, Department of Homeland Security, Part 105, Maritime Security: Facilities. http://ecfr.gpoaccess.gov/cgi/t/text/text-idx?c=ecfr&sid=52524729af4fc03a9556266fcc691b5d&rgn=div5&view=text&node=33:1.0.1.8.52&idno=33 (accessed July 11, 2008).

Code of Federal Regulations. 2003d. Title 33, Navigation and Navigable Waters, Chapter I, Coast Guard, Department of Homeland Security, Part 105, Maritime Security: Facilities Part 105, Subpart C, Section 105.305, Facility security assessment. http://edocket.access.gpo.gov/cfr_2003/julqtr/33cfr105.305.htm (accessed July 11, 2008).

Fischer, Robert J., Edward Halibozek, and Gion Green. 2008. *Introduction to security.* Amsterdam: Elsevier.

International Maritime Organization. 2002. FAQ on ISPS Code and maritime security. http://www.imo.org/Newsroom/mainframe.asp?topic_id=897#levels (accessed July 11, 2008).

International Maritime Organization. 2004. International Ship and Port Facility Security Code. http://www.worldtraderef.com/WTR_site/ISPS.asp (accessed July 8, 2008).

U.S. Coast Guard. 2003. Facility security plan development guide. http://homeport.uscg.mil/cgi-bin/st/portal/uscg_docs/MyCG/Editorial/20061206/FSPPamphlet.pdf?id=386315960a140d4050e6c1875f2a214b2a0d20f2 (accessed July 10, 2008).

U.S. Coast Guard. 2004. Facility security plan review common discrepancies. http://home-port.uscg.mil/cgi-in/st/portal/uscg_docs/MyCG/Editorial/20061006/FSP%20Review--Most%20Common%20Discrepancies.doc?id=b1de130acd35cf2a2def3c11e340039aea4b5c52 (accessed July 10, 2008).

U.S. Coast Guard. 2008. U.S. Coast Guard maritime security (MARSEC) levels. http://www.uscg.mil/safetylevels/whatismarsec.asp (accessed July 11, 2008).

7

ACCESS CONTROLS

Granting access into port facilities is a challenge without severely disrupting passenger operations, commerce, international trade, and recreational and tourist-related port business. Ports present an attractive target for terrorists and developing criminal conspiracies due to their component role in national and local economies. They contain important assets and infrastructure, which, if damaged, could cause significant loss of life, as well as damage to the port facility, economy, and the environment. The importance of developing comprehensive port access control systems and protocols cannot be understated. As the basic function of security is to protect the target environment from harm, the foundation of this effort is the establishment of an effective regimen of control over who and what will be permitted to enter the environment. As the access control infrastructure in Figure 7.1 suggests, port facilities must strike the right balance between efficient throughput and knowing precisely who and what is coming in.

Even in residential settings, access is controlled by developing best practices to screen those desiring to enter. When the doorbell rings, residents want to know who is there before opening the door. Children are taught to practice good security and safety when they are alone or when someone knocks at the door. If unfamiliar third parties are permitted entry, they have (hopefully) been prescreened to ensure there are no risk factors in their backgrounds that portend some future harm. Although we cannot always be certain that every risk has been eliminated, we perform due diligence by initiating at least some fundamental background check about the boarders, vendors, delivery people, and maintenance and repair people whom we allow entry to our residences, our secure environments. Similarly, by instituting controls to identify, screen, and monitor people and vehicles entering ports, a major layer of security is added to mitigate the vulnerabilities of the open systems nature of seaports.

This chapter discusses two major components essential to comprehensive port access control: *identification and credentialing* and *restricted-area access controls*. Identification and credentialing is the process that provides seaports with a systemic way to identify and control who has authorization to enter a seaport. Restricted-area access controls comprise physical infrastructure, procedures, systems, and guidance for screening, monitoring, and controlling access into the facility. The primary methods for restricting access, such that those with criminal intent are excluded, are to identify them before access is granted and to conduct screening activities during access. By providing staff

Figure 7.1 Access control systems at port facilities must ensure a balance between security and throughput.

with the tools and guidance for screening, port management will succeed in reducing the risks associated with allowing people entry into critical areas of the port.

7.1 Port Vulnerabilities Associated with Access Controls

7.1.1 Frequency of Access

Ports must be aware of who and what is coming on to the property at all times. A major dynamic affecting port vulnerability is *frequency of access*. Those people who access the port most frequently may develop an intimate knowledge of port operations and geography, including knowledge of security systems, guard forces, and access controls. The port's first line of defense in developing effective access controls in its Port FSP must be in knowing who is entering the port and why. Knowledge of port operations is a valuable tool in the terrorist and criminal arsenals. Many communities depend on convenient and ready access to waterways and proximity to intermodal rail and surface transportation systems. There may be no other way to bring in goods and commodities. Terrorists and criminals look for ways to cripple local, regional, and national economies. Criminal conspiracies can develop on seaports due to the ability of regular patrons to identify ways to defeat security mechanisms, such as by becoming familiar with systems, schedules, employees, and methods of access.

Terrorist organizations model their activities after classic smuggling operations to probe for weak links in port security systems. Smuggling is a way by which terrorists can use the maritime domain to transfer weapons and explosives into or out of seaports. Port security can impact the ability of terrorists to use vessels and port facilities to smuggle weapons by minimizing the ability of potential criminals to access the port. Those people intent on exploiting ports to conduct criminal activity or on developing them as targets of terrorism will use their knowledge of ports and their operations to find weaknesses in their security systems. The ability to locate gaps in security may enable terrorists to develop targets of opportunity.

A port's vulnerabilities to terrorist attacks are exacerbated by the amount of death, injury, and destruction that can be accomplished through the exploitation and use of hazardous materials and/or weapons of mass destruction. Some methods for using access control processes to mitigate frequent access vulnerabilities and prevent infiltration by criminal conspiracies are as follows:

- Criminal history background checks of employees and port users.
- Employer authorization letters validating employee-employer relationships.
- Strict enforcement of port identification credential regulations.
- Close screening of vehicles and pedestrians entering the port facility.
- An alert and responsive security guard force.
- Close scrutiny of identification credential information.

7.1.2 Advance Notice Requirements

Ports and port facilities provide natural transportation and trade interfaces between bodies of water and the communities they serve. It is a natural occurrence for major cities and towns to develop in locations where the shipping is able to access either natural or man-made port facilities. Seaports provide interfacing communities with significant commerce, economic development, and sources of employment. Port access controls protect the port's interface with its host city, region, or state, by minimizing infiltration of criminal elements. *Advance notice* of vessel arrivals, cargo shipments, general deliveries, and passengers is another dynamic that, if understood properly, provides port security management with a useful tool in mitigating the port's access vulnerabilities. In addition to knowing who is coming onto the seaport, it is critical to know what vessels, vehicles, and cargo will be coming to the port and when. By having advance notice of vessel arrivals, seaports will be in a position to assess and evaluate changes in threat levels associated with the type of vessel, type of cargo, number of passengers and crew, countries of origin of crew, and countries of registration for ships interfacing with the port.

In the United States, several regulatory devices have been developed and implemented to assist port security with reducing vulnerabilities associated with port-transportation interfaces. One mechanism is the U.S. Customs and Border Protection's

Passenger and Crew Manifest Rules (Federal Register 2005). With some exceptions, these rules require electronic submission of manifests at least ninety-six hours before vessels enter a U.S. port. Operators must compare travel documents presented by passengers with the manifest information submitted. The U.S. Coast Guard (2008) established the National Vessel Movement Center to track notice of arrival information from ships entering U.S. ports. Notification can be made via the Internet using an electronic form. For cargo, the MTSA of 2002 required the mandatory submission of cargo manifest information to U.S. Customs and Border Protection. In 2003, that agency published regulations pursuant to the Trade Act of 2002 that require advance transmission of electronic cargo information for both arriving and departing cargo. Considering the push by the U.S. DHS to better screen for threats, port security management does have a number of effective resources as potential agency partners in reducing threats associated with incoming material and individuals.

7.2 Identification and Credentialing

Insufficient access controls represent a critical vulnerability for ports for which identification and credentialing processes become essential components of the Port FSP. Port employees and frequent visitors, such as itinerant labor, vendors, and service workers, must be identified to control and limit their access to the facility. Port identification cards represent the basic level of access control for the port to know who and what is coming onto the facility. Port management must identify the people and their associated organizations who conduct business at its facilities. In addition to knowing who will be coming to the port on a frequent basis, effective screening must occur to ensure that people applying for port credentials are authorized to do so by their employer organizations.

7.2.1 Photo Identification Credentials

The issuance of a photo identification credential to each person authorized access is a key component of port access control. Individuals must be required to possess and display a photo identification credential, namely, a badge or card, at all times when accessing or working within port restricted–access areas. The basic structure entails the issuance of identification credentials to employees and visitors; a classification system for various port restricted–access areas; and color-coding to indicate the type of access authorization. Ports must also consider procedures for card issuance, production processes, the reporting of lost or stolen credentials, and proper badge inspection criteria, and the impact of government regulations on the issuance of credentials.

Photo identification badges can be very effective control mechanisms if they include an accurate and current photograph of the holder, name, date of birth, a physical description (height, weight, eye and hair color), the employer's name, and a unique identification number. Employees, visitors, and others with frequent access to port facilities, must be required to wear and visibly display the photo identification badge so that they can be identified at all times. The identification badge is not just for when the employee is going through the access control point, but for all times that the person is in the port facility.

7.2.2 Fingerprints and Criminal History Background Checks

Some ports have instituted a process of issuing port identification credentials only to individuals who have been subjected to a criminal history background investigation. If permitted by enabling legislation, it is especially important to consider developing this capability to filter out and deny access to those with a propensity to engage in criminal activity. National, state, and/or local laws may require certain controls preceding the issuance of port identification credentials. In the United Kingdom, approximately two hundred thousand airport employees who work in restricted areas must undergo a criminal background check, but the requirement only covers crimes committed in the United Kingdom. Concerns raised about extending these checks to foreign-born airport workers' home countries suggest that efforts to develop criminal background checks as a precondition of access credentialing will require considerable international cooperation (BBC News 2008). Port security managers should review existing regulatory and statutory documents to ensure compliance with credentialing requirements. For example, in the state of Florida, all deepwater seaports are required by state law to screen applicants for port identification cards to exclude people with certain types of crimes in their backgrounds. Florida law requires people who regularly access seaports to undergo a fingerprint-based, criminal history background check prior to card issuance (Florida Statutes 2007). The statute lists several offenses and conditions, such as trafficking in narcotics, which limit the ability of certain people with felony criminal backgrounds to work on or access port restricted areas. The prescriptive Florida approach to port security regulation was used as a model for certain aspects of post-September 11 federal security legislation, such as "the USA Patriot Act, covering hazardous materials transport; the Aviation and Transportation Security Act, covering airport jobs; and the Maritime Transportation Security Act, covering the nation's seaport jobs" (Collins Center for Public Policy 2006, p. 7). Other jurisdictions may wish to integrate similar control mechanisms into their credential issuance protocols to restrict certain people with a propensity toward criminal behavior from receiving a valid seaport access credential.

7.2.3 Transportation Workers Identification Credential

The predominant U.S. federal legislation related to port security, the MTSA, established the groundwork for the Transportation Workers Identification Credential (TWIC), a national identification card. TWIC is administered by the Transportation

Security Administration and the U.S. Coast Guard. The TWIC is designed to provide a uniform means of identifying workers in national transportation industries, not only in maritime and ports, but in aviation, rail, trucking, and related sectors. TWICs will be issued to merchant mariners, as well as workers who require unescorted access to secure areas of ports, vessels, and outer continental shelf facilities. It was originally estimated that 750,000 workers, including longshoremen, truck drivers, and port employees would require a TWIC. The program is being planned to incorporate biometric technology to enable agencies to positively identify the individual presenting the credential for access. Issuance will be dependent on immigration-, criminal-, and terrorist-screening checks and the provision of a fingerprint for biometric identification.

In 2007, the U.S. Coast Guard issued an NVIC entitled, "Guidance for the Implementation of the Transportation Worker Identification Credential (TWIC) Program in the Maritime Sector." This NVIC details the enrollment and issuance process and provides guidance on TWIC implementation. In early 2008, the U.S. House of Representatives, Coast Guard Subcommittee of the House Transportation and Infrastructure Committee, held a hearing to determine the status of the TWIC program. Reports of progress were generally positive; however, implementation issues, including a revised estimate that 1.5 million people might require the card, have delayed complete implementation and raised maritime industry worries about the impact of this program on port commerce and operations. As of January 2008, TWIC programs were operating in fifty-four U.S. ports, including two of the largest, Los Angeles–Long Beach and New York–New Jersey, with 110,000 TWIC enrollments and 12,000 credentials issued (BPS Newsletter 2008). By mid-2008, concerns about the TWIC program bureaucracy (e.g., busy phone lines, crowded enrollment facilities, repetitive background checks, and the $132.50 cost of the card) continued to proliferate, but 353,187 employees had pre-enrolled, with about 90,000 cards issued (Hall 2008).

One important concern for port security management is the possibility of having to maintain concurrent operations of both TWIC and existing port credentialing systems. The U.S. Coast Guard is implementing TWIC in port facilities on a rolling basis. The compliance dates for facilities vary and depend on when enrollment processes are completed in a particular COTP Zone (Blank Rome LLP 2007). The U.S. DHS (2008) advised that the final compliance date for the TWIC program will be April 15, 2009, and is working with maritime industry officials to effect TWIC implementation. As the time frame for TWIC implementation depends to some extent on port infrastructure, systems, and organizational capabilities, theoretically, there could be an undetermined amount of time before TWIC can be fully implemented, since the deadline has already been extended. Ports may have to consider maintaining dual credentialing systems until it is certain that TWIC will be ready for a full operational phase.

Another important concern for Port FSOs and managers, primarily associated with developing infrastructure, is the functionality of TWIC biometric readers at port access points.

Biometrics refers to methods for uniquely recognizing humans based upon one or more physical traits, such as through the use of fingerprints, voiceprint identification, and retina scans. For port security professionals, adapting existing access control systems to biometrics suggests a need to understand the latest biometric technologies, including their vocabularies, applications, parameters, and basic features. The operation of biometric card readers able to read individual fingerprints and media across a spectrum of port-operating environments will require considerable analysis by port security. Card readers must be installed at all locations such that pedestrians, vehicle drivers, and passengers have ready access to biometric reading devices. Access control systems may be designed to enable pedestrians and vehicle occupants at access gates to present fingerprints and credentials without interacting directly with a human gate operator. Decisions regarding access-point architecture and systems design must balance cost, efficiency, and gate throughput time against risk assessments and security concerns, in particular port environments and facilities. Alternative reader systems may include portable or handheld devices that can be used in different locations or for vehicles with multiple occupants. The Port FSO should consider the spectrum of vehicles that will be accessing the port (e.g., buses, labor shuttles, large delivery vehicles). There may be obvious safety, throughput, and access issues regarding wheelchair users or handicapped drivers and large vehicles with multiple occupants. Port development and maintenance staff may require specialized equipment and expertise to be able to build proper enclosures for mounting TWIC readers in suitable locations. The wiring and placement of computer equipment and cabling within existing or planned security gatehouses and kiosks will be based on available space and competition with electronic routing requirements. Gatehouse space constraints as well as current operational requirements will be key factors in considering the purchase and installation of new access control systems required by TWIC. Outlying or temporary port access gates may have no infrastructure, power, or connectivity in place with which to interface between TWIC servers and readers.

7.2.4 Credentialing Procedures

Port security must institute procedures for employees and visitors to receive photo identification for display prior to having access granted to a restricted access area. Employee identification cards should be issued upon initial employment and be revalidated on a periodic basis. Personnel management procedures should be in place to provide controls for ensuring that employees return their identification cards upon separation or upon change of responsibilities, such as reassignment to another work location or changes in employers. Identification badges for employees and visitors should be issued only upon production of verifiable, government-issued photographic identification (e.g., a passport, a driver's license). Visitor identification credentials should indicate whether the visitor must be escorted or is permitted unescorted access. Procedures should include the following:

- Permanent identification cards are issued to employees who are expected to have regular and frequent access to seaport restricted access areas. The credential is issued for a predetermined period, for example, one year, with a clearly identifiable expiration date.

- Temporary identification cards may be issued to individuals whose period of employment or regular access to the seaport is for a limited duration. For example, an employee hired to work on a temporary basis, or for a project expected to last for a limited time, may be issued a credential for access that expires on a given date, for example, one month from the date of issuance.

- Visitor passes may be issued for a one-time entrance to a seaport's restricted access area. Visitors can be business visitors or vendors or personal visitors (e.g., friends/family of crew or employees). Visitor credentials should be specific as to whether the access is escorted or unescorted, and what entity is responsible for the escort. Procedures for the issuance of visitors' credentials should include instructions on the displaying or wearing of the badge (e.g., above the waist, not covered by clothing), security of the badge (e.g., how to report it lost or stolen), and where/if to return the credential upon exiting the seaport.

7.2.5 Credentialing Classification Systems

The purpose of a credentialing classification system is to designate the type and extent of access an individual may be granted to the seaport based on the need for a person to be in a particular area. Classification categories for seaport restricted access areas include the following:

- Permanent employees who work at the seaport: These individuals would have the widest level of access based on their having been preauthorized by port management in coordination with port-employing organizations. Permanent employees may have the widest level of access, but the port may further restrict access as to the locations and times during which the employee is required to work. For example, access may be limited or prohibited during an employee's off hours or when a particular port facility or operation is closed.

- Day workers or casual laborers: Many ports depend on a significant amount of temporary employees, day laborers, or casual workers. Often, these employees do not have regular employment and are only hired when there is a need to supplement the normal operations with additional workers. A credentialing system may designate a classification for this category of worker to distinguish them from the regularly scheduled workforce. Procedures must exist for the issuance of temporary labor identification badges specific to particular restricted access areas, including logs and records for temporary labor badges reported lost or stolen. Seaports must develop procedures for issuing temporary labor identification credentials. Office staff should be able to issue credentials based on predetermined needs. Logbooks or computer records must be maintained to control lost, stolen, or unreturned temporary labor credentials.

- Employees of companies with business at the port but who do not access restricted access areas on a regular basis: Seaports may have organizations operating at the port whose operations do not require employees to be in the restricted areas of port operations. Travel agencies, cruise lines, cargo handlers, restaurants, shops, and the like may operate at the port, but it may not be necessary for employees to be in the areas of the docks, wharves, berths, or cargo-handling areas. Credentialing categories may restrict access to these employees to public or nonrestricted areas of the seaport.

- Ships' crew members: Often, ships' crew members, especially if from other countries, may not be in possession of sufficient crew identification credentials. Crew members may be issued a limited form of seaport identification to enable them to transit through the seaport between the vessel and the public (nonrestricted) areas.

- Cruise or ferry passengers: Passengers should be in possession of authorized tickets or boarding documentation before being permitted access to terminals and ship-loading areas. If practical, seaports can issue passengers a temporary credential identifying them as passengers for the purpose of transiting between the public and restricted areas of the seaport.

- Visitors: Visitor credentials can be categorized in terms of escorted or unescorted access, and whether the visit is business or personal. Large groups of visitors may be separately categorized to ensure appropriate controls, movement, and escort throughout the visit.

7.2.6 Credential Coding

Identification cards should be coded in a manner so that a visual inspection of the card indicates the access authorization for the cardholder. The use of colors as a coding mechanism is one way for security and port employees to readily identify the classifications, areas, and levels of access a credential provides. Employees responsible for access control should have a ready means (e.g., post orders, charts, computer guides) for visually verifying the level of access when presented with an identification credential.

7.2.7 Production Processes

Identification cards should be produced by a process that allows them to be durable and resistant to alteration or tampering. Credentials, if not durable, can become faded, distorted, or unreadable. Card production systems and processes should produce credentials that are laminated and resistant to deterioration or distortion. Efforts to alter credentials can be thwarted by using media that make tampering efforts obvious. Credential screening personnel should be provided with training and orientation to enable them to spot altered or distorted credentials, and procedures should be in place to require people with distorted cards to return them for reissuance.

7.2.8 Credential Sequencing

Port identification cards should be issued by serial number. By issuing credentials in sequence, port administrators build in control processes to improve identification of lost or stolen credentials and to improve accountability and inventory controls. Accountability for issued badges strengthens the port's ability to resolve discrepancies and minimizes the ability of criminals and terrorists to convert stolen cards for illegal uses. One issue for management is ensuring that staff responsible for ordering identification card stock be cognizant of maintaining awareness of card sequencing. Especially in systems that have embedded electronic data, card stock ordering can be a significant cost if attention to sequencing in ordering is not maintained.

7.2.9 Lost or Stolen Credentials

Procedures must be developed to require the reporting of lost or stolen port identification cards. Cardholders must be instructed to officially report lost or stolen credentials. Seaports may wish to require that an official police report accompany a request for the reissuance of a lost or stolen card. Official documentation substantiates a cardholder's request for reissuance and provides law enforcement authorities with a mechanism for tracking credentials throughout the criminal justice system.

7.2.10 Role of Port Users in Credentialing Programs

Port users, most importantly port employees, can also reduce risk and vulnerabilities by assisting the seaport in controlling the ingress/egress of vehicles, vessels, cargo, and people. Port identification cards may be issued to regular port users and personnel, and it is essential to ensure that cardholders adhere to the rules as follows regarding issued credentials:

- Ensure credentials are current. Expired credentials will likely prevent a person from accessing a port's restricted access areas. The use of expired credentials contributes to undermining the security of the port. All employees should be cognizant of the expiration date and take steps to renew the credential before it expires.
- All employees must possess and visibly display the issued port credential. Users should be prepared to present the credential for inspection to security

personnel when requested. When credentials are not visibly displayed, users may be stopped and questioned as to their business in a particular area.

- Management must enforce the rules. Managers and staff responsible for groups of employees must ensure all staff adhere to the rules concerning port credentials. There should be no tolerance for users not possessing and displaying a valid port credential. When numerous people are observed not displaying credentials, the impression is that there is no enforcement. Efforts to undermine the credentialing system create an environment of lax security.

- There must be zero tolerance for violators. Port users and employees who refuse to follow established identification procedures should be prohibited from working or entering port facilities.

7.2.11 *Visualizing and Inspecting Access Credentials*

To improve the identification and credentialing system, seaport security and operations personnel must be instructed in the proper visualization and inspection of access credentials.

- Observing the information contained on the credential: Name, date of birth, employer, physical description, expiration date. Credentials should include vital information unique to the cardholder. Inspecting personnel should be trained to compare the data against the person presenting the credential to make identification certain. Doubts about the validity of the credential may be resolved by the screener asking the cardholder pertinent questions (e.g., How old are you?), without the cardholder looking at the credential for the answer.

- Comparing photograph and description to person presenting the credential: An essential screening tool is to ensure that the photograph and physical description matches the cardholder. A good opportunity for a Port FSP drill is to have security staff practice screening individuals at checkpoints. *Red-teaming*, whereby an inspection team takes the perspective of an adversary to assess weaknesses in existing plans and operations, can utilize people carrying different credentials to attempt access at various port screening points. The goal should not be to antagonize or scare staff, but to train them to look at each and every person and credential closely, especially the ones for people who gain frequent and regular access.

- Recognizing counterfeit or altered credentials: Screening personnel should be thoroughly familiar with the makeup and composition of the authorized port credential(s) to be able to spot altered or unauthorized documents. Intelligence information indicating how other documents have been altered should be presented in training so that employees have a basis for understanding how documents can be altered.

7.2.12 Visitor Controls

The Port FSP should provide clear procedures, rules, and regulations for controlling the access of visitors to the port's secured, controlled, and/or restricted areas and facilities. Visitor control issues and concerns include:

- Visitors should be invited guests of specific port businesses, tenants, or agencies.
- Visitors should be authorized access only to areas specific to their port business.
- Visitors should be restricted from unauthorized roaming around the port.
- Visitors should be required to provide valid government-issued photo identification, such as a current driver's license or passport, to obtain port credentials.
- Visitors should be required to undergo port vehicle or pedestrian screening activities at any security checkpoint.
- Temporary identification credentials should be valid only for the period required to be on the port or expire at a predetermined time.
- Temporary credentials should be displayed on the outermost garment on the upper body and be readily visible at all times.
- Visitors' vehicles should be provided with an identification document (e.g., mirror hang, placard, temporary decal).
- Visitors driving vehicles should be instructed to observe No Parking zones, fire lanes, or other restricted vehicle areas.
- Visitors entering restricted access areas must display a port-issued credential and be escorted at all times by an individual with a restricted access area badge for that location.
- While on port property, all people are subject to local, state, and federal regulations.
- Visitors should be instructed to report any suspicious activity to port security and/or local police.

7.2.13 Visitor Brochure

Visitors to the port facility should be provided with a brochure orienting them to the facility, but most importantly, educating them on security and safety issues. The following are examples of the types of security information that should be provided to port visitors who are issued temporary identification credentials.

- A statement of the port's security and safety policies
- Identification form requirements for people wishing to enter restricted access areas, including examples of acceptable identification (e.g., government-issued, include current photograph, etc.)

- A statement on the port's security screening policies and locations of screening points
- Information on the port's security organization
- Information concerning port law enforcement organizations
- A map of port roadways, terminals, and restricted and public access areas
- Information concerning public transportation, including locations of parking lots, shuttle or bus stops, and taxi stands
- Information on conditions for obtaining entry to port restricted access areas
- Requirements for visitors to report to port security
- Requirements for visitors to have authorized business on the port
- Entry into restricted areas only upon direction by authorized port staff
- Provisions for both escorted and unescorted access into port restricted access areas
- Provisions for wearing high-visibility clothing and safety equipment in industrial operations areas
- Restrictions on smoking
- Restrictions on firearms, dangerous weapons, and hazardous materials
- Restrictions on the use of cameras and video and audio recording equipment
- Restrictions on the use of mobile computing devices, cellular telephones, and personal data devices
- Information concerning domestic animals or pets on port facilities
- A statement on the port's exposure to liability for lost property, damage, or injury on port property
- Information on the use and parking of motor vehicles on port property
- Specific information for vessel passengers or for the drop-off and pickup of vessel passengers and crew
- Information concerning requirements for the delivery and reception of cargo shipments
- Information concerning how to report emergencies or request assistance from port security and law enforcement organizations
- Instructions for contacting port security and/or law enforcement regarding suspicious people, behavior, vehicles, packages, and potential health or safety concerns
- Information for contractors or vendors performing services on port facilities

7.3 Restricted Area Access Controls

Access control systems represent that component of port security in which the Port FSO makes determinations as to what people, vehicles, and materials will be permitted to enter the seaport. Access controls include, but are not limited to, requiring identification cards for employees and visitors; requiring advance notice of deliveries; and the screening of vehicles, pedestrians, and cargo.

7.3.1 Balancing Access Control and Port Commerce

Access into port facilities is a challenge without severely disrupting port operations. Port management must develop access control criteria that will strike a sensible balance between security and commerce. Severe access controls that constrain the ability of the port to operate effectively may encourage port users to seek alternatives. Identification of the proper access control restrictions includes participation by port users in a process to develop realistic security mechanisms. As such, cooperative leadership among port users is essential in developing realistic access controls.

7.3.2 Identifying and Defining Restricted Access Areas

Port management must define and identify the restricted access areas of the port facility so that all people are aware of areas where only those with proper authorization are permitted access. Restricted areas should include, but are not limited to, the following areas:

- Cargo storage or staging areas. This includes cargo container yards, cargo warehouses or sheds, and areas where cargo is prepped or staged for transit. The objective is to impede people's abilities to tamper with or compromise the security of cargo to deter theft, smuggling, and improper or illegal import/ export of goods.
- Docks, berths, wharves. Only those people with a need to be there should be allowed access to work areas adjacent to vessels. Major concerns relate to access to cargo, vessels, provisions, passenger luggage; the ability to smuggle contraband; and the introduction of improvised explosive and parasitic devices in support of terrorist activities. Figure 7.2 illustrates passenger luggage, which has been inspected by security, staged on the dock for loading onto a passenger vessel. The security and protection of the interface areas between the port facility and the vessel is critical in maintaining the integrity of articles such as these.
- Fuel storage or transfer yards. Some seaports may have significant fuel storage and transfer facilities, such as those illustrated in Figure 7.3. Major fuel transfer seaports may be regional receiving facilities for certain basic products, such as aviation fuel and gasoline. Only those people with a need should be allowed access to fuel storage facilities to protect the facilities themselves and to deter terrorists and criminals from converting fuel into a weapon of mass destruction.
- Passenger cruise and ferry terminals. Terminals represent the interface between the port facility and the passenger-carrying vessel. The restricted access area should be defined to ensure protection of the passengers and the

Figure 7.2   Passenger luggage staged on a dock prior to vessel loading.

vessel. Only passengers and authorized employees should be permitted access to passenger terminals.

Port restricted access areas should be clearly marked, posted, and delineated to identify them as locations requiring special authorization to enter. Signage and other visual media should provide clear and accurate warnings and information. As illustrated in Figure 7.4, signs should be minimal, easy to read and understand, and convey relevant information concerning applicable laws, ordinances, and regulations to inform people about penalties for entry into a restricted access area without authorization. Borders or barriers between the restricted and nonrestricted access areas must be clear and unambiguous.

7.3.3 Gates and Gate Access Controls

Restricted access area controls are comprised of physical infrastructure, procedures, systems, and guidance for screening, monitoring, and controlling access into the facility. These controls emphasize the physical barriers and protective measures that the seaport can integrate into its security protocols to further control access into the port. Gates and gate access controls represent the most important physical access control components for seaports. Seaport security is enhanced by constructing and maintaining physical gates, infrastructure, processes, and systems for establishing primary access and control points for entering seaport restricted access areas.

05/26/2003

Figure 7.3   Port fuel storage and transfer facilities require specific access controls.

- Gates: those points of access between the restricted and nonrestricted access areas of seaports. Gates may be used for vehicular and/or pedestrian traffic. Gates should be constructed and situated so that they provide for the most efficient balance between security and commerce, given the level of security in place at the seaport.
- Gates Access Controls: the systems and processes effected to control access through the gate. These may be comprised of any or a combination of the following: gate arms, camera systems, access control systems, identification and credentialing media readers, security guards, alarms and alarm monitoring systems, gatehouses, communications systems, lighting, and other physical barriers.

7.3.4 Preventing and Deterring Access to Restricted Areas

Breaches of security can be directly attributable to port failure to prevent unauthorized people from accessing the designated restricted access areas. Pedestrians who walk past posted port security officers without challenge, or vehicles able to avoid scrutiny in entering restricted areas, represent vulnerabilities the port facility must promptly address. Statutorily authorized agencies, such as the U.S. Coast Guard, can issue

Figure 7.4 Signage posted advising of port restricted area.

discrepancy reports, levy fines, and even close ports down entirely in the event a port fails to adequately protect its facilities from unauthorized access. Port security management and staff must be held responsible for their actions. Staff assigned to access points must be comprehensively instructed and supervised to scrutinize approaching vehicles and people wishing to access the port facility. Supervisors are directly responsible for ensuring that access control procedures are being strictly adhered to by their assigned officers at all access points. Continuing breaches of security related to access control is a signal for the Port FSO to conduct training with all security staff to review and emphasize procedures for preventing and deterring access to the restricted areas. Emphasis should be on how important it is for all staff to be attentive to their positions and responsibilities.

7.3.5 Controlling Vehicles in Restricted Access Areas

Vehicular access to the port's restricted access areas, such as common cargo dock areas, gantries, wharves, and so forth, should be severely restricted in the Port FSP. Federal, and perhaps also state and local, port security regulations may specifically prohibit personal vehicles, as well as people without specific business, in restricted access areas of the port. All docks, wharves, berths, and cargo-operating areas should be designated restricted, and with possibly some exceptions, no personal vehicles should be allowed. Ports may have to consider FSP provisions for special situations, such as the following:

- Construction, repair, maintenance, or service workers driving personal vehicles or operating or transporting special equipment or tools
- Vessel-provision delivery vehicles (smaller business operations, e.g., food vendors, messengers, and contract repair personnel, may have employees driving their personal vehicles, as opposed to commercial vehicles, as part of their delivery services)
- Vehicles making supply deliveries to companies with offices in restricted areas
- Commercially marked utility vehicles (e.g., water and sewer, electric company)
- Vehicles that may require close access along fence lines, adjacent to cargo containers, in gantry areas, alongside vessels, or in other undesignated parking areas
- Vehicles requiring access to restricted access areas that do not have registered port-issued parking permits or decals
- Parking on wharves (the U.S. Coast Guard and other regulatory agencies may consider the wharf to mean the entire area between waterlines and fences or other boundary delineators)
- Interterminal transfers of vehicles and cargo

7.3.6 Temporary Restricted Area Vehicle Authorization Documentation

Certain operations within port facilities will have a need to admit individuals with their vehicles on a temporary or itinerant basis. For example, construction activities may require personnel to be shifted from one job site to another, or vessels at a pier may require specialized repairs necessitating equipment from a vendor who has not already received a permanent access credential. Employees and vehicles that normally access a port's restricted area should be vetted in advance and provided with permanent credentials; to control the temporary access of vehicles into restricted areas, the port security agency should develop a form for temporary access that can be issued to the drivers of vehicles.

Figure 7.5 provides a temporary restricted area vehicle access credential template, which can be adapted by port facilities to fit a variety of purposes. For example, the documentation, in the form of a letter, may authorize temporary commercial or construction vehicle access and parking to areas adjacent to a cruise terminal or wharf area for the purposes of construction and other critical maintenance or repair work. The language can be modified to specify that authorization does not permit parking in illegal areas such as near fire hydrants, in tow-away zones, and so forth. The port facility can also specify that the vehicle be properly identified by visibly displaying the issued document and that all drivers, occupants, and workers involved with the activity must have a valid port-issued access credential or temporary visitor pass. The documentation can also articulate specific restrictions, such as requiring that fluorescent

---

WORKZONE AUTHORIZATION LETTER

DATE and TIME of AUTHORIZATION: March 16, 2008, 3:00 p.m – 4:00 p.m.
LOCATION AUTHORIZED: Oceangoing Cargo Terminal, Dock 7
COMPANY: New World Propeller Service, Inc.
DRIVER/PORT IDENTIFICATION NUMBER: John H. Doe/ Temporary Day Pass # 051608-25
OCCUPANT(S): Robert L. Jones/Temporary Day Pass # 051608-26
VEHICLE: 2002 International Truck, Red, FL tag #XYZ-123

Pursuant to Port of _____ security procedures, this letter authorizes temporary commercial/construction vehicle access to and parking in the specified restricted access areas for the purposes of construction and other critical maintenance or repair work. This authorization does not permit parking in illegal areas such as fire hydrants, tow-away zones, etc. The vehicle must be properly identified by visibly displaying this letter and all drivers and occupants involved with the activity must have Port Identification (Valid *Port Credential or ID or Temporary Day Pass*). Fluorescent cones shall also be placed around the vehicle or vehicles performing work at the cruise terminal. The vehicle driver/occupants must be escorted into, at, and out of the restricted access area by: (SPECIFY CONDITIONS OR OTHER ESCORT REQUIREMENTS)

Prior to accessing or parking in any restricted access area, commercial/construction vehicles are required to be screened and have credentials verified at the Vehicle Inspection Station, located at:
_____. This station is open daily from 6:00 a.m. to 4:00 p.m.

If it is necessary to verify validity of this letter, or in the case of a related emergency, notify: (PORT FACILITY SECURITY AGENCY)

Shift Commander   Telephone Number: _____
Port Security Department

Chief   Telephone Number: _____
Port Security Department

_____
Signature/Title (Chief of Port Security or Authorized Designee)   Date

Vehicle Inspection Verification		
Vehicle License Plate Number	Security Officer Name/Signature	Date/Time

Figure 7.5 Temporary Restricted Area Vehicle Access Credential Template.

cones be placed around the vehicle or that vehicles remain at specified locations for limited times.

7.4 Vehicle and Pedestrian Screening

People and vehicles accessing seaports must be subjected to screening activities designed to deter the infiltration of weapons, materials, and contraband that could be used to commit acts of terrorism or criminal activity at seaports. People and vehicles must be required to pass through a screening checkpoint to access a designated restricted area, such as a vessel dock or a cargo yard. Security screeners should be posted to screen the individual and anything he/she may be carrying. Screeners should be trained to look for items and materials that could harm the port facility. Obvious weapons include such items as guns, knives, and clubs, but screening protocols should include training and instruction in detecting less obvious items that could be converted for use as weapons. The aircraft hijackers who committed the September 2001 terrorist attacks were able to introduce common box cutters through the airport screening points, which were then used to subdue passengers and crew. Screeners should also be trained to look for materials that, although not weapons themselves, could be used as weapon components. The possession and transportation of hazardous materials on ports must be balanced against the purpose of the visit. Certain materials, although dangerous, are commonly used in port operations (e.g., welding equipment and gases for vessel and equipment repairs) and must be screened and controlled while being used on port property.

7.4.1 Suspicious Indicators in Screening

A good access control program includes an understanding of human behavior and physical opportunities for compromising security. A facility's potential for compromise is reduced by identifying personal motives and minimizing opportunities for threats. Access control screening involves recognizing characteristics and behavioral patterns of people who are likely to commit unlawful acts at seaports. All port users and employees, but especially staff with primary responsibilities for authorizing access, should be aware of and concerned about people seeking access to, seeking information about, photographing, or inspecting any of the following:

- General layout of port facility. Ask questions about people seeking details about the physical layout of the seaport. What is that person's business on the port? Is he or she affiliated with a bona fide port user organization?
- Location of actual or potential access points. Knowledge of ways to enter port facilities would provide a criminal or terrorist with vital information. Be suspicious about people who seem to be conducting surveillance or watching entry and exit points on and around the seaport.

- Seaport protective measures. These include guard postings and patrols, monitoring equipment, communications capabilities, data processing, alarms, lighting, and police response. A seaport's security system is dependent upon protecting sensitive security information. If people are asking questions about security mechanisms and processes, attention must be paid to the reasons why that information is being asked. Port users should report any suspicious activity or requests for information to police and/or security authorities at the seaport.
- Numerical strength and functions of security personnel. This kind of information should never be disseminated. Individuals seeking information about seaport guard strength and locations should be referred to security authorities for evaluation.
- Security doors and barriers. Inquire about and be alert for people conducting physical inspections of security physical access controls. They may be trying to assess the strength and vulnerabilities of doors, gates, fences, and so forth.
- Utilities and power-generating equipment. Only people who are identified and authorized should be permitted to access and inspect utilities and power-generating equipment.
- Vessel mooring areas, berths, navigation aids. Be alert for private watercraft operating in the waters adjacent to seaports. Are they conducting appropriate recreational or commercial activities, or are they assessing port operations, navigational aids, berthing capabilities? Report suspicious marine activities to the designated law enforcement or security waterside patrol forces.
- Fire and rescue capabilities. Terrorists and criminals may attempt to assess the response capabilities of first responders. Report any suspicious questions, activities, and incidents to police and/or security.
- Roadways and transportation infrastructure. Be alert for people and vehicles that appear to be circling seaport property repeatedly with no discernible reason. Repeated observations of the same people or vehicles, including aircraft, should generate a report to law enforcement or security to investigate.
- Levels of supervision and management of security and port operations staff. Information about the supervisory activities and management capabilities of seaport operations and security staff should be closely guarded. Do not answer questions from strangers or over the telephone that provide critical data about staffing, budgets, reports, plans, and so forth. Refer inquiries to the appropriate seaport staff for determination of whether the information should be provided.

7.4.2 Screening Equipment

Specialized equipment, such as metal detectors, x-ray machines, and hand wands assist port security in screening people, personal effects, ships' provisions, noncontainerized cargo, and vehicles. Screening individuals and vehicles can be enhanced by integrating equipment into the security regime geared toward assisting security personnel in detecting illegal or dangerous objects. Metal detectors can be set up to detect the presence of metallic objects on people. Stationary metal detectors can be supplemented by handheld devices, which guards can use to screen individuals more closely. X-ray devices can be used to examine the personal effects, bags, and other hand-carried items. Vehicles carrying cargo containers can be routed through stationary or mobile systems designed to provide imagery of container contents.

7.4.3 Delivery of Vessel Provisions

United States federal seaport security regulations contained in the MTSA of 2002 mandate that 100 percent of the vehicles delivering provisions to vessels be screened prior to delivery to the vessel. U.S. Coast Guard (2003, par. 2.6) NVIC 11-02, "Recommended Security Guidelines for Facilities," provides the following specific considerations for seaports constructing vessel-provisions screening protocols:

- Ensure checking of ships' provisions and package integrity
- Prevent ships' stores from being accepted without inspection
- Prevent tampering
- Prevent ships' provisions from being accepted unless ordered
- Ensure searching the delivery vehicle
- Ensure escorting delivery vehicles within the facility
- Verify and inspect ships' provisions, transport vehicles, and storage areas
- Require advance notification as to type of provision, driver details, and vehicle registration
- Designate restricted areas to perform inspections of provisions
- Ensure screening of delivery vehicles
- Ensure that the ships' provisions entering the seaport match the delivery documentation
- Develop inventory control procedures

Since the implementation of MTSA, U.S. ports have had to develop processes to manage advance notice of vessel provisions deliveries for cruise and cargo vessels required by the statute. Efforts have included manual systems requiring a substantial amount of labor and paperwork. There are systems and technology available using Web-based or proprietary software that may meet the MTSA vendor security requirements. Using a password-protected, online, or server-based platform to manage vendor access information, client representatives can electronically authorize vendor access to port facilities by selecting stored information from various secured lists. These systems may be developed to interface directly with cargo and cruise lines' provisions management systems. Ports and port users will need to coordinate in systems development to accept the information provided through this online application in lieu of manual systems, and the Port FSP will need to integrate these systems in its documentation subject to review by appropriate regulatory agencies. Port FSOs can obtain product demonstrations of these applications, which can greatly enhance ports' abilities to organize and process advance notices of vessel provisions deliveries. Costs may be negotiated between ports and port users to share the burden of new technologies developed for these systems.

7.5 U.S. Coast Guard–Recommended Access Control Measures

U.S. Coast Guard (2003) NVIC 11-02, "Recommended Security Guidelines for Facilities," provides guidance on developing security plans, procedures, and measures for port facilities. The U.S. Coast Guard publishes NVICs to provide guidance for seaports in developing security plans, procedures, and security measures. Port FSOs can use these NVICs and other published regulations and notices as mechanisms for developing and implementing security access control measures and activities, in concert with regular risk assessment activities. NVIC 11-02 can be used by seaport security management as a guide to effecting restricted area access controls and processes. These measures include the following:

Limiting the number of access points. Seaports effect access control by minimizing the number of places a person or vehicle may enter the seaport. Permanently closing unused gates and concentrating traffic into only the minimum number of gates necessary enables the facility to concentrate its resources on the areas most needed to be secured.

Monitoring or securing all access points. Through a combination of access controls (human, physical, electronic), seaports must ensure they have all potential entry points monitored and secured.

Identifying and searching/inspecting all vehicles, people, bags, deliveries, articles, or packages entering the facility. A primary component of any access control system is knowing who and what is coming onto the seaport. Identification and credentialing systems are the first step in knowing who is coming into the port. Screening procedures to identify personal effects, vehicle contents, cargo, provisions, and other materials are needed to ensure the port identifies all materials entering the port.

Denying access to those who refuse to submit to security verification at a point of access. Seaports must have established procedures to disallow entry to people who refuse to submit themselves and/or their vehicles to access control checks. People refusing to comply should also be referred to appropriate law enforcement personnel for investigation and follow-up.

Restricting access to authorized and essential personnel and providing methods of identification for employees and visitors. Credentialing systems are essential for allowing access by employees and frequent visitors. Access controls must be in place to only allow access to authorized personnel in possession of valid credentials.

Establishing parking procedures and designating parking areas. Controls on the movement of vehicles within the port are essential aspects of an access control system. Seaports must designate parking areas and ensure that only the vehicles so authorized are permitted in the designated areas. Seaports should also establish parking permit or decal systems to enable management to identify the owners of vehicles allowed to access the seaport.

Allowing only authorized personnel to have access to vessels. Effective port access controls must include steps to ensure that only crew, ticketed passengers, and authorized service delivery personnel have access to vessels.

Prescheduling arrivals of vessels and work conducted at the facility. Controlling the arrival of vessels at ports entails awareness of what vessels are expected and when. Unauthorized or unexpected vessels must be controlled so that the port is aware of the security conditions at all times. Additionally, seaports must control the work operations by having precise schedules for cargo and other ship operations. Prescheduling work activities enables the seaport to know whom to expect to be on the seaport at preset times.

Erecting fences or other barriers to designate a perimeter. Physical demarcations of the seaport perimeter provide a visual cue, as well as a physical separation, so that people clearly understand the boundaries between the public and restricted areas of the seaport.

Implementing procedures for escorting visitors, contractors, vendors, and other non-facility employees. Seaports effect positive access controls when they implement methods for escorting nonregular access individuals through the seaport. Port user organizations that have a need for visitors, contractors, and others must take responsibility for escorting these individuals through the seaport.

References

BBC News. 2008, May 8. Airport staff avoid crime checks. http://news.bbc.co.uk/2/hi/uk_news/7389219.stm (accessed July 4, 2008).

Blank Rome LLP. 2007. Coast Guard/TSA issue TWIC final rule: Final rule postpones card reader requirement and addresses certain challenges facing the program. Maritime Developments Advisory. http://www.blankrome.com/index.cfm?contentID=37&itemID=1215 (accessed July 14, 2008).

BPS Newsletter. 2008. House hearing held on TWIC program. PortSecurityNews.com. http://portsecuritynews.com/news/templates/registered.asp?articleid=1892&zoneid=29 (accessed January 31, 2008).

Collins Center for Public Policy. 2006. Florida's restrictions on employment opportunities for people with criminal records. http://www.collinscenter.org/usr_doc/OffEmp.pdf (accessed May 23, 2008).

Federal Register. 2005. 70 Fed. Reg. 17820, Electronic transmission of passenger and crew manifests for vessels and aircraft. http://web.nbaa.org/public/ops/intl/apis/apisfinalrule040705.
pdf (accessed July 14, 2008).

Florida Statutes. 2007. Florida Statute 311.12, Seaport security standards. http://www.leg.state.
fl.us/statutes/index.cfm?App_mode=Display_Statute&Search_String=&URL=Ch0311/
SEC12.HTM&Title=->2007->Ch0311->Section%2012#0311.12 (accessed July 13, 2008).

Hall, Mimi. 2008, May 19. Problems beset worker ID program. *USA Today*. http://www.usatoday.
com/news/washington/2008-05-18-workerid_N.htm (accessed July 4, 2008).

U.S. Coast Guard. 2003. Navigation and vessel inspection circular (NVIC) no. 11-02:
Recommended security guidelines for facilities. http://www.uscg.mil/hq/g-m/nvic/11-02.
pdf (accessed July 13, 2008).

U.S. Coast Guard. 2007. Navigation and vessel inspection circular (NVIC) no. 03-07: Guidance
for the implementation of the Transportation Worker Identification Credential (TWIC)
program in the maritime sector. http://www.uscg.mil/hq/cg5/nvic/pdf/2007/NVIC%20
03-07.pdf (accessed July 14, 2008).

U.S. Coast Guard. 2008. National vessel movement center. http://www.nvmc.uscg.gov/index.
html (accessed July 14, 2008).

U.S. Customs and Border Protection. 2003. Trade Act of 2002: Advance electronic information.
http://www.cbp.gov/xp/cgov/trade/trade_outreach/advance_info/ (accessed July 14, 2008).

U.S. Department of Homeland Security. 2008. DHS realigns TWIC compliance date. http://
www.dhs.gov/xnews/releases/pr_1209745179774.shtm (accessed July 14, 2008).

8

PHYSICAL SECURITY ISSUES IN THE PORT FACILITY

8.1 Managing Physical Defenses in a Competitive Environment

Physical security measures consist of those resources and systems that provide the seaport with deterrence capabilities in preventing crime as well as the introduction of potentially dangerous people, vehicles, and materials into the port. Within the context of the present discussion, it would be prohibitive to analyze every conceivable physical security resource. There are multiple texts that provide port security professionals with detailed technical information on materials, windows, doors, locks, keys, alarm systems, lighting, and the myriad of other physical security hardware available for the port facility. Rather than dissect hardware, this discussion is grounded in those fundamental physical security management issues that are likely to confront the Port FSO on a regular basis. To be sure, the Port FSO must review relevant government regulations and industry conventions to fully appreciate the standards that most port facilities must develop and adhere to. But, perhaps more important than knowing which specific type of padlock to put on a gate or whether the parking control system decals should be on the inside or outside of vehicles is understanding from a managerial perspective what physical security issues are predominant and how decisions affecting physical security can be made effectively.

In general, port management operates on a plane driven by maritime market directions and the ability of the port to meet its customers' needs. For instance, all one needs to do to appreciate the competition among ports in the container-shipping business is to take a look at a map of the southeastern coast of the United States. Moving from south to north, the deepwater ports in Miami, Fort Lauderdale, West Palm Beach, Jacksonville, Savannah, and Charleston are just a few of the U.S. ports that engage in some type of cargo-shipping business. While each port has its unique market niche, operating conditions, and business models, the fact is that the world's container-shipping fleet has many choices it can make when it comes to deciding which port to do business with. If the Port of Miami cannot handle an increase in container capacity, Port Everglades, just twenty-five miles north, may be able to. The reality is that shippers and cargo operators make decisions based on what works best for their customers and their business models. If containers coming off ships in one port are being delayed by ground-level traffic management issues, it may be just as easy for them to move their deliveries to another port.

For this reason, the Port FSO must have a collateral appreciation, not just for the physical security plans to be emplaced, but also for how those plans will affect market decisions by the port's key customers. For the most part, port directors will probably not concern themselves with ground-level, physical security issues, until and unless those issues constrain the port's ability to compete successfully in the market. When conflicts surface, for example, when a cargo terminal operator is prevented from moving freely about the port property to shift containers or repair equipment due to locked gates, strictly enforced access controls, or new credentialing requirements, it will be the port director who will be receiving heated telephone calls and e-mails about the failure of security to appreciate the business operations necessary for the movement of freight. Thus, the Port FSO must be cognizant of how physical security decisions in the port facility affect port operations in the aggregate. While the FSO may be acting rationally, and perhaps with sound legal support, to integrate comprehensive crime-prevention measures, those decisions must consider the impact on port clients in terms of increased expenditures for the human and physical resources that port users may be incurring as a result of hardware and systems security issues. Thus, the following discussion offers a survey of some of the more salient physical security issues that require considered managerial review as the Port FSO and port management work collectively with port users to affect security of the port.

8.2 Standard Operating Procedures

Obviously, developing and writing the Port FSP is of paramount importance as the port affects its strategy to mitigate the identified risks. A concurrent responsibility is to document how the FSP will be implemented in a practical way. Much of this documentation will be procedural in nature. A "Standard Operating Procedure (SOP) is a set of written instructions that documents a routine or repetitive activity followed by an organization. The development and use of SOPs are an integral part of a successful quality system as it provides individuals with the information to perform a job properly, and facilitates consistency in the quality and integrity of a product or end-result" (U.S. Environmental Protection Agency 2007, p. 1). SOPs provide a ready reference and resource for the staff in terms of the framework and substance of Port FSP implementation. For example, both the IMO's ISPS Code and the U.S. MTSA port facility regulations require ports to effect procedures and conditions related to baseline and heightened levels of security in the port facility. Because certain levels of security require certain actions, the Port FSO must develop mechanisms to implement these actions at the staff level. Thus, if at MARSEC level 2 a Port FSO must ensure and update the Declarations of Security it has with vessels in port, then staff must be assigned to facilitate these updates. The SOPs provide the security staff with the background, enabling legislation, organizational constructs, and procedural steps with which to effect implementation of the Port FSP. SOP "terminology is less important than content and implementation . . . Courts tend to assess liability based on factors such as:

- Systems in place to develop and maintain SOPs . . .
- Compatibility with regulatory requirements and national standards
- Consideration of unique departmental needs
- Adequacy of training and demonstration of competence
- Procedures used to monitor performance and ensure compliance" (Federal Emergency Management Agency and U.S. Fire Administration 1999, p. 2).

Thus, the Port FSO must consider SOPs from the perspective of one providing assertive guidance to staff that directs them as far as the capabilities of the port's security systems, compliance with relevant laws and regulations, acquisition of port resources, training, and compliance procedures. Failure to provide this level of direction in essence could affect the port's liability in the event of a catastrophe or failure in security that could be attributed to lax oversight and supervision of staff.

The Port FSO must review the FSP and consider those aspects that require procedural documentation. For example, SOPs must be in place to effectively control access to the port. This process begins with developing and communicating clear and basic directions for security personnel and port users. Other critical areas of port security that will likely require SOP documentation include, but are not limited to, the following:

- Establishment, organization, and operations of port security steering committees
- Conducting crime threat, terrorism threat, and vulnerability assessments
- Security guard force operations manual and procedures
- Emergency mobilization and response plans
- Communications procedures between the port security force and external local, state, and national law enforcement agencies
- Restricted area access control systems using identification and credentialing documents
- Controls on visitors in restricted areas of port facilities
- Formal guidelines for computer and information security
- Firearms and weapons restrictions

While it may not be practical to develop procedures for every conceivable event, the more the Port FSO can establish rational directions for staff to follow, the more effective Port FSP implementation will be.

8.3 Perimeter Security

Perimeter security refers to detecting, assessing, and tracking intruders and/or threats related to the facility perimeter, which is the area contiguous to and surrounding the target security environment. Physical security devices along the perimeter can include one or more of a combination of intrusion detectors, alarms, barriers, lighting, structural materials, procedural controls, and human resources. There are many ways to facilitate effective perimeter security, and in fact, the Port FSO will likely discover that there is a wide assortment of both traditional hardware and technological devices and systems available. Port FSOs must consider the various port facility operations, configurations, and layouts, as well as the port's proximate locations to adjacent waterways and metropolitan areas in planning its perimeter security. For example, the Port of Miami is an island port connected by a primary roadway bridge to the central downtown area. While it may appear to be a simple process to secure the perimeter of an island, which is surrounded by water on all sides, it can become complex when a port adjoins a highly developed roadway infrastructure, high-end residential and commercial development, world-class tourist destinations, a major city sports arena, and busy recreational and commercial inland waterways. Thus, perimeter security must be assessed in consideration of each port's unique business and operating features and its geographic features and relative place in the larger environment.

Individual components of port perimeter physical security depend on the environment and general location of the port facility. Issues related to technology and port security management will be discussed in a later chapter, but for the present discussion, the development of a well-planned perimeter security strategy should precede hardware purchase. Whatever devices and systems the Port FSO elects to develop for perimeter security, the best strategy will be one that is focused on the wise use of the environment in concert with the most efficient mix of physical and human resources to inhibit criminal activity and harm on the port facility.

8.3.1 Crime Prevention through Environmental Design

The term *defensible space* was developed by architect Oscar Newman (1996) in the early 1970s. It refers to the restructuring of a residential environment's physical layout so as to enable inhabitants to control the surrounding areas, including the streets, grounds, lobbies, hallways, and corridors, and to preserve the stability of inhabitants' lifestyles. The idea of constructing neighborhoods with defensible space as a way of preserving a community's security was further explicated as a theory of criminology by C. Ray Jeffrey (1971). Known as crime prevention through environmental design (CPTED), the theory suggests that crime can be prevented by instituting controls over human behavior. By using concepts and strategies associated with urban planning and environmental engineering, society can design its homes and businesses for safety and security by building in devices to affect what people will or will not do in given environments. CPTED builds on the relationships between crime, fear of crime, and the use of environmental constructs to reduce the probabilities of criminal activity occurring in given locations. It is "focused upon the interaction between human behavior and the 'built environment,' including both natural and constructed elements. The physical design of an environment can facilitate surveillance and access control of an area and can aid in creating a sense of property awareness (territoriality)" (Collins, Ricks, and Van Meter 2000, p. 252).

CPTED is a strategic concept that may help the Port FSO understand the relationship between effective planning and implementation of efficient physical security regimens. There are four overarching CPTED strategies that the Port FSO can draw from in effecting perimeter security:

1. Natural Surveillance. By maximizing visibility of the target environment, potential intruders can be easily observed and deterred from committing criminal activity. Visibility-enhancing features include such things as unobstructed doors and windows, pedestrian-friendly sidewalks and streets, building entryways, and illumination at night.
2. Natural Access Control. Potential intruders perceive an increased risk of detection when facilities are designed to effectively distinguish the public property from the private areas. Thus, access ways, walkways, streets, and building entrances are designed so that there are clear lines of demarcation that separate the public and private areas.
3. Territorial Reinforcement. Creating a sense of control over a designated space discourages potential intruders from invading that space. Techniques include defining property lines and separating public and private space through landscaping, pavement designs, gateway treatments, and fencing.
4. Maintenance. By maintaining landscaping and other facility features such as lighting and building surfaces, inhabitants build on the other three CPTED strategies. Figure 8.1 illustrates damage to a kiosk and fence line related to a severe storm at this port facility container storage access point. While events like this are often unpredictable, port management's ability to effect quick repairs to secure the facility contribute to the perception that the port is aware of and on top of destabilizing conditions. Likewise, routine activities such as cutting the grass, trimming the fence lines, and keeping the lights working properly all contribute to the perception that the environment is under surveillance and that the owners are in control.

In residential security applications, CPTED principles are applied when homeowners critically assess the use of landscaping, lighting, pavement lines, and similar boundaries to establish a secure sense of place about the home. Thus, the admonition to cut back the overgrowth of shrubs that obscure windows and the placement of spotlights to illuminate the property at night are part of an overall strategy that gives potential intruders the impression that someone at home means to protect what he/she

Figure 8.1 Damaged infrastructure at the port facility requires quick repairs to maintain effective perimeter security.

owns. Similarly, businesses use CPTED strategies to reinforce perceptions that the environment is under scrutiny, suggesting that any criminal activity will be observed by the owners. In small retail establishments, the use of see-through windows unobscured by advertising and the placement of cash registers so that they can be observed from the outside are devices that contribute to the perception of surveillance of an establishment. In the port environment, CPTED strategies can be applied as a layering construct to reinforce perimeter boundaries by defining the port's space, such as the use of well-marked, high-visibility access roadways, preventing vehicles and pedestrians from moving freely onto non-trafficway port properties, channeling traffic to and from defined restricted and secured access areas, and using physical and man-made barriers to deter transit into high-threat or nonpublic locations.

8.3.2 Fencing

Perimeter fence lines should be clearly established and maintained so as to provide a physical and visual means of preventing and/or controlling access into port facilities. Fences are barriers that define property lines and establish notice to potential intruders that the area beyond the fence is different and requires some type of authorization to access. Fences alone however, while effective psychological barriers, are not necessarily physically insurmountable. They define the boundary, but they may not be effective deterrents to intrusion. Port FSOs will have to carefully survey the port facility to determine which types of fencing will be effective in keeping intruders away from the cargo terminals and other restricted areas. When considering types of fencing, there are many options available in terms of materials and components, but probably the most economical and practical will be one or a combination of three types:

1. Chain-Link. Chain-link fencing usually consists of galvanized or coated steel wires, available in various gauges, that are bent and connected to each other in zigzag patterns. It is generally considered to be strong, long lasting, and economical. Port FSOs considering using chain-link fencing for restricted access areas should use No. 1 or heavier gauge wire with small mesh openings. While chain-link fencing provides an effective visual barrier, the smaller openings work to deter the transfer of items across the fences. This may be especially important in facilities where the threats of contraband smuggling or thefts from cargo containers are higher. In fact, in facilities where there is a significant risk of the transfer of contraband, for example, between a busy dock area and a public, nonrestricted area, the Port FSO may wish to consider a double line of fencing to create a sort of "no man's land." The interval between the fences creates another layer of security that can often be easily observed to detect intruders.

2. Barbed Wire. This is a type of fencing in which sharp metal protrudes along regular intervals on a strand of metal wire. Multiple strands are often used in tightly stretched, straight-line patterns. Barbed wire is not typically used as a stand-alone fence but rather in conjunction with other fencing or wall systems, often at the top to deter intruders from climbing over it. When it is used, attention must be paid to the height at which the barbed wire is placed. If it is too low, it may be easily scaled or cut.

3. Concertina Wire. Also known as barbed tape, concertina wire consists of flat metal wires embedded with sharp barbs webbed together into large coils. The wire is quite flexible and difficult to penetrate. In the port facility, coils of concertina wire can be placed at the bottom and/or top of chain-link fencing to provide an added measure of impenetrability. Figure 8.2 depicts the use of concertina wire in conjunction with a wire-metal fence. Notice the concertina wire is positioned on a 45-degree vertical metal guard at the top to effect an added measure of defense.

In many port facilities, the type of operations will affect decisions related to fencing materials, composition, and construction. The U.S. Customs and Border Protection (2006), in specifying requirements for the Customs-Trade Partnership Against Terrorism (C-TPAT) program, requires that perimeter fencing enclose the areas around cargo-handling and storage facilities, container yards, and terminals, and that fencing be regularly inspected for integrity and damage. Fencing in commercial ports is subject to damage from normal operations. In Figure 8.3, notice how the top rail of

Figure 8.2   Concertina wire used in conjunction with metal fencing in a port facility.

this fence has been dislodged, probably due to equipment and containers being backed into the fence.

In most facilities, fences should be reinforced at the bottom with strong ground supports to minimize the opportunities for intruders to slide underneath them. In busy commercial ports, fences should be reinforced with hard barriers or earthen berms to prevent damage or intrusion by wheeled vehicles, cargo containers, and other large pieces of equipment. In some facilities, it may be necessary to use barrier walls instead of fencing, or perhaps a combination barrier wall-fence, to provide additional strength in locations where fencing is susceptible to breach or damage. The decision to use reinforcing fence barriers should be based on identifying those locations on the port where fencing is subject to chronic damage. Site inspections should be able to identify locations where barriers will be more effective. Notice in Figure 8.3 how

Figure 8.3   Cargo terminal fencing damaged by repeated contacts with cargo-moving equipment.

concrete barriers have been placed at the bottom of the fence in an effort to mitigate this damage from occurring. The downside of the placement of the barriers, as in this example, is that they could also be used by an intruder to scale the fence. For this reason, consideration must be given to the form of the barrier wall-fence combination to reduce the chances that the barrier could be climbed. Some ports may wish to consider fence alarm systems that can be programmed to sense various types of movement. These systems may be monitored locally, from a central control point, or via mobile security patrols who can respond immediately to alarms. Alarm sensors, however, may be triggered by nonintrusion events, such as high winds, animals, or other routine activity in the environment.

In developing physical security requirements for seaports in the State of Florida, the legislature created a number of prescriptive standards that can be adopted by Port FSOs in other areas as baseline guides for perimeter security. In particular, the fencing standards in Florida provide a concise set of fencing guidelines for restricting access to secure areas of port facilities.

Fencing should be 8 feet high, 9 gauge galvanized steel, of 2 inch wide chain link construction topped with an additional 12–18 inches of barbed wire outrigger consisting of 3 strands of 9 gauge galvanized barbed wire at a 45 degree outward angle above the fence. Bottom of fencing should be no more than 2 inches from hard surface of concrete or asphalt. This surface should be sufficiently thick to prevent access from underneath. The exterior and interior sides of the fence should be cleared and uncluttered by not less than 5 feet to ensure that the integrity of the fence is not compromised. For high risk ports only: Reinforcement of the fence line with a barrier (e.g. ditch or berm) is recommended to enclose wheeled operations involving containers on chassis or truck loaded with consolidated cargo overnight.

(State of Florida 2000, Standard 6)

8.3.3 *The Small Vessel Threat and Waterside Security*

"There are simply too many boats, too many boaters, and too many potential targets to think that this is a risk that can be managed only through the activities of the federal government. . . ." That was the message from U.S. DHS Secretary Michael Chertoff addressing the April 2008 gathering of the National Marine Manufacturers Association American Boating Congress on the subject of the small-boat threat to the homeland security of the United States. Prior to this, in 2007, the National Small Vessel Security Summit engaged private, commercial, and government stakeholders on the security threats posed by small vessels in the U.S. maritime domain. That conference identified a number of critical issues concerning the potential threat from small vessels facing both the public and private sectors (Homeland Security Institute 2007, pp. 5–9):

- The need for a National Small Vessel Security Strategy
- The terrorism threat posed by the comparatively less regulated recreational boating community versus the commercial vessel sector
- The need for the federal government to conduct and convey systematic threat and risk assessments
- The burden of restrictive federal regulations on boaters and other small vessel operators
- The need for a culture of partnership and trust within and across the boating community
- The need for adequate funding and resources for the U.S. Coast Guard
- Training to enhance coordination, cooperation, and communications among federal, state, local, tribal, and territorial authorities
- Improved intelligence collection, analysis, and dissemination
- Expanded education and outreach to citizen stakeholders
- Improved boater situational awareness
- Enhanced mechanisms to report suspicious boating activities
- Controversy over the application of federal commercial vessel Automatic Identification System requirements to the recreational boating community
- Operator and vessel identification limitations
- Technologies and operational procedures to detect radiological and nuclear threats

- Reassessment of security zones

In his 2008 address, Secretary Chertoff went on to cite a U.S. Coast Guard report of some thirteen million registered and one million unregistered recreational vessels in the United States. He indicated there were three thousand small commercial vessels, three thousand fishing vessels, and four hundred thousand recreational vessels "in the vicinity of important maritime infrastructure" in the United States. He identified four major threat categories associated with small vessels:

1. A small vessel used as a waterborne improvised explosive device (similar to a USS *Cole* attack scenario)
2. A small vessel used to smuggle weapons into the country
3. A small vessel used to smuggle terrorists
4. A small vessel used as a platform from which a standoff weapon (e.g., rocket-propelled grenade) could be launched

It is no wonder that the U.S. government is concerned enough about this potential threat to the maritime sector that it is advocating a plan for improving small vessel safety protocols by asking states to create and enforce safety regulations for recreational boaters and have them keep an eye out for and report any unusual behavior on the water (Sullivan and Lindlaw 2008).

Provisions of the U.S. MTSA require port facilities to implement security measures and have the capability "to continuously monitor, through a combination of lighting, security guards, waterborne patrols, and automatic intrusion-detection devices, or surveillance equipment, as specified in the approved FSP (Facility Security Plan), the: (1) Facility and its approaches, on land and water; (2) Restricted areas within the facility; and (3) Vessels at the facility and areas surrounding the vessels" (Code of Federal Regulations 2003b, Section 105.275). Prior to the September 2001 terrorist attacks and the enhanced interest of the government in maritime security, the responsibilities for port waterside security were spread across a variety of public and private sector agencies. Ports themselves may not have taken a direct responsibility in securing the waters adjoining the port, believing that public law enforcement, including the U.S. Coast Guard, as well as state and local law enforcement agencies, provided the bulk of waterborne security for their jurisdictions, including seaports. With the passage of the MTSA in 2002, the U.S. Coast Guard, as the statutorily authorized federal agency enforcing port security regulations, began to push the responsibility of waterside port security onto the port facilities from the perspective that the ports themselves must assume the onus (and costs) for implementing MTSA provisions requiring a waterborne security capability. This certainly has had the impact of forcing port facilities to factor new and previously unnecessary marine patrol assets and waterside security capabilities into their Port FSPs.

Port security measures may restrict the use of waterways adjacent to and inside port facilities. A question for the Port FSO will be to determine if there is a local or federal security zone for marine interests in waters surrounding the port. Is it enforced? If so, what agency is responsible for patrol and enforcement? Is it posted? Large, clearly marked signs should be posted along the port's perimeter warning boaters of any restricted waterside areas and no-trespass zones. Seaport security controls and local legislation may be designed to restrict regular access to the seaport's docks, berths, slips, and maneuvering waters. An effective waterside access control system may include human and physical resources deployed both on land and in the water. Figure 8.4 illustrates an example of a deployable in-water gate system protecting access to docking areas in the waters of this port facility. The objective of this device is to impede the ability of small surface and underwater crafts or people from approaching the secure areas of docks and vessels in ports. Devices and systems such as this may not be practical in all port facilities, especially those in which the docks run parallel to busy inland waterways. In many ports, a combination of physical security devices, land-based security, waterborne patrols, and/or camera, sonar, and radar technology may be necessary to protect the waterside perimeter of the port facility.

The Port FSO will be duty-bound to consult with the cognizant U.S. Coast Guard COTP, as well as local, state, and federal law enforcement agencies, to determine the threat levels generally existing in the maritime security zone in which the port resides. Given the variety of ports and waterways in the United States and around the world, different facilities will require different and scalable waterside security measures. The

Figure 8.4   This deployable in-water access gate protects the port's docks and vessels from waterborne intruders.

existence of any federal, state, or local marine exclusion zones will certainly be a factor in the Port FSO's planning. For example, the COTP has the authority under federal law to restrict access to certain waters under certain conditions. Within the port facility, the Port FSO may be held responsible for implementing plans to affect security of these exclusion zones when they directly impact port operations. In this case, the ability to deploy waterborne assets such as small vessels operated by armed law enforcement or security officers may be necessary. Recreational and nonport watercraft may approach the port waterside perimeter or seawall and may cause a police and security response. Marine patrol assets of the port and/or local, state, and federal law enforcement agencies may provide directed waterside patrol of the port's waterside perimeter and inspections of below-water dock areas, vessel hulls, and infrastructure support columns on a regular basis. At the announcement of increases in security levels at the facility, the Port FSO may have to coordinate with marine patrol-equipped agencies to increase the levels of waterborne patrols to the port facility.

Port FSOs tasked with developing port waterborne patrol capabilities, whether via the use of assigned police personnel, proprietary security staff, or contracted security services, must have a baseline understanding of job and equipment specifications to effectively procure and implement waterborne security assets and staff. These specifications should include a number of important components including a general knowledge of the following items as specified in the MTSA (Code of Federal Regulations 2003a):

- Current security threats and patterns
- Recognition and detection of dangerous substances and devices
- Recognition of characteristics and behavior patterns of people who are likely to threaten port security
- Techniques used by intruders to circumvent port security measures
- Security-related communications
- Knowledge of port emergency procedures and contingency plans
- Operation of security equipment and systems
- Inspection, control, and monitoring techniques
- Relevant provisions of the Port FSP
- The meaning and consequential requirements of different MARSEC levels
- Waterborne patrol methods
- Report writing and log and record keeping
- Identification of port security problems and specific trouble areas
- Federal security procedures related to U.S. Customs and Border Protection, U.S. Immigration and Customs Enforcement, and U.S. Coast Guard requirements
- State, local, port authority, and port facility police/security procedures
- Hazardous materials, response, and first aid
- Use of force and weapons for use in a water environment
- Explosives; nuclear, biological, and chemical response

- Terrorism response procedures

Patrol boat and equipment requirements and specifications will vary according to prevailing jurisdictional, maritime, weather, and general operating conditions, but the following are general recommendations:

- Minimum length: 23 feet
- Minimum propulsion: 200 horsepower, minimum of two engines
- Minimum equipment: VHF radio, radar, global positioning system, compass, depth finder, remote spotlight, public address system, security/police light bar or strobes, audible emergency siren, safety equipment (fire extinguisher, first aid kit, flares, boat hook, life preservers), marine head, computer equipment capable of monitoring port facility cameras and waterside surveillance system
- For equipment used in providing waterborne patrol services to the port facility, maintain documentation for maintenance, calibration, and testing of equipment
- Vessel personnel to be equipped with two-way radios with the capability to promptly reach backup support and communicate with port land-based security staff

The acquisition and implementation of a waterborne patrol component to the Port FSP will require a considerable amount of research in terms of risk assessment, security planning, product differentiation, and human resource capabilities. Marine patrol assets are an expensive proposition for any organization. Since port management will be taking a big step in acquiring these assets, Port FSOs would do well to consider a variety of organizational methods of providing this capability. Inter-agency agreements with law enforcement agencies, outsourcing, and resource sharing arrangements are alternatives the Port FSO should consider in developing the waterborne security component. The availability and growth of technological innovations for both surface and underwater surveillance systems for commercial ports is another aspect of the perimeter security equation that may affect the Port FSO's decision making regarding waterborne security.

8.4 Parking Control

Parking control on the port facility is a physical security device that provides another layer with which to manage the ingress and movement of vehicles. Parking areas should be located outside of fenced operational areas, particularly those areas that are designated as restricted. Keeping personal vehicles out of cargo and other operational areas minimizes the opportunities for the illegal transfer of cargo and contraband. The vehicle in Figure 8.5 has been parked underneath a gantry crane in the cargo operations area of this port. Notwithstanding the obvious safety hazards of parking directly underneath a crane, the Port FSO must vigorously enforce parking regulations to ensure that vehicles such as this one are not being used to transfer contraband or

Figure 8.5   Personal vehicle parked in cargo operations area underneath gantry crane.

stolen cargo from or into the restricted areas of the port facility. This of course will be a challenge in many port facilities due to the limited land availability and operational requirements. There actually may be a need for certain vehicles to be able to transit and park in cargo operations areas to perform the functions associated with port-vessel interfaces, such as crane maintenance and repairs, the carriage of safety equipment and tools, and the ability of supervisors to respond immediately to operational necessities and emergencies. Ports with significant cargo terminal operations may have large numbers of employees who must be able to obtain access to the operational areas. Ports may be able to address the restrictions on the parking of personal vehicles by providing off-port parking and shuttle services or by utilizing an employee-only bus transportation service such as those used in many airports.

Employees exiting restricted cargo and passenger facilities should be required to pass through a controlled area under the supervision of port security personnel. The continuous monitoring of the movement of vehicles and staff provides an observational layer of security that deters illegal activity. Employees visiting their motor vehicles during work shifts, such as during lunch and work breaks, should be required to notify management or security personnel. Employees working in port operational or cargo areas should be restricted from visiting their vehicles unless authority is given by management. Access to port employee parking areas should be restricted by a permit system that enables port management to identify the owners of vehicles. All vehicle owners should be properly identified and credentialed. In all systems of parking control, effectiveness will be gauged according to how strongly the regulations are enforced. Ports with systems and controls in place but with lax enforcement will be tasked to justify the security of the facilities when challenged by government regulators. Beyond that, ports that fail to enforce their own regulations invite intrusions and behavior that may compromise port safety and security. A judicious system of enforcement using scalable levels of sanctions, such as warnings, fines, withdrawal of parking privileges, towing and removal, and the like, will alert the port community that port security is important and that compliance with parking regulations and vehicle restrictions is a necessary component of the culture of security within the facility. Once the Port FSO obtains the cooperation of port organizations and employees in controlling parking, the facility will move toward a more confident level of operational security.

8.5 Access Points

The primary consideration in locating access points in port facilities is finding the most effective balance between securing the port while allowing the appropriate levels of access to enable the seaport to operate in an efficient way. Too few access points, while ideal from a security perspective, may inhibit port operations to the point where customers will be reluctant to engage in commercial operations. On the other hand, an ill-defined and haphazard collection of access points into restricted areas may expose the port to infiltration and challenge it to provide more staff and resources to effectively screen and control movement into the facility. Finding the correct balance is a process of risk analysis, threat assessment, identifying critical infrastructure, cooperative leadership, and good planning. In all respects, the Port FSO will benefit from working cooperatively with the port's organizational users and development staff to engineer the proper balance of access and security. Considerations must be given to the best use of an access point. For example, a port's primary business may be driven by the need to have large trucks accessing cargo areas to deliver and receive containers. In this environment, access may need to be controlled by a series of vehicle lanes, gates, credentialing systems, and staff to be able to accommodate large vehicles in the numbers projected. It is important, however, to consider the likelihood that the facility may also need to accommodate smaller vehicles, as well as pedestrians. For safety purposes, the port would not want pedestrians to mix with large truck traffic, so the staff must engineer access points to segregate them. In Figure 8.6, this port has developed a pedestrian-only crew gate to control access to docked vessels. By doing so, it is unnecessary to have crew members intermingle with vehicles and provisions, which are screened separately at another access point. Separate gates for personnel and vehicle traffic provide both safety and security. By channeling pedestrian traffic through a separate gate, security staff can better control the movement and screening of individuals.

Figure 8.6 A pedestrian-only access gate safely identifies and screens vessel crew members entering the restricted dock area.

The Port FSO must constantly evaluate the number, placement, and composition of access points into restricted areas. Gates that are not being used should be permanently sealed to eliminate opportunities for criminals and unauthorized people to enter the facility by breaking locks or bypassing poorly controlled barriers. Essential, high-use gates should be secured by extra padlocks, case-hardened steel chains, or deadlocking bolts. Gate locking mechanisms must be strong and designed for maximum security consistent with the level of usage. For example, gates that are used by multiple port users, where it is necessary for port staff to respond before they are opened, should have strong locks and chains that resist tampering and deterioration. For added security, chains can be welded directly to the gate. The Port FSO may consider equipping gates with a recording system to document inspection stops by security personnel during routine patrols. Security patrols of seaport gates are necessary to ensure gates are secured when not in use and are not being compromised. Recording systems, either manual or computer-based, provide port management with assurance that patrols are regularly inspecting the security of the gates. Gates equipped with alarm systems will provide an added layer of protection and may be necessary in particularly sensitive or high-value cargo locations of the facility. Manned gatehouses should be minimally equipped with electric power, telephony, computer capabilities, and other communications devices to enable security staff to access credentialing systems, make inquiries, and report incidents.

Additional layers of protection can be added by the use of *bollards*, which are vertical posts used to control or direct vehicle movement through access gates. Some bollard systems can be quite sophisticated. Using hydraulics or electric power, bollards can be built in-ground and raised or lowered below a road surface on command. They are effective for responding to increasing threat levels, securing sensitive areas, and controlling access when and where varying levels of security are needed. Other barrier systems, such as gate arms, metal wall barriers, and raised metal teeth, are available for both permanent and temporary installations that can be integrated into access point infrastructure to further restrict or deter entry. In port facilities where gate operations may require more flexibility due to construction activities, repairs, berth shifting, and wharf availability, Port FSOs can procure a supply of concrete barriers, such as those

Figure 8.7 Barrier systems provide flexibility and enhance physical security when managing access into restricted areas.

illustrated in Figure 8.7. These barriers are relatively manageable in terms of placement and movement (e.g., with forklifts) and provide effective barriers in certain situations, or while the port develops a more permanent barrier system. Barrier systems are also available using plastic materials that can be filled with water when emplaced, and drained for easy transport.

References

Chertoff, Michael. 2008, April 28. Remarks by Homeland Security Secretary Michael Chertoff at the National Marine Manufacturers Association American Boating Congress. U.S. Department of Homeland Security. http://www.dhs.gov/xnews/speeches/sp_1209472037198.shtm (accessed July 19, 2008).

Code of Federal Regulations. 2003a. Title 33, Navigation and Navigable Waters, Chapter I, Coast Guard, Department of Homeland Security, Part 105, Maritime Security: Facilities Part 105, Subpart C, Section 105.210, Facility personnel with security duties. http://edocket.access.gpo.gov/cfr_2003/julqtr/33cfr105.210.htm (accessed July 24, 2008).

Code of Federal Regulations. 2003b. Title 33, Navigation and Navigable Waters, Chapter I, Coast Guard, Department of Homeland Security, Part 105, Maritime Security: Facilities Part 105, Subpart C, Section 105.275, Security measures for monitoring. http://edocket.access.gpo.gov/cfr_2003/julqtr/33cfr105.275.htm (accessed July 19, 2008).

Collins, Pamela, Truett A. Ricks, and Clifford W. Van Meter. 2000. *Principles of security and crime prevention*. 4th ed. Cincinnati: Anderson Publishing.

Federal Emergency Management Agency and U.S. Fire Administration. 1999. Developing effective standard operating procedures for fire and EMS departments. FA-197. http://www.usfa.dhs.gov/downloads/pdf/publications/fa-197-508.pdf (accessed July 17, 2008).

Homeland Security Institute. 2007. Report of the DHS national small vessel security summit. HSI Publication Number RP07-12-01. Arlington, VA: Homeland Security Institute. http://www.dhs.gov/xlibrary/assets/small_vessel_NSVSS_Report_HQ_508.pdf (accessed July 17, 2008).

Jeffery, C. Ray. (1971). *Crime prevention through environmental design*. Beverly Hills, CA: Sage.

Newman, Oscar. 1996. *Creating defensible space*. Washington, DC: U.S. Department of Housing and Urban Development. http://www.huduser.org/Publications/pdf/def.pdf (accessed July 18, 2008).

State of Florida. 2000. Port security standards compliance plan, standard 6, fencing. Florida Statute 311.12(1)(a), Seaport security standards.

Sullivan, Eileen, and Scott Lindlaw. 2008, April 27. To stave off terror, feds issue safety strategy for boaters. Associated Press. http://ap.google.com/article/ALeqM5j8zyZYvgdcfCVKb4-NyCb-JZV-ywD90AFV7G0 (accessed April 27, 2008).

U.S. Customs and Border Protection. 2006. C-TPAT security criteria sea carriers. http://www.cbp.gov/linkhandler/cgov/trade/cargo_security/ctpat/security_criteria/sea_carrier_criteria/sea_carrier_criteria.ctt/sea_carrier_criteria.doc (accessed July 17, 2008).

U.S. Environmental Protection Agency. 2007. Guidance for preparing standard operating procedures. EPA QA/G-6. http://www.epa.gov/QUALITY/qs-docs/g6-final.pdf (accessed July 17, 2008).

9

SECURITY FORCE MANAGEMENT

9.1 Security and Human Resources

Organizations use human resource management activities to further the operation's competitive position by recruiting and developing capable employees and managers and by developing staffing plans and actions focused on contributing to the economic (i.e., bottom-line) success of the organization. Within the port organizational framework, the essential and major focus should be on the continued improvement of the commercial ventures in support of the port's mission, goals, and objectives. The more efficient and flexible the port is, the more effective it will be in meeting the demands of global competition in transporting goods and people and in contributing to the economic well-being of the communities they serve. This chapter's discussion is concerned with the managerial development of the security force in port organizations. A fundamental aspect of developing human resources in any organization is the improvements that people make to the overall productivity. A constraint in assembling a competent divisional workforce is that managers may have relatively little control over the larger port organization's capital, materials, and procedures. This is an especially salient concern for security managers. Security, perceived as an overhead cost to organizations in general, must always be working to justify expenditures that may not contribute directly to overall productivity. Security managers must work cooperatively with human resource managers to support employee development as they pursue the organization's strategies.

Organizations improve through more effective and efficient uses of their resources, particularly their human resources. The organization's human resource management objectives will be benchmarks against which the security force's programs and activities will be critiqued. For example, port leadership may establish a strategic goal for the port to increase its cargo operational capacity over a three-to-five-year period. To accomplish this, the port may develop objectives for streamlining operational throughput and increasing capacity. Within a heightened security environment, though, government regulations and concerns about threats to the global supply chain may constrain a port's ability to increase throughput. This may manifest itself in the hiring of additional security staff, increased security screening, additional checkpoints, delays associated with the imaging of cargo containers, and similar risk mitigation strategies. The security manager's challenge will be to recruit and develop a competent security force, committed not only to security objectives but also to the core business objectives of the commercial enterprise. Human resource management should thus be a cornerstone element of the security manager's force management strategies.

There are four recognized human resources management objectives (Werther and Davis 1996), which the port security manager must internalize in the development of an integrated security force:

1. Organizational objective. Human resource management exists to contribute to organizational effectiveness. Human resource management is not an end in itself, but it is a way to work with a department in meeting its personnel needs. Constructive and cooperative practices that engage both human resource and security managers in identifying the correct job tasks, specifications, and classifications for port security staff accomplish this objective.

2. Functional objective. Human resource management must be consistent with organizational needs and demands. In other words, human resources should not be more or less sophisticated than the organization itself, but should be in sync with the needs of the organization. To the extent that human resources and security can align their personnel needs with that of the port's strategic direction, the better it will function to provide the necessary human capacity.

3. Societal objective. This is the effort that organizations must make not only to be socially responsive but also to minimize the negative impact of this task on the organization. Port security and human resource managers must develop capacities for recruiting and hiring personnel who understand not only the security needs of the port, but that security functions must complement the port's mission of economic stability and sustenance for its stakeholders.

4. Personal objective. Organizations must assist employees in achieving their personal goals in order to maintain high levels of individual motivation and job satisfaction. Notwithstanding the contributions security employees make to overall security effectiveness, management must consider how well it establishes and maintains an environment that capitalizes on security staff initiative and creativity.

Meeting these objectives will result in greater contribution of the human resources function to the port's bottom-line and to the needs of the security department in developing an effective force for mitigating threats to the port.

9.2 A Framework for Managing and Leading the Security Force

Management is a "process of working with and through individuals and groups and other resources to accomplish organizational goals" (Hersey and Blanchard 1988, p. 2). Managers guide supervisors and employees so that they may achieve optimal results in the performance of activities designed to accomplish the organizational mission. They help employees to actively and creatively confront and resolve issues. The central challenge for port security managers in developing a responsive and flexible security force is contributing to the port organization's improvement in the face of significant constraints. Changing demands of workers, international and domestic competition, ethical lapses in judgments, government and legal requirements, and workforce diversity issues are just some of the dynamics port security managers will have to work through as they develop force competencies. Within the context of developing this framework, the port security manager is responsible to:

- Plan, organize, direct, and coordinate workforces
- Minimize conflict
- Maintain effective interpersonal relationships
- Identify and resolve supervisory problems
- Direct employees in meeting departmental objectives
- Be aware of employees' mental and physical health conditions
- Maintain appropriate social standards and employee demeanor
- Develop normative and measureable performance standards
- Be aware of and proficient with counseling and disciplinary procedures
- Be aware of concepts of budgeting and planning
- Understand personnel handling procedures (e.g., compensation, benefits, labor relations)

The key to establishing this framework within the port security organization will be in how well the leadership develops the middle-management function. This position may be called many different things, such as sergeant, lieutenant, commander, or supervisor; but whatever its nomenclature, the middle manager's role is crucial to establishing the necessary linkages between line operations and senior management. If the security mid-level manager is not embraced by port security leadership as "part of the team," the organization's strategic vision, mission, and values will not successfully filter down to operational levels, where the actual work of port security gets done. In public law enforcement, particularly since the recent push toward community- and problem-oriented policing, police middle managers have been viewed as vitally responsible for using human resources effectively to solve problems in their communities. It is the police middle manager's role to provide a creative atmosphere for problem solving. Community and problem-solving policing models require a less traditional management style, one less reliant on tight supervision and control, with more emphasis on management that liberates employees to make decisions and provide input for the organization's output (Sparrow 1993).

Many security organizations adopt a quasi-military approach to force management, similar to that of public police agencies. It is logical to propose that managers and supervisors engaged in solving problems associated with threat management in ports can identify with the importance of establishing close communications and coordination between line activities and management strategy. Witham (1987) suggested that police organizations need *transformational leaders* to successfully meet modern law enforcement challenges. In this approach, organizational leadership assertively develops and cultivates a vision and works aggressively to instill that vision in employees and managers. This transformation of the leader's role, from one of controlling employee behavior to encouraging creativity, innovation, and risk taking, is seen as a way for organizations to develop better strategies for responding to community and stakeholder needs. Couper and Lobitz (1988) identified leadership as the critical factor in moving law enforcement agencies toward a style of policing that emphasizes quality, commitment to staff, and the development of a people-oriented working environment. The traditional, "professional," incident-driven model of policing emphasizes adherence to rules and procedures and control over employees and is characterized as being closed to outsiders. Conversely, Couper and Lobitz highlighted the characteristics of a new style of policing emphasizing the movement toward quality in policing: a problem-solving model; teamwork; community orientation; data-based decision making; asking and listening to employees; the leader as coach and teacher; creativity, innovation, and experimentation; trust in employees; reliance on employees' skills; improving processes when things go wrong; and an organization open to the community. Goldstein (1990, p. 149), an early advocate of problem-oriented policing, emphasized the importance of a style of leadership that creates a supportive organizational environment:

> A working environment in which great stress is placed on controlling employees results in a lack of dignity for those at the bottom and often adversely affects productivity. This condition can be corrected by the new sense of importance, independence, and prestige that comes from a relationship with management built on mutual trust and on agreement that an officer has the freedom to think and act within broad boundaries.

One of Goldstein's central themes is the shift from a traditional leadership model, stressing authority and control of employee behavior, to a more flexible style, allowing for greater employee input into decisions. His reasoning is that if officers are to be more effective in solving community crime problems, they must be given the freedom to examine alternatives, recommend solutions, and take risks.

There are parallels to be drawn from the research on leadership in law enforcement to managing port security forces in a homeland security environment. One of the true realities of any organization is that the ground-level, line employees are the ones closest to the issues and problems. Even on a factory assembly line, the production worker is typically in the best position to see where the process may be negatively affected by poor materials or timing. In seaports, line-level security staff are in the best position to see the issues and problems posing threats to the port: dockworkers not wearing port identification in restricted areas, alarm systems failing to adequately notify necessary resources, or operational and training issues affecting security force response capabilities. Force management and leadership must tap into the knowledge of the security force and use it to develop successful fixes to constraints inhibiting effective port security. Using Sparrow's (1993) model, the power of the middle manager in port security forces can be articulated as:

- Having the ability to establish and develop close relationships among line staff and senior management
- Engaging security personnel to identify with the organizational vision in applying effort to security tasks, but with an eye toward achieving efficiencies in operational capacities
- Using a knowledge of organizational culture (i.e., its strengths, weaknesses, and receptivity to innovation) to engage personnel in the security mission in creative and successful ways
- Using knowledge to accomplish tasks and work within the system to develop and acquire resources
- Understanding agency resource capabilities in terms of being able to go to senior port management to identify and advocate for resource and equipment improvements needed to meet new risks and changing security needs
- Paying attention to details associated with security operations
- Becoming familiar with the bureaucracies of the port's various stakeholders and associated security and law enforcement agencies
- Most importantly, knowing when to shift management styles, by applying appropriate controlling and/or coaching strategies in solving human resource and security operational issues

Management of security force operations should begin with a clear statement of the organization's mission. A sample *mission statement* is, "The organization provides security services to the port and serves as the command and control authority for personnel employed by the port security force." Once a mission is articulated, security force transformational leadership strategies should engage and empower staff in developing security plans and risk mitigation approaches. This can be accomplished as follows:

- By involving supervisors and line staff in planning
- By maintaining consultative relationships to motivate staff in meeting goals
- By developing clear links of rewards to performance in implementing change
- By training staff in the skills needed to be creative and successful
- By articulating and adhering to the port organization's vision
- By providing clear mandates for changes needed to achieve results
- By obtaining needed resources for staff to achieve results

Traditional models of policing developed as a result of labor-intensive jobs requiring management techniques based on compliance with rules and regulations with little employee input (Enter 1991). While bureaucratic organizational models and autocratic leadership styles likely predominate in many law enforcement and security regimes, they do not facilitate the problem-solving roles required to effectively lead the way in solving many port security challenges facing the organization.

9.3 Staff Planning and Budgeting

Developing an effective and efficient port security staff will largely be a function of planning and budgeting. "A budget is a plan for the accomplishment of programs related to objectives and goals within a definite time period, including an estimate of resources required, together with an estimate of the resources available. . ." (Smith and Lynch 2004, p. 38). Budgets are planned for a specific time period for which management estimates the resources required. Estimates include revenues and expenditures. The primary role of the security budget is to translate the port's security plan into the dollars needed in the environment to compensate the staff, and purchase and maintain the equipment and infrastructure deemed necessary. Budgets provide the organization with a way to hold staff accountable for plans and for working within the confines of anticipated port revenues and expenditures. The decisions a port security manager will make concerning the types and numbers of security staff to hire must be balanced against the alternative uses of the port's available financial resources. Given that security has traditionally been conceptualized as an overhead expense not contributing to economic bottom-lines, the security manager may have to defend budgeting and staffing decisions that draw resources away from port investments that could be used to grow port capacity and develop competitive edges in trying to attract business. Budget decisions not only involve anticipated benefits, but they also represent *opportunity costs*. In other words, if the port security manager requests an additional $1 million to hire a given number of additional security guards and supervisors to comply with a government security regulation, the anticipated benefit is that the staff will be trained and developed to effectively implement the Port FSP. Other port organizational elements may argue that the opportunity cost to the port is that the $1 million could be spent on enlarging the berthing space adjacent to a passenger cruise terminal in order to accommodate the larger-sized vessels that the industry is building. The practical cost (unless alternative funding is identified and procured) is that companies with larger vessels will do their business at another port. Thus, port security, despite the emerging understanding that it does contribute to organizational productivity, will still have to compete with the other component port organizations, such as marketing, development, and maintenance, to advocate for the necessary funding with which to staff the security function.

9.3.1 Staffing Needs Assessment

To achieve rational planning in the budgeting process, and to provide justifications for requested funding, a port security staffing needs assessment should be conducted. Port security and law enforcement staffing levels could be determined by using traditional officer-to-population ratios, but staffing levels and allocations should really consider other relevant data such as response times, crime levels, threat assessments, and specific service needs in particular functions. In private sector applications, security staffing may be more sensitive than public law enforcement agencies to equipment and infrastructure needs, such as surveillance tools, access control systems, and physical security requirements. In conducting the needs assessment, the Port FSO, or manager responsible for developing budget requests, should consider both public law enforcement and proprietary/contract security personnel needs. The first consideration should be to identify the positions necessary for the security force's peak effectiveness. Critical vacancies must be prioritized and filled first, before desired support or administrative positions. To assist with the staffing needs assessment, a simple post staffing chart (see Figure 9.1) can be developed, which identifies critical security assignments and responsibilities, as well as the functional level of security or law enforcement required for the assignment. These tools also assist in estimating and budgeting for personnel costs.

With the assistance of human resource management staff, job-task analyses can be conducted to determine the tasks, duties, and responsibilities needed for each security job. Information about jobs can be systematically collected, evaluated, and organized to establish the optimum combination of task functions for each identified position. Workload analyses will also help the Port FSO develop an understanding of positions that could be eliminated or consolidated to achieve efficiencies. It must be remembered that security at many port facilities may be the responsibility of several public sector agencies and private companies. Local law enforcement and private security services provide a variety of security and ancillary services including command and control; access-gate control and screening of pedestrians, and commercial and private vehicles; parking enforcement; traffic control; revenue collection; random and

PORT LOCATION-FUNCTION	NUMBER OF EMPLOYEES	SCHEDULED DAYS	SCHEDULED HOURS	TOTAL HOURS/WEEK
Terminal A Interior Security	1-Police Officer (P)	Mon, Wed	0600-1800	1-P @ 24 = 24
Terminal A Traffic Control	2-Security Officer (S)	Mon, Wed	0600-1800	2-S @ 24 = 48
Terminal A Waterside Patrol	1-S	Mon, Wed	0600-1800	1-S @ 24 = 24
Commercial Vehicle Inspection Station	1-P 1-S	Mon through Sun	0600-2400	1-P @ 126 = 126 1-S @ 126 = 126 Total = 252
Gate #1 Access Control	1-S	Mon through Fri	0600-1900	1-S @ 65 = 65
Cargo Area Security	3-S 1-Security Supervisor (SPV)	Mon through Sun	0000-2400	3-S @ 168 = 504 1-SPV @ 168 = 168 Total = 672

Figure 9.1 Port Facility Security Post Staffing Chart.

directed police and security patrols; criminal investigations; and administrative services to the port facility. In addition to these, security staffing may be provided by private security services contracted by the port's user organizations, such as passenger lines and cargo terminal operators. Given the variety of organizational and funding structures associated with the provision of security and police services to port facilities, security and law enforcement staffing needs must be identified and assessed to support budget requests.

9.3.2 The Debate over Private Security versus Law Enforcement

There is somewhat of a bias toward the use of public law enforcement in providing significant levels of homeland security. Witness the growth of dedicated homeland security units, bureaus, and sections in local police departments around the United States since 2001. Cleveland, Ohio, Mayor Jane Campbell referred to police as being part of the "domestic army—the troops who will be called upon to respond to the next terrorist attack" (Hall 2004, par. 1). Authorized federal, state, and local law enforcement officers are distinguished from private sector security agents in one major respect: police have the power to enforce the law by making arrests for criminal law violations. Private security officers, on the other hand, may possess one of three kinds of power and authority:

1. The same authority possessed by a citizen or property owner
2. That obtained by deputization or commissioning from a public law enforcement agency
3. A mix of civilian powers and special prerogatives added by statute, ordinance, or governmental regulation (Fischer, Halibozek, and Green 2008)

The limitations of private security officers in terms of their legal authority precipitate a preference for the use of public law enforcement agents in many security environments. The power of making a citizen's arrest typically allows a private security officer to protect the interests of an employer's property, but it is generally a good idea to either have an arrest warrant in hand, or to leave formal arrests to authorized public law enforcement personnel. In retail settings, private security officers usually have legal grounds to briefly detain suspected shoplifters for a reasonable investigation, but they still have to be turned over to the police for arrest and prosecution. No laws prevent a private security officer from conversing or asking questions of a willing participant. The U.S. Constitution's Miranda restrictions on custodial interrogations only apply to public sector agencies, so private security officers asking suspected intruders and violators questions about their actions are not violating a person's rights. Ports, however, may be private, public, or quasi-public organizations. Given that security or law enforcement officers may be acting within the scope of their government-authorized official duties while performing security functions on ports, security managers must clearly articulate policies and procedures for all security staff regarding detention, arrest, and interrogation. The use or threat of physical force to coerce someone to answer questions is always prohibited. There is also a distinction between searches conducted by public police and those by private security since the Fourth Amendment of the U.S. Constitution does not apply to searches by private people (Fischer, Halibozek, and Green 2008). Given the vagaries of the law, as well as the lack of standardized rules across numerous jurisdictions, it is no wonder that there is a preference for the use of police over private security.

Notwithstanding a desire to have relatively more highly trained and better compensated (and hence more expensive) law enforcement personnel engaged in critical infrastructure protection, there is an argument to be made that the private sector can provide credible and reliable security services as part of a port facility's overall plan. Since the September 2001 terrorist attacks particularly, there has been worldwide growth in the use of private security in many sectors. In the war in Iraq for example, more than twenty thousand armed expatriates were estimated to be working for private security companies in 2005 (Fidler). Overall, employment in security occupations is growing faster on average than all other occupations (Fischer, Halibozek, and Green 2008). Even though only about half of the states in the United States have imposed training standards on private security, the security profession has been an ardent advocate for increased training and professional standards for security personnel. ASIS has been leading the cause for security professionalism since the 1950s with a comprehensive agenda for security training and certification. ASIS offers a broad curriculum of training programs to the security industry. While not specifically geared toward port security operations and management, ASIS nevertheless is an essential resource for port security managers developing force management capabilities. ASIS training programs include a regular agenda of national and international security conferences. For example, the 2008 ASIS International 2nd Asia-Pacific Conference, "Dynamic Solutions for Emerging Challenges," held in Singapore, featured a comprehensive agenda addressing key security topics, both region-specific and of global interest, including natural disasters, protection of intellectual property, terrorism, avian flu, transit security, port security, and supply chain security. ASIS also offers a regular series of regional workshops, online degree programs, and virtual forums, many of which have direct and tangential applications for port security. ASIS offers many industry-specific classroom programs in locations across the United States and Canada. Some examples of the types of training provided are physical security design, applications, and technology; video security technology; crisis management; asset protection; and threat assessment.

Around the world, the push for security professionalism and standards is gaining momentum. In the United Kingdom, the 2001 Private Security Industry Act facilitated a system for the statutory regulation of the private security industry, including the following:

- Licensing individuals in specific sectors and to approve security companies
- Maintaining governmental review of the private security industry
- Monitoring the activities and effectiveness of those working in the security industry
- Conducting inspections
- Establishing standards of conduct, training, and supervision
- Making recommendations to improve standards (Office of Public Sector Information 2008)

Clearly, there is an impetus and urgency for increased professionalism in security that has not been limited to the United States. There is recognition that homeland and infrastructure security must engage resources from both the public and private sectors. While public sector law enforcement is certainly a critical component of facility security planning, total or unbalanced reliance on government criminal justice agencies may not be in the port's security, commercial, and/or economic best interests. A port facility's choices regarding the force composition necessary to implement the Port FSP will depend on unbiased risk assessment, legislative constraints, political will, resource availability, funding, and to a large extent, the internal and external pressures from agencies and organizations that have concerns and interests about port security and the stability of the maritime domain.

9.3.3 The Debate over Proprietary Security versus Contract Security

Another major decision for ports developing or changing their security force structure and organization is whether to operate a proprietary security operation, contract out for services, or develop a hybrid of the two. The movement in private security is toward hybrid security operations; however, any individual or company challenged to consider the reduction of risk or prevention of loss will have to understand the fundamentals of security organization and management. Port directors and their FSOs must carefully evaluate the fundamental management concerns associated with the operation of an in-house, or proprietary, security operation. Is the port prepared and capitalized to support the compensation and benefits packages that may be necessary to engage a skilled, competitive workforce? Are the managerial competencies present to lead the security staff in a transformative way to engage them creatively in facility security planning and implementation? Is a proprietary force flexible enough to respond to changing MARSEC and threat levels, or does the port need to contract out to engage external security services to provide for anticipated increases in security during emergencies? Port leadership must carefully have this discussion, especially concerning the appropriate placement of security operations within the port organization. The important relationships to focus on are those concerning the key tasks involved in the integration of the security function with the port's core business function. Essential questions management must consider as the port contemplates the type of security organization are as follows:

- What do port management envision as the mission and role of the port security force?
- What will be management's considerations when force agents implement and enforce security measures in the port facility?
- Will security measures be seen as inhibiting port operations or as a value-added component to port productivity?
- How should port management organize the security function within the larger organization?
- What basic activities will be associated with the organizational functions of security?
- What is involved in organizing the security function in an organization?

Management will have to assess the comparative costs and the projected effectiveness of proprietary and contracted approaches balanced against the important question of whether security can be truly and totally integrated into the organization. Consider the following hypothetical situation: The port's information security manager receives information from technical staff that a computer server's firewall has been breached. In identifying potential losses that might be experienced, one is the compromise of access control data (e.g., personal identification data in the credentialing system). This compromise is quantifiable, as are the costs and lost productivity associated with repairing the firewall. The loss calculation may vary, depending on whether the Port's FSO and information security manager must rely on in-house or external staff, resources, and expertise. In any organization, management must assess costs and benefits of decisions made in support of the core business function. The use of proprietary or contract security and technical services will affect the nature of this decision making from both practical and financial perspectives. In any event, the use of contract security services in place of existing port law enforcement or proprietary security staff may be subject to considerable review and require approval of amendments to the Port FSP by the U.S. Coast Guard and other state or local regulatory agencies.

9.4 Developing and Maintaining Force Competencies in Port Security

9.4.1 Port Security Personnel Training

The adequacy of private security training generally has traditionally been low for the simple reason that there have been no uniform standards for training courses with respect to content, length, method of presentation, instructor qualifications, and student testing. To illustrate, consider the standardization of training required for police officers to be certified. In the United States, there is typically an agency of state government that administers legislative requirements for the training and certification of law enforcement personnel. According to the U.S. Bureau of Justice Statistics, in local police agencies serving one hundred thousand or more residents, new police recruits completed, on average, about sixteen hundred hours of academy and field training (Training Network 2007). Comparatively, there are very few, and nonstandardized, training and certification requirements for private sector security agents. For example, several studies of the adequacy of private security training have been conducted, including one by Cunningham, Strauchs, and Van Meter (1990), known as the Hallcrest Report II, which "noted that the typical private security guard received only four to six hours of preassignment training" (Fischer, Halibozek, and Green 2008, p. 112). In the United States, there are approximately eight hundred thousand sworn federal, state, and local police officers (U.S. Department of Justice 2008), but the burgeoning and complex security industry is a $100 billion-a-year business (ASIS 2005). Given the present homeland security emphasis on critical infrastructure security, do these numbers suggest a need to improve the standardization, levels, and amounts of training provided to private security officers? Essential questions that the port security manager must consider in developing a sound and professional security force are as follows:

- How does the quality of training for port security personnel compare with that of the police, as well as with comparable private security organizations in industry, the external community, the region, the state, the nation, and the world?
- How important is a college education to the level of professionalism, qualities of leadership, and opportunities for advancement required and desired for security managers in a port environment?
- What subjects and procedures should be included in the port security training program?
- What is the current status of federal and state regulation of ports and the security industry, and how does that impact the competencies required of the port's security force?

It should go without saying that security officers in any organization must be properly trained for the tasks and responsibilities they will be assigned. Whichever systems are in operation at ports to control the access and flow of people, vehicles, ships, and cargo, they will only be as good as the people who operate and maintain them. The security officer is the most vital link in the entire system. The manner in which the officers perform their duties can mean the difference between an effective operation, one that adds value to the commercial enterprise, or the collapse of even the most sophisticated and expensive systems. Security personnel must participate in effective security training and educational programs to appreciate the need for effective security measures. Security officers should be properly trained to understand why security systems and plans are necessary as a precursor to implementation. Training is imperative for both proprietary and contracted security force personnel. Preliminary training for newly hired personnel is essential prior to actual assignment to operational posts. Pre-employment classroom training may be required for certification by the governmental entity having jurisdiction over the seaport. As well, in-service and refresher training are needed for experienced personnel to practice skills, learn new systems, and exercise plans and procedures. Management must implement a continuous program of in-service training to update security personnel with new or revised information and techniques. Continuing instruction should include the latest trends and techniques in security maintenance and crime prevention.

Both the ISPS Code and its U.S. counterpart, the MTSA of 2002, have specified a standard for training of port security personnel. The MTSA, as codified in Title 33, CFR, Part 105 (2003) requires port facility personnel with security duties to have knowledge, through training or equivalent job experience, in the following:

- Current security threats and patterns
- Recognition and detection of dangerous substances and devices
- Recognition of characteristics and behavioral patterns of people who are likely to threaten security
- Techniques used to circumvent security measures
- Crowd-management and control techniques
- Security-related communications
- Knowledge of emergency procedures and contingency plans
- Operation of security equipment and systems
- Testing, calibration, and maintenance of security equipment and systems
- Inspection, control, and monitoring techniques
- Relevant provisions of the FSP
- Methods of physical screening of people, personal effects, baggage, cargo, and vessel stores
- The meaning and the consequential requirements of the different MARSEC levels

These, of course, are minimum training requirements as provided for by U.S. federal legislation and regulation. It is therefore recommended that port security managers concerned about staffing competencies and the implementation of a comprehensive Port FSP consider additions to the training curriculum. Naturally, all training curricula should be guided by a needs assessment, as well as an objective evaluation of the specific port operational systems, local and state legal requirements, and funding resources of each particular port. The purpose of the *training needs assessment* is to examine the operation to identify missing knowledge, skills, and abilities for staff to perform their assigned tasks. A gap for which training may provide the bridge has been characterized as a *gap analysis* (Rouda and Kusy 1995), that is, the difference between the organization's desired levels of proficiency (where improvements are needed) and the current staff readiness condition. After an assessment of operational priorities and a determination of where opportunities exist for training to provide the necessary efficiencies, the port security staff training curriculum might include the following in addition to the MTSA-required training, as appropriate to each port facility:

- Patrol methods, to include training in fixed, random, and mobile directed patrols, and in both reactive and proactive methods
- Report writing (investigations, incidents, accidents, daily and weekly activities, log maintenance, and record keeping)
- Identification of security problems and specific areas of trouble
- Transportation logistics, cargo handling, storage, and documentation procedures
- National/federal government security procedures, including relevant customs, immigration, and coast guard requirements
- State and local, including port authority, police procedures
- Hazardous materials incident response, storage, and transportation procedures
- First aid, cardiopulmonary resuscitation, and the use of automated defibrillator devices
- Use of force and weapons, including appropriate certifications in both lethal force (firearms) and less lethal force (batons, chemical agents, electric stun guns, etc.) devices
- Use of security and restraint devices (e.g., handcuffs)
- Weapons of mass destruction, including explosives, nuclear, biological, chemical, and incendiary
- Fundamentals of terrorism and extremism in relation to homeland security and domestic preparedness
- Freedom of speech, public assembly, and civil rights
- Civil disturbances and labor unrest
- Computer and information security
- Ethics and professionalism
- Legal procedures and authority, including civil and vicarious liability, limitations on arrest, detention, interviews and interrogation, and search and seizure
- Fire prevention and protection, including the use of fire extinguishers, fire hoses, emergency equipment, and personal protective devices
- Traffic and parking enforcement, control procedures, and authority
- Environmental, occupational, and industrial safety procedures and regulations
- Emergency operations and response, including building and facility evacuation procedures

It must be remembered that training will not be a solution for all organization problems. Breaches of security can occur not only because personnel may not be effectively trained in a particular system or procedure, but also because they may be poorly supervised, sick, unmotivated, or simply lackluster performers. In all respects, when considering the expenditure of scarce monetary resources on a training program, the port security manager must also assess operational conditions aside from lack of knowledge, skills, and abilities that may be contributing to system deficiencies. If supervision, management, and/or procedural controls are not in place to direct staff properly, all the training in the world will not help.

9.4.2 *Written Directives*

Effective security force management requires a system of written directives documenting objectives, rules, policies, and procedures for security force implementation of the Port FSP. Also referred to as SOP (Standard Operating Procedure) or an operations manual, written directives should clearly specify and describe the makeup of the organization and completely document the operating standards for the security force. Components for a written directive system for port security staff should minimally include the following:

- Organization Statement. A simple organizational statement might say: "The Port Security Department is an operational element of the Port of __ under the command of a Chief of Security, reporting to the Port Director." By clearly articulating the organizational makeup, all security personnel are made aware of their position in the organization and the relationship of the security force to the larger seaport community.
- Statement of General Procedures. This might indicate that port security force operations require the publication of SOPs to ensure effective and efficient operations.
- Roll Call Information Board. This should be maintained in each security force office location. Supervisors should review the roll call information daily with their assigned personnel and acknowledge that they have done so by affixing their initials and date on each new information item. This serves as a control mechanism for management to ensure that information conveyed from within the organization is reaching its intended audience.
- Periodic Inspections. Procedures should exist for periodic inspections of security personnel and equipment to ensure continued capability.
- Periodic Instruction. Procedures should also exist for periodic instruction to continually update and upgrade the training of security personnel.
- Statements of Personnel Responsibilities. These are used to articulate the port security force management's clear statements of the responsibilities of all positions in the organization. For example: "The Security Sergeant is responsible for the supervision and coordination of the assigned element. The sergeant directs subordinates' operational activities, relays orders and assignments from

higher authority, and ensures that departmental goals and objectives are being met in the work of assigned personnel."

- Post Orders. Post orders are developed for each specific security assignment in the port facility. The orders specify the tasks for each assigned function or post and provide guidance to employees as to their required actions. Post orders should be produced in such a way that they provide a ready and usable reference guide for security officers. Personnel will be reluctant to read or consult manuals and directives that are cumbersome, voluminous, and difficult to use. The best directives are those that are concise, portable, and manageable within the operating conditions of the workforce.
- Dissemination. When disseminating written directives to staff, it is essential to maintain a control and follow-up system to ensure understanding and implementation. If a system of written directives is being used, staff should be required to acknowledge receipt of new or revised directives by signing receipts or logs that indicate so. In addition, security supervisors should conduct orientation and review sessions with staff to review new or revised directives to ensure staff understanding and to resolve any confusion in implementation.

Written directives developed to implement a Port FSP may be considered as Sensitive Security Information, or SSI, a term referenced in the U.S. MTSA of 2002. Not all written directives issued to port security personnel may be SSI. The Port FSO will have to determine which written directives meet the SSI criteria when disseminating to staff. Under Title 49 of the CFR, the U.S. Transportation Security Administration has the authority to designate as SSI any information obtained or developed in carrying out security requirements that would be detrimental to the security of transportation if that information was disclosed. Due to concerns about maritime transportation security, the Transportation Security Administration has designated maritime FSPs as SSI. Only covered people with a need to know may handle SSI materials. Covered people include owners or operators of a maritime facility that are required by the MTSA to have a security plan. Certainly, members of the port security force may have a need to know certain aspects of the FSP; thus, written directives conveying this information may be considered SSI. In handling SSI documents, including Port FSP written directives, security staff must adhere to the following restrictions:

- If the SSI is in their possession, they must prevent unauthorized disclosure.
- When the individual is not in physical possession of the SSI, it must be stored in a secure container such as a locked desk or file cabinet or in a locked room secure from unauthorized access.
- To preclude recognition or reconstruction of the information, a covered person must destroy the SSI completely when it is no longer needed.
- If a covered person becomes aware that SSI may have been compromised by release to unauthorized people, he/she must promptly inform the local U.S. Coast Guard COTP (U.S. Coast Guard 2004).

In all cases where written directives have been designated as SSI, a written statement should be included on the documentation clearly identifying it as such. A sample SSI statement on Port FSP-related written directives and correspondence is:

Warning: This document contains Sensitive Security Information that is controlled under the provisions of 49 CFR Part 1520. No part of this document may be released without the written permission of the Undersecretary of Transportation for Security, Washington, DC, 20590. Unauthorized release may result in civil penalty or other action.

Naturally, administrative controls must be established by the Port FSO to systematically and regularly review all security-related correspondence for the SSI designation.

9.5 Security Force Operations and Patrols

Security officers must perform high-visibility patrols of all port-controlled facilities. Special attention should be given to roadways, terminals, and parking areas where passenger, employee, and vehicular traffic is heaviest, considering the day and time. Officers must also frequently patrol the waterside, dock, berth, pier, cargo, container storage, and gantry crane areas. Specific operational assignment functions may include, but are not limited to, the following:

- Monitor or secure all access points as identified by the Port FSP, and as assigned by the Port FSO
- Monitor, respond to, and investigate incidents of unattended luggage, vehicles, packages, and items that may pose a security threat to port facilities and personnel
- Search or inspect vehicles, people, bags, deliveries, articles, or packages entering the port facility as prescribed in post orders
- Deny access to those people refusing to submit to security verification at access points and refer to appropriate law enforcement personnel for investigation and follow-up
- Restrict access to port restricted access areas to only authorized and essential personnel
- Enforce parking procedures and control the movement of vehicles within the port facility
- Inspect fences and other physical security barriers and devices to ensure soundness of port perimeter security
- Escort visitors, contractors, vendors, and other nonfacility personnel through the port facility as required
- Operate equipment (e.g., metal detectors, x-ray machines, handheld wands) to assist in screening people, personal effects, ships' provisions, noncontainerized cargo, and vehicles

- Conduct 100 percent screening of vehicles making deliveries of provisions to vessels in accordance with the U.S. MTSA requirements
- Control and restrict access of noncredentialed port visitors
- Monitor the movements of people, vehicles, and cargo throughout the port facility to ensure compliance with local, state, and federal port security regulations
- Operate closed-circuit television, surveillance, and access control systems
- Patrol parking lots, terminals, business premises, and cargo areas to prevent unauthorized entry and detect violations of established security regulations and procedures
- Stand guard at gate entrances and permit entrance to only authorized people and vehicles
- Stop suspicious people in restricted areas and question identity and nature of activities
- Detain people entering or leaving the port facility without the required authorization
- Maintain logs of vehicles and people entering security areas; check identification; dispense and collect passes
- Control and direct traffic using the port's road network to expedite the flow of traffic with maximum safety
- Summon law enforcement officers and assist in related criminal investigations and arrests
- Assist police, fire, and other first responders in response to port emergencies
- Operate mobile radio equipment, telecommunication devices, and patrol vehicles
- Prepare incident reports and logs in accordance with organizational rules, regulations, and procedures
- Maintain order and assist people with inquiries and problems
- Investigate and report port employees violating port-specific security procedures
- Handle investigations and dispositions of lost or unclaimed luggage and other personal property
- Make reports to supervisors on all unusual circumstances
- Monitor, inspect, and investigate intrusion, fire, and utility monitoring alarm systems

The Port FSO should work cooperatively with port security managers, administrative staff, and most importantly, line-level security officers and supervisors to engage them in ideas, suggestions, and contributions in developing task functions relevant to port operations.

References

American Society for Industrial Security. 2005. Career opportunities in security. http://www.asisonline.org/careercenter/careers2005.pdf (accessed August 28, 2008).

Code of Federal Regulations. 2003. Title 33, Navigation and Navigable Waters, Chapter I, Coast Guard, Department of Homeland Security, Part 105, Maritime Security: Facilities Part 105, Subpart C, Section 105.210, Facility personnel with security duties. http://edocket.access.gpo.gov/cfr_2003/julqtr/33cfr105.210.htm (accessed July 24, 2008).

Couper, D. C., and S. H. Lobitz. 1988, April. Quality leadership: The first step towards quality policing. *The Police Chief*, pp. 79–84.

Cunningham, William, John J. Strauchs, and Clifford W. Van Meter. 1990. *The Hallcrest Report II: Private Security Trends 1970–2000*. Boston: Butterworth-Heinemann, as cited in: Fischer, Robert J., Edward Halibozek, and Gion Green. 2008. *Introduction to Security*. 7th ed. Burlington, MA: Butterworth-Heinemann.

Enter, J. E. 1991. Police administration in the future: Demographic influences as they relate to management of the internal and external environment. *American Journal of Police*. 10:65–81.

Fidler, S. 2005. World: Steady growth expected for private security industry. Corpwatch. http://www.corpwatch.org/article.php?id=12638 (accessed January 14, 2008).

Fischer, Robert J., Edward Halibozek, and Gion Green. 2008. *Introduction to security*. 7th ed. Burlington, MA: Butterworth-Heinemann.

Goldstein, Herman. 1990. *Problem oriented policing*. Philadelphia: Temple University Press.

Hall, M. 2004, November 29. Police, fire departments see shortages across USA. *USA Today*. http://www.usatoday.com/news/nation/2004-11-28-police-shortages-cover_x.htm (accessed July 24, 2008).

Hersey, Paul, and Kenneth H. Blanchard. 1988. *Management of organizational behavior: Utilizing human resources*. Englewood Cliffs, NJ: Prentice-Hall.

Office of Public Sector Information. 2008. Private Security Industry Act 2001. 2001 Chapter 12. http://www.opsi.gov.uk/acts/acts2001/ukpga_20010012_en_1 (accessed July 24, 2008).

Rouda, R. H., and M. E. Kusy. 1995. Needs assessment: The first step. Technical Association of the Pulp and Paper Industry. http://www.alumni.caltech.edu/~rouda/T2_NA.html (accessed May 1, 2000).

Smith, Robert W., and Thomas D. Lynch. 2004. *Public budgeting in America*. 5th ed. Upper Saddle River, NJ: Pearson Prentice Hall.

Sparrow, M. 1993. Integrating distinct management styles: The challenge for police leadership. *American Journal of Police*. 12:1–6.

Training Network. 2007. Law enforcement training. http://www.hr-training-network.com/products/law_enforcement.shtml (accessed January 14, 2008).

U.S. Coast Guard. 2004. Sensitive security information regulations under 49 U.S.C. 114 (s) and 49 CFR 1520.7 (k) (Transportation Security Agency Regulations). Homeport. http://homeport.uscg.mil/cgi-bin/st/portal/uscg_docs/MyCG/Editorial/20061206/SSI_3.pdf?id=cc7d53da2662ed13da6e6ae0697e8f6ee3a3007a (accessed July 10, 2008).

U.S. Department of Justice. 2008. Law enforcement statistics. Office of Justice Programs, Bureau of Justice Statistics. http://www.ojp.usdoj.gov/bjs/lawenf.htm (accessed August 28, 2008).

Werther, William B., and Keith Davis. 1996. *Human resources and personnel management*. 5th ed. Boston: Irwin McGraw-Hill.

Witham, D. C. 1987. Transformational police leadership. *FBI Law Enforcement Bulletin*. 56:2–6.

Vessel and Cargo Operations

10.1 Vessel Operations

The passenger cruise vessels in Figure 10.1, docked in this port, may hold as many as three- to four-thousand passengers and crew each—and these are not the largest ones in the market today. The *Freedom of the Seas*, launched in 2006 by Royal Caribbean Cruises Ltd., has a total passenger occupancy capacity of 4,375. With a crew complement of 1,360, and assorted vendors and shore-based staff and guests on board, it is conceivable that almost 6,000 people may be on board this vessel during its port turnover days. Another Royal Caribbean vessel, the *Genesis*, under construction in Finland and scheduled for launch in 2009, is projected to be the world's largest passenger cruise vessel with a passenger capacity estimated at 6,400 (Wise 2007). This number does not include crew and shore-based support staff and vendors who will be interfacing with the vessel during port calls. Considering that ports routinely handle multiple cruise vessels during their turnovers, it is not unusual to have many thousands of people, as well as the vehicles used to transport passengers, luggage, and provisions, transiting the port facility on any given day.

For all intents and purposes, large vessels such as these essentially become floating structures connected to port facilities by passenger gangways, cargo-loading equipment, fueling operations, and ancillary service networks. Potential threats to the vessel become threats to the port facility. Fire, on-board emergencies, criminal activity, even simple disturbances may pose a threat not only to the vessel and its occupants but to the interfacing terminal and port facilities. Thus, it is a necessary task for the Port FSO to ensure that vessel security and port facility security are synchronized and coordinated. From the perspective of the Port FSO, vessels in port represent another component of port infrastructure that must be protected. Distinct from port facilities, vessels have their own infrastructure, personnel, threat assessments, vulnerabilities, plans, and security considerations. To compound this, when vessels arrive in port, they must be managed via a terminal facility that, depending on port governance and organization, may have a distinct infrastructure and security-planning agenda. Considering the many activities that occur between the vessel and port, it is clearly apparent that high levels of coordination are necessary to effectively manage security for port-vessel operations.

02/03/2003

Figure 10.1   Passenger cruise vessels in port.

10.1.1 Security Planning Considerations for Vessels

The Port FSO's management of security requirements for in-port vessel operations must be approached from the perspective of coordinated risk reduction: How can the Port FSO synchronize efforts with Vessel Security Officers (VSOs) and the Terminal Security Officer to reduce the risks from international terrorism, general criminal activity, and natural and man-made hazards? As with Port FSP development, the agenda must include identification of potential security problems, potential solutions and strategies, and the human and physical resources that will be required. Preparations must include identifying port operational and administrative systems that may have to be changed or developed to fund and develop port facility-vessel security precautions. This may necessitate systemic hardening of port infrastructure, port-vessel interfaces, and renewed emphasis on the vetting of crew, staff, guests, and visitors to the vessel while in port. To ensure continuity of port and vessel operations and business, the Port FSO must work closely with the ship operators, the VSO, and the Terminal Security Officer to refine and test coordinated security planning, preparation, and response capabilities.

In the heightened homeland security environment, threats to vessels from terrorism and sabotage top the list of concerns facing the shipping industry. In 2001, the International Chamber of Shipping recommended that ship operators appoint an officer to be responsible for the security of each individual vessel: "The officer's responsibilities include advising the master on the threat assessment for the voyage and agreeing on the ship's response; detailed contingency planning; encouraging security awareness and vigilance on board the ship; and reporting all occurrences and suspected occurrences of unlawful acts" (2001, par. 1). With the 2004 adoption of the ISPS Code, there is now an international requirement for passenger vessels and for commercial vessels greater than five hundred gross tons to have a Ship (i.e., Vessel) Security Officer designated on each ship. The VSO, who reports to the ship's master, is designated as responsible for the security of the ship, implementation and maintenance of the Vessel Security Plan, and coordination with the ship operator's Company Security Officer and Port FSOs. In the U.S., the MTSA of 2002 has a similar requirement for VSOs. Both the ISPS Code and the MTSA provide specifications of the functions and responsibilities for VSOs. The MTSA's requirements, as codified in Title 33, CFR (2003a), Part 104, for the VSO are as follows:

(a) General.
  (1) A VSO may perform other duties within the owner's or operator's organization, provided he or she is able to perform the duties and responsibilities required of the VSO for each such vessel.
  (2) For manned vessels, the VSO must be a member of the crew.
  (3) For unmanned vessels, the same person may serve as the VSO for more than one unmanned vessel. If a person serves as the VSO for more than one unmanned vessel, the name of each unmanned vessel for which he or she is the VSO must be listed in the Vessel Security Plan (VSP).
  (4) The VSO of any unmanned barge and the VSO of any towing vessel interfacing with the barge must coordinate and ensure the implementation of security measures applicable to both vessels during the period of their interface.
  (5) The VSO may assign security duties to other vessel personnel; however, the VSO remains responsible for these duties.
(b) Qualifications. The VSO must have general knowledge, through training or equivalent job experience, in the following:
  (1) Those items listed in Sec. 104.210 (b)(1) and (b)(2) of this part;
  (2) Vessel layout;
  (3) The VSP and related procedures, including scenario-based response training;
  (4) Crowd management and control techniques;
  (5) Operations of security equipment and systems; and
  (6) Testing and calibration of security equipment and systems, and their maintenance while at sea.
(c) Responsibilities. In addition to those responsibilities and duties specified elsewhere in this part, the VSO must, for each vessel for which he or she has been designated:
  (1) Regularly inspect the vessel to ensure that security measures are maintained;
  (2) Ensure maintenance and supervision of the implementation of the VSP, and any amendments to the VSP;

(3) Ensure the coordination and handling of cargo and vessel stores and bunkers in compliance with this part;

(4) Propose modifications to the VSP to the Company Security Officer (CSO);

(5) Ensure that any problems identified during audits or inspections are reported to the CSO, and promptly implement any corrective actions;

(6) Ensure security awareness and vigilance on board the vessel;

(7) Ensure adequate security training for vessel personnel;

(8) Ensure the reporting and recording of all security incidents;

(9) Ensure the coordinated implementation of the VSP with the CSO and the relevant Facility Security Officer, when applicable;

(10) Ensure security equipment is properly operated, tested, calibrated and maintained; and

(11) Ensure consistency between security requirements and the proper treatment of vessel personnel affected by those requirements.

In addition to an understanding of the role of the VSO, the Port FSO must be aware of the likely threats facing vessels. Much of this knowledge will be developed in consultation with the ship operators. Since the VSO is typically a crew member aboard ship, vessel owners and operators with ships that call on port facilities regularly should develop a relationship with the security management in each port of call. It is in these regular dialogs and communications where port users and port representatives can build a database of potential threats and risk mitigation problem sets. Obviously, the Port FSO will have to work from a baseline understanding of the threat environment facing vessels calling on specific port facilities. Pate, Taylor, and Kubu (2007, pp. 20–21) articulated several vessel-specific terrorist threat scenarios from their review of the maritime transportation research literature, as follows:

- Cargo containers used to smuggle terrorists or nuclear, chemical, or biological weapons or components
- General-use vessels such as tugboats or fishing and supply ships used to transport weapons
- Large cargo ships used as collision weapons to destroy waterfront infrastructure and facilities or to deliberately sink in shipping channels
- Vessels hijacked for ransom to support political violence
- Fuel-carrying vessels deliberately exploded in port
- Vessel attacks designed to disrupt world oil trade and cause environmental damage
- Seizure of or attacks on passenger vessels to cause mass casualties by food supply contamination, explosive detonation, or ramming with a fast-approach, small attack craft
- Attacks on military vessels and port facilities used by military vessels

Beyond the threats associated with terrorism, the Port FSO must also consider the general and specific crime threats that may confront port facilities engaged in various types of vessel operations:

- Murders, sex crimes, robberies, or assaults on passengers and crew both on-board vessels and while transiting port facilities.
- Property crimes against vessel passengers while on board and in port, for example, thefts of luggage and personal belongings, vehicle thefts, and burglaries.
- Vessel crew and passengers smuggling narcotics and other contraband through port facilities.

In 2007, the FBI advised the U.S. Congress on voluntary reports of alleged criminal incidents by member organizations of the Cruise Lines International Association, the official trade group representing North America's cruise industry. The voluntary reporting system was organized, with U.S. Coast Guard participation, to better understand the extent of crime occurring on board passenger cruise vessels. There are also mandatory incident-reporting requirements under MTSA and other federal law, but these voluntary industry reports represent a reasonable aggregation of likely criminal threats involving passengers and crew on board vessels transiting port facilities.

There are eight reporting categories in the Cruise Lines International Association framework: homicide, suspicious death, missing U.S. national, kidnapping, assault with serious bodily injury, sexual assault, firing or tampering with vessels, and theft greater than ten thousand dollars. Of the 207 voluntary reports made during the first five months of the program, there were no reports of homicides, suspicious deaths, or kidnapping; four reports of missing U.S. nationals; thirteen reports of assaults with serious bodily injury; forty-one reports of sexual assault; thirteen reports of theft involving more than ten thousand dollars; and one report of firing or tampering with vessels. The remaining 135 incidents, 65 percent of all reports, involved less serious matters such as simple assault, low-dollar loss theft, fraud, suspicious activity, bomb threats, sexual contact, or activity that was not criminal in nature. Of the 207 incidents reported, 16 (8 percent) occurred while a passenger was ashore outside of the United States, and 39 (19 percent) were responded to and/or investigated by law enforcement other than the FBI. According to FBI Deputy Assistant Director Salvador Hernandez, "Incidents on board ships when investigated by the FBI are documented through investigative files under the 'Crimes on the High Seas' classification. Of the 207 incident reports, the FBI opened 18 investigative files. This number is consistent with the number of 'Crimes on the High Seas' cases opened annually for the past five years" (2007, par. 13). Looking at these numbers realistically, the Port FSO should be able to work constructively with ship operators to factor in precautions that must be taken to manage criminal and other incidents involving passengers and crew. It may be that a port facility will only handle limited passenger vessel ports-of-call. In cases like this, the likely threat probability may be very low. In other facilities however, such as major passenger cruise and ferry ports, the volume of passengers may require more significant dialog with ship operators to manage regular reports of crime occurring on board vessels in and around the port facility.

10.1.2 Coordinating Security between the Port Facility and Vessels

From the Port FSO's perspective, risk management considerations involving significant passenger operations must consider the general threat of crime to passengers on board vessels in port. While the Port FSO and his/her staff may not be directly responsible for investigating or managing these incidents when they occur within port facilities, the port will likely be involved in ancillary or supporting roles in assisting either passengers or the investigating law enforcement agencies. It is not unusual for allegations of incidents aboard passenger vessels to attract media interest, and this may be an issue for port management when inquiries from news agencies are made directly to port officials. Is the port facility organized with a media liaison staff person or public information officer that can coordinate the release of information with port security and vessel representatives? Similarly, port security staff may be pressed to support the ship operator's needs for emergency medical assistance, fire and rescue, police support, crime scene investigators, and the like. Does the Port FSP consider various scenarios involving the coordination of shore- and vessel-based personnel and systems? The best strategy for the Port FSO is to begin and maintain regular dialog with the ship operator, Company Security Officer, VSO, and Terminal Security Officer to establish the necessary port-vessel protocols when managing criminal allegations while ships are transiting port facilities. This advance planning will serve to provide standard operating procedures for notifications, response, and investigations of crimes in port. To this end, the Port FSO, security, and management staffs must work closely with federal, state, and local law enforcement agencies so that investigations are coordinated and managed efficiently.

Another important area of coordination between port security and vessel security is communications. As many law enforcement and first responder agencies in the same area have different communications protocols, systems, and infrastructure, the ability to effect direct communications between port and vessel security organizations may require focused attention. An ideal approach would be for the Port FSO to provide port-of-call vessels with a direct radio or telecommunications capability with port security. Emergencies occurring within the port or on board vessels could immediately be managed and coordinated if all parties had the ability to communicate with a central command center. Alternatives to direct radio communications are monitored, computer-based communications (e.g., e-mail, text messaging), mobile or fixed telephone service, and in the event of power loss, messenger service.

A direct interface between the port facility security staff and the harbor and waterway pilots servicing vessels for the port will also be a critical security node in terms of the port's situational awareness and readiness. Pilot boats, such as those illustrated

Figure 10.2   Pilot boats used to transfer harbor and waterway pilots to vessels entering port facilities.

in Figure 10.2, are used to transport harbor and waterway pilots to and from large vessels approaching and departing port facilities. Because vessel masters do not often have a close familiarity of the unique operating conditions of local waterways in each port of call, pilots are used to navigate local port approaches and waterways for arriving and departing vessels. The pilots use these smaller vessels to approach alongside ocean-going vessels, and the pilots transfer via a ladder or lower-level gangway. Given the close proximity and connections that waterway pilots have with the maritime assets approaching and departing ports, there is an opportunity for port security to co-opt this operational relationship to improve the situational awareness on the waters adjoining the port facility.

This situational awareness could also assist port facilities in responding to suspicious activity on the waters adjoining port facilities. For example, on April 12, 2002, members of the environmental group Greenpeace, protesting illegal logging in South American rain forests, illegally climbed aboard the *APL Jade*, a cargo ship believed to be carrying mahogany from Brazil (Murdock 2003). Two individuals were able to board the cargo vessel, which was approaching the Port of Miami, Florida, from a smaller craft that pulled alongside the larger vessel, similar to how waterway pilots transfer to and from piloted vessels. The event, occurring not long after the September 2001 terrorist attacks, illustrated the vulnerabilities large commercial vessels have to being boarded illegally by people who might have an intent to harm the crew or use the vessel for criminal purposes. The U.S. Coast Guard was able to apprehend the intruders in this case; however, port security officials must consider similar threat scenarios involving vessels at sea and in proximity to port facilities. Thus, the ability to have a coordinating presence and communications with waterway pilots operating in these waters would be a significant asset to the port's security posture.

While port security staff may elect to establish direct communication and planning linkages with the working pilot group(s), it may be advantageous to also engage port berthing operational staff in these security linkages. Because operational decisions concerning vessel moorings and berths might also affect or otherwise engage port security, port management may accomplish multiple operating objectives by controlling both operational and security decisions involving vessel movements within one command framework. Under MTSA, but truly as a matter of necessity, at all MARSEC levels the Port FSO must have the capability to communicate with vessels transiting the port. Engaging port operations staff in this process ensures coordination of information transmission and a more stable security planning environment. From a coordination perspective, it is the Port FSO's responsibility to build relationships with vessel operations staff, berthing personnel, pilots, terminal operators, private proprietary or contract security staff, public safety, and law enforcement agencies to ensure that the port is prepared to receive vessels with the appropriate security measures in place.

10.1.3 Declaration of Security

The Port FSO must ensure adequate interfaces and coordination of security plans and the mitigation of security threats between the port facility and vessels that transit the port, including the execution of the necessary Declarations of Security (DoS) as required by the ISPS Code and U.S. MTSA regulations. Under U.S. MTSA regulations (Code of Federal Regulations 2003b), a DoS is an agreement executed between the VSO and the Port FSO. It is the mechanism for ensuring that all identified security issues are shared and addressed and that security will be in place as long as the vessel is in the port facility. At MARSEC level 1, the ship's master or VSO, or a designated representative, of any cruise ship or manned vessel carrying certain dangerous cargoes in bulk must complete and sign a DoS with the FSO or the designated representative of any interfacing port. They must coordinate security needs and procedures, and agree upon the contents of the DoS for the period of time the vessel is at the facility. The written DoS must be signed upon a vessel's arrival, before any passenger embarkation or disembarkation or cargo transfer operation. At MARSEC levels 2 and 3, the vessel master, VSO, or designated representative must sign and implement a DoS with the FSO of any facility on which it calls, prior to any cargo transfer operation or passenger embarkation or disembarkation. At MARSEC levels 1 and 2, VSOs of vessels that frequently interface with the same port facility may implement a continuing DoS for multiple visits, provided that:

- The DoS is valid for the specific MARSEC level,
- The effective period at MARSEC level 1 does not exceed 90 days, and
- The effective period at MARSEC level 2 does not exceed 30 days.

When the MARSEC level increases beyond the level contained in the DoS, the continuing DoS becomes void, and a new DoS must be signed and implemented. The U.S. Coast Guard COTP may, at any time and at any MARSEC level, require any manned vessel subject to MTSA regulations to implement a DoS with the Port FSO prior to any vessel-to-vessel or vessel-to-facility interface when he or she deems it necessary.

The written form of the DoS should minimally include the length of time that the DoS is valid, covered activities (e.g., mooring, loading cargo, fuel operations), the security levels of both the ship and port facility, and the initials of the VSO and the Port FSO as agreement that the specific activities will be done in accordance with the approved security plan. Specific actions to be addressed on the DoS form may include documentation of and agreements concerning restricted areas' authorized access requirements, cargo operations, vessel provisioning, passenger embarkation and disembarkation, baggage handing, communications, and any other activity considered relevant by the concerned parties in maintaining effective port-vessel security. The Port FSO must ensure that respective vessel and port facility security responsibilities are clearly articulated via an agreement on the contents of the DoS.

10.1.4 Passenger and Crew Security

Under U.S. MTSA regulations, the Port FSO must ensure that dangerous substances and devices are not permitted onto port facilities. To this end, passenger and crew security becomes a planning priority as the Port FSO considers the necessary screening and inspection protocols associated with vessels transiting the port. In 2008, it was reported that British intelligence agents learned of al-Qaeda plans to attack cruise ships in the Caribbean using small watercraft loaded with explosives. Reports have also surfaced concerning the use of fraudulent crew identities enabling potential terrorists to work on cruise ships and then take over and destroy them by sinking or starting a fire (Maritime Terrorism Research Center 2008). Assuredly, security planning involving vessel passengers and crew must be a prime consideration for port security managers. Procedures and systems addressing personnel screening and access to vessels in port facilities must be developed. All port access control systems should be designed to provide high levels of security for vessel passengers and crew, as follows:

- Systems should be designed to restrict and detect prohibited weapons, incendiaries, or explosives aboard passenger vessels, on people or in luggage, cargo, and ships' provisions.

- Vessel gangway security, including photo identification and electronic systems, should be designed to prevent unauthorized boarding and reboarding after port calls.
- Timely and accurate passenger and crew manifests are basic tools used by port security, customs and immigration, and port operations staff to provide ports with certain specific information as to the individuals expected to be in the seaport.
- Training for ships' crews in security-related duties provides another layer of security to ensure wider awareness of security concerns while vessels are in port. Orienting crew to the access control requirements for the seaport also assists in obtaining cooperation and compliance with port access control requirements (e.g., identification display, screening requirements).
- Coordination of ship and terminal security measures when ships are in port is a key component of developing continuity of access controls between vessels and seaports.

Passengers, crew, and other people accessing restricted areas such as secure terminals and vessels may be required to pass through a screening checkpoint. These checkpoints must be staffed by security personnel trained to screen and, if necessary, to search people prior to accessing restricted areas. Passenger and crew screening checkpoints may include the following provisions:

- X-ray Machine. People should be required to place items being carried for passage through an x-ray machine. Laptop computers should be removed from their carrying cases, and outer garments (e.g., coats, hats) should be removed and placed in a tray provided by the screening staff.
- Metal Detector. People should be required to walk through a fixed or portable metal detector. Individuals should remove any items from their clothing and pockets that could set off the alarm (e.g., belts, loose change). A secondary screening may be necessary if the detector senses metal. Entry should be denied if an individual refuses to be screened.
- Handheld Metal Detector. Handheld metal detectors (hand wands) are used to identify materials that caused the primary metal detector to alert. They are also useful for applications in port locations where large portable or fixed metal detectors are impractical and for inspecting packages and letters for metal objects.
- Secondary Screening. Individuals may be selected for random additional screening. Secondary screening may also be necessary following a primary screening, such as when a metal detector alarms. Carry-on baggage of individuals selected for secondary screening should be opened and examined. These individuals should not be permitted to leave the screening area with personal items or baggage that has not been opened and examined.

- Explosive Trace Detection. Equipment is available to conduct explosive trace detection inspections of baggage separate from the x-ray machine. This equipment may be necessary in port facilities with significant passenger cruise activity, especially in those ports where passengers transit directly to airports from seaports with their baggage checked through by designated airlines.
- Pat-Down Inspection. A pat-down inspection can be used in addition to a handheld metal detection screening to detect the presence of dangerous items or weapons on a person. Pat-down inspections should be limited to a cursory pat-down of an individual's outer garments. Port security personnel, unless authorized by law, should not engage in extensive pat-downs of individuals or invasive body searches.
- Limited Screening. Individuals may be required to open parcels, bags, and packages for a visual inspection. Security staff may also request people to open coats and outer garments, turn pockets inside-out, and remove hats for visual inspection.

10.1.5 Military Vessel Visits to Commercial Port Facilities

Specific security plans and procedures for military vessels visiting commercial port facilities must be developed well in advance of each visit. General security considerations for military vessel visits should include provisions for dates/times of the visit, berthing and mooring information, ship agent contact, provisioning instructions, planned special events, visitor and public access restrictions, vehicles permitted shipside, and scheduling of police/security patrols. For visits by U.S. military vessels and for visits by foreign military vessels in U.S. ports, the Naval Criminal Investigative Service will be involved in advance security planning. The Naval Criminal Investigative Service is the U.S. Navy's law enforcement and counterintelligence element, which works with local, state, federal, and foreign agencies to counter and investigate terrorism, espionage, computer intrusions, and many other criminal offenses. It is the navy's primary source of security for U.S. Navy personnel and assets, which it supports with protective services and vulnerability assessments of military installations and related facilities, including ports, airfields, and naval exercise areas. The Port FSO will coordinate military vessel security plans with the Naval Criminal Investigative Service, as well as with local police, other federal agencies including the U.S. Coast Guard, and the private sector security and port operational elements that will be involved during military port visits. Security planning considerations should include the following:

- Dates and times of visit
- Locations of port waterway entry and departure, berthings, and moorings
- Plans and arrangements for refueling while vessel is in port

- Designation of port security and/or law enforcement personnel to meet military vessels upon arrival and offer assistance, including a port facility security briefing for vessel officers and crew
- Names and contact information for designated ship agent(s)
- Dates and times of disembarkation and embarkation for crew members, visitors, and provisioning
- All provisions and vehicles to be screened at designated port facility vehicle inspection stations
- Plans and provisions for parking for vehicles (e.g., rental, government vehicles) of ship officers and crew
- Restrictions on vehicles parked dockside along the vessel
- A list of crew members, visitors, and provisions to be furnished to security officers assigned to the dock access control gate for access control
- Names of all nonmilitary personnel (e.g., ship visitors) to obtain temporary port visitor passes
- Arrangements for specific and/or requested military and law enforcement force protections (e.g., waterside patrols, explosive detection canines and screening for underwater and dock locations, special weapons teams for periods of heightened alert or unique threats)
- Screening and credential checks of port operations staff working in military vessel dock locations
- Identification of and planning for scheduled events taking place on the ship (e.g., VIP receptions, public visitors)
- Security officers and supervisors to monitor the dock areas and staff for compliance
- All security and law enforcement personnel assigned to receive copies of special post orders and security protocols
- Cost estimates of any extra security or law enforcement to be developed for review and approval by appropriate port and military management

10.2 Cargo Operations

10.2.1 U.S. Government Initiatives to Secure Cargo

U.S. Customs and Border Protection is the federal agency responsible for examining foreign cargo entering the United States through its seaports. In 2005, the agency articulated the scope of the challenge of trying to secure cargo within the global maritime transportation network:

- Sea containers move 90 percent of international commerce.
- The number of containers is increasing.
- Over a hundred million containers are shipped internationally every year.
- An ocean-going cargo ship can carry up to eight thousand containers.

- In fiscal year 2004, ten million containers entered the United States, nearly a million more than in fiscal year 2003, and two million more than in fiscal year 2002.
- The number of trade entries processed by U.S. Customs between 1996 and 2004 increased 75 percent.
- U.S. Customs predicts continued growth of 7 percent a year.
- The number of vessel containers in circulation will increase by 14 percent each year.

Shortly after the 2001 terrorist attacks on America, U.S. Customs began the Container Security Initiative. In this program, U.S. Customs agents work with foreign government customs services to examine high-risk cargo containers at foreign seaports before they are loaded onto U.S.-bound vessels. The initiative has four core elements as the foundation for the success of this program (U.S. Customs and Border Protection 2005):

1. Computerized intelligence and manifest information to identify those containers that pose a risk for terrorism
2. Prescreening of high-risk containers at the port of departure
3. Use of nonintrusive inspection technology (e.g., gamma-ray, x-ray machines) to examine containers
4. Tamper-evident cargo containers

The Container Security Initiative was initially deployed in twenty foreign ports with the highest volume of U.S.-bound shipping containers (i.e., two-thirds of all maritime containers shipped to the United States). According to the United States Department of Homeland Security (2008), there are now fifty-eight foreign ports participating in the initiative, representing 85 percent of the container traffic coming to the United States. To participate in the Container Security Initiative, foreign ports must:

- Have both nonintrusive inspection technology and radiation-detection equipment in place to inspect cargo;
- Establish an automated risk-management system to identify potential high-risk containers, validate threat assessments, and substantiate container selection examination criteria;
- Be willing and able to share data, intelligence, and risk-management information with U.S. Customs officials;
- Assess and address port infrastructure vulnerabilities; and
- Maintain programs to identify and address employee security or integrity violations in order to prevent internal conspiracies (U.S. Customs and Border Protection 2005).

In 2003, U.S. Customs and Border Protection implemented new regulations requiring that cargo carriers provide a declaration or manifest of cargo destined for or passing through the United States no later than twenty-four hours before loading at a foreign port. Known as the 24-Hour Rule, its intent is to provide some ability for the government to evaluate the risk of vessels carrying weapons of mass destruction before cargo is loaded onto vessels (Steamship Mutual 2003). The rule pertains specifically to sea containers and requires shippers to provide detailed descriptions of the container contents. This allows U.S. Customs to analyze the container content information and identify potential terrorist threats before its arrival in the United States (U.S. Customs and Border Protection 2003).

The Customs-Trade Partnership Against Terrorism (C-TPAT) is another federal program administered by U.S. Customs and Border Protection (2007a). It is designed to strengthen port security by developing better security practices related to the importing of cargo containers into U.S. ports. C-TPAT is a voluntary initiative. Launched in 2003, it relies on relationships between government and businesses involved in cargo shipping, such as importers, carriers, manufacturers, and licensed customs brokers, to enhance security throughout the international supply chain. The program requires participating businesses to ensure the integrity of their security practices and to communicate and verify the security guidelines of their business partners within the supply chain. Under the program, validated port elements and cargo carriers may receive reduced customs scrutiny of their cargo by submitting a security plan that meets U.S. Customs and Border Protection's minimum standards. Through 2007, sixty-nine hundred businesses received validation for participation in the program. Specific benefits to C-TPAT member businesses include the following:

- Reduced numbers of U.S. Customs inspections
- Priority processing for U.S. Customs inspections
- C-TPAT Supply Chain Security Specialists work with companies to develop international supply chain security practices
- Potential to participate in U.S. Customs importer self-assessment programs
- Potential to attend supply chain security training seminars

Like many new initiatives, heretofore undeveloped security programs sometimes require reexamination and tweaking to ensure program goals and objectives are being met. In 2008, the U.S. Government Accountability Office, the investigatory arm of Congress, reported that C-TPAT was experiencing some problems verifying that C-TPAT members' security practices met minimum criteria. On Congress's behalf, the Government Accountability Office examined the progress being made by U.S. Customs in its benefit award policies for C-TPAT members, the validation of members' security practices, and management and staffing challenges. Issues that surfaced in the Government Accountability Office's assessment included the testing of member companies' supply chain security practices not typically being done by Customs, and questions about companies being certified for reduced Customs inspections before they fully implemented any additional security improvements requested by the government (Yen 2008). As with all security planning, there is always a need to reassess and reevaluate outcomes to ensure a consistent level of productivity in mitigating the threats.

The Megaports Initiative, administered by the U.S. National Nuclear Security Administration, is a program established in 2003 in which the U.S. government engages foreign countries to emplace radiation detection equipment in their seaports. According to the U.S. National Nuclear Security Administration (2008), seventy-five ports have been identified for participation in this effort, which represents a U.S. multiagency strategy to mitigate the global threat of terrorists' use of the maritime domain to smuggle or use nuclear material and weapons. The International Atomic Energy Agency (2006) reported 103 incidents of illicit trafficking and other unauthorized activities involving nuclear and radioactive materials in 2005. Although most of these incidents involved low-grade nuclear materials, the report emphasized that even the small number of incidents involving highly enriched uranium represents security vulnerabilities at the facilities that handle this material. Given the threat that the misappropriation of highly enriched uranium poses to world security, this effort to develop a comprehensive layer of security across the international shipping environment is significant. The training of personnel and the funding and procurement of detection equipment to screen for the presence of radioactive materials in foreign ports are designed to enable security officials to examine cargo in ports and take appropriate action before cargo is transferred onto vessels. As part of this international effort, U.S. Customs and Border Protection (2007b) launched efforts to strengthen the screening of shipping containers destined for the United States. The Secure Freight Initiative is a joint partnership between the U.S. DHS, the Department of Energy, and the Department of State, in which U.S. Customs is field testing the use of integrated scanning technology. Initial testing is occurring in three foreign ports: Port Qasim, Pakistan; Puerto Cortes, Honduras; and Southampton, United Kingdom. Containers are scanned for radioactive substances and x-rayed to display their contents, with the data and images transmitted back to the United States in real time for analysis and comparison with cargo manifest information to assess the containers' risk levels.

10.2.2 Cargo Security in the Port Facility

Notwithstanding the efforts of many government agencies to strengthen the security and integrity of cargo transiting the worldwide maritime domain, from a port operational perspective, security controls within ports themselves must provide for integrity in the ground-level cargo handling systems. As with any business that depends on a secure infrastructure to be viable in a competitive marketplace, a port facility must develop practices that ensure cargo—whether in shipping containers or in assorted barrels, sacks, and boxes (see Figure 10.3)—can be reliably transported through and stored within its facilities. Eighty percent of cargo thefts are the result of a series of minor thefts (Fischer, Halibozek, and Green 2008). The implication of this figure for the Port FSO is that the concern is not only the possible loss of a forty-foot cargo

Figure 10.3   Break-bulk cargo in assorted containers at a port facility's screening point.

container but also the aggregate losses that might occur from employee theft, pilferage, shoddy accounting, information theft, and a host of other criminal activities. Anything of value can be the subject of cargo theft. Certainly, popular products such as computers, miscellaneous electronics, prescription drugs, jewelry, cigarettes, liquor, and designer clothing will top the list of targets for theft. In port facilities, however, the worldwide scope of commodities and products that come in and out each day represents a smorgasbord from which potential thieves, terrorists, and schemers can pick and choose. A containerful of straw baskets or a pallet of bagged cat litter may not be at the top of the list of potential targets, but to a small-basket or cat-litter business exporting inventory into a new market, the loss of even a small percentage of product could represent the difference between operational liquidity and bankruptcy. Therefore, it is crucial that the Port FSO work collectively with cargo terminals, shippers, and law enforcement to reduce the opportunities for pilferage and theft within the port facility and develop security controls for cargo moving into, around, and out of the facility. To this end, port facilities have a responsibility to their clients, to the maritime industry, and to the community at large to develop strong cargo reception, storage, and release processes that provide confidence in the movement of cargo through the port and reduce the chances for fraud, illegal conversion, and theft.

As discussed previously, internal criminal conspiracies within port facilities represent a significant security threat and challenge for the Port FSO. With respect to the potential for cargo theft, thieves will attempt to build relationships with cargo terminal employees to learn and exploit the terminal's vulnerabilities. Terminals with poor security (e.g., guard patrols neglecting to make security rounds, nonexistent or inadequate surveillance technology, or even poor lighting within storage yards at night) become opportunities for potential criminal activity. The ability to co-opt port facility and cargo industry employees' access to restricted cargo areas and develop specific knowledge of port law enforcement and security activities should be a major focus for Port FSOs in developing risk-reduction strategies. A potential smuggler's ability to facilitate and monitor illegal shipments concealed inside the cargo of legitimate shippers is another potential area of concern for the Port FSO. To address the threat from internal criminal conspiracies, the Port FSO must work for the full cooperation of terminal operators and employees. Much of this can certainly be accomplished through the development and implementation of strong credentialing and access control systems. Beyond this, however, there must be focused understanding of the security mission and coordination between port security and cargo operations to neutralize this threat.

The U.S. MTSA (Code of Federal Regulations 2003c) addresses the requirement for port facilities to develop security measures for handling cargo. These are not prescriptive measures, in the sense that they do not specifically advise port facilities how to accomplish cargo security; but the federal regulations do require that the Port FSP ensure cargo handling security measures that:

- Deter tampering
- Prevent cargo not meant for carriage from being accepted and stored
- Identify cargo interfacing with the port facility
- Have cargo-control procedures at facility access points
- Identify cargo accepted for temporary storage in restricted areas
- Restrict cargo from entering without a confirmed date for loading
- Ensure cargo is released only to carriers specified in cargo documentation
- Coordinate security measures with shippers and responsible parties
- Have a continuous inventory and location of all dangerous goods or hazardous substances from receipt to delivery
- Ensure cargo entering the facility is checked for dangerous substances and devices, at rates specified in the Port FSP, through visual and/or physical examinations, use of detection devices, or canines
- At MARSEC level 1, ensure cargo, cargo transport units, and cargo storage areas are routinely checked prior to and during cargo handling operations to deter tampering, match delivery and cargo documentation, screen vehicles, check container seals, and use other methods to prevent tampering
- At MARSEC level 2, implement additional security measures, such as conducting checks for dangerous substances and devices; intensifying checks to ensure only documented cargo enters the facility; intensifying vehicle screening; increasing frequency and detail in checking seals and other methods to

prevent tampering; segregating inbound and outbound cargo; increasing frequency and intensity of visual and physical inspections; limiting the locations where dangerous goods and hazardous substances, including certain dangerous cargoes, can be stored

- At MARSEC level 3, ensure additional security measures, such as restricting or suspending cargo movements or operations, being prepared to cooperate with responders and vessels, and verifying the inventory and location of any dangerous goods and hazardous substances

Port FSOs and security management must develop specific provisions for effecting at least the minimum level of cargo security required by the U.S. MTSA. The U.S. Coast Guard, in reviewing Port FSPs and plan amendments, will not tell the Port FSO specifically how to accomplish the MTSA-required levels of security; however, the agency does provide guidance, including recommendations for cargo security and screening, in several published and available NVICs, including the following:

- NVIC 11-02, Recommended Security Guidelines for Facilities
- NVIC 03-03, Implementation Guidance for the Regulations Mandated by the Maritime Transportation Security Act of 2002 for Facilities
- NVIC 06-04, Voluntary Screening Guidance for Owners or Operators Regulated Under Parts 104, 105, and 106 of Subchapter H of Title 33, Code of Federal Regulations

Figure 10.4 provides a checklist the Port FSO can use to conduct an assessment of the cargo security management practices existing in the port facility as a preliminary step to developing Port FSP cargo security provisions and for coordinating security plans with cargo terminal operators and other port users.

In all cases, the Port FSOs should consult with the U.S. Coast Guard COTP to factor in information from area maritime security risk assessments and recommendations available from NVICs and from Coast Guard personnel responsible for port facility security. Just as important is the quality of the continuing dialog and coordination with port cargo stakeholders and users to develop reasonable security strategies. Not only must the port have solid security plans for cargo handling and storage, but it must address industry concerns regarding security delays associated with cargo and container vehicle processing and traffic management. Port facilities should share industry concerns for effecting improvements to cargo processing times. Signage, traffic controls, and cargo gate processing technology should be implemented to improve the queuing and staging of container vehicle traffic across the roads and into the lanes leading to the port facility's cargo gates. A full-time cargo gate manager should be designated to maintain oversight and take responsibility for operations at main cargo gates to ensure gate processing times are optimized and delays are minimized. Conduct an analysis of gate processing times to establish a benchmark stan-

Cargo Delivery and Reception Procedures

- Issue gate passes to persons upon verification of identification.
- Verify company names on vehicles and equipment.
- Release cargo only to carriers in delivery orders.
- Verify truck driver and company before cargo release.
- Restricted area access only to authorized personnel.
- Protect shipping documents from unauthorized use, tampering, and theft.
- Check container seals for integrity and verify seal number against documents.
- Check vehicle interiors for stolen merchandise and unauthorized occupants.
- Obtain legible signatures from drivers accepting delivery.
- Closely inspect delivery documents and verify cargo shipments.

Lading and Unlading

- Move cargo directly to and from railcars, trucks, vessels, and port storage locations.
- Check seals on container shipments prior to arrival, departure, and transfer.
- Open empty containers for examination, then reseal and store door to door.

Storage of Loose Cargo

- Stack loose cargo parallel to fences and walls with unimpeded views of perimeters.

Documentation

- Electronic transmission of cargo manifests to U.S. Customs in advance of vessel arrival.
- Inspect bills of lading prior to cargo acceptance.
- Ensure accurate descriptions of type, weight, and amount of cargo.
- Develop security procedures to protect documentation from tampering.

Control, Inventory, and Reconciliation

- Develop accurate cargo lists and location charts.
- Segregate import, export, and domestic cargo.
- Segregate delivery and receiving operations.
- Report cargo shortages and overages.

Figure 10.4 Cargo Security Management Checklist.

High Value Cargo

- Store high-value cargo in segregated areas with separate logs and procedures.
- Place containerized high value cargo placed in high locations to limit access.

Seals and Sealing Practices

- Inspect seals when containers enter and leave facilities.
- Develop reporting and inventory procedures for tampered or broken seals.
- Seal unsealed shipments at point of entry with notation of seal numbers on documents.
- Provide secure storage and documentation of seals.
- Regularly inspect seals, numbers, dates, times, and places of examinations.

Equipment Controls

- Institute controls on access and keys to mules, trucks, forklifts, and loaders.
- Secure equipment in designated areas when not in use.

Audit and Management Controls

- Institute procedures for investigating unauthorized removal of cargo.
- Identify and correct security breaches resulting in unauthorized removal.
- Conduct regular staff inspections of cargo security management procedures.

Source: Adapted from U.S. Maritime Administration. 2002. Port Security Assessment Field Report. Washington, DC: Inter-American Port Security Training Program.

Figure 10.4   (continued)

dard for present operations, and for future operations when new access gate facilities are planned or become operational.

A primary responsibility for cargo processing is to control and identify those vehicles authorized to deliver cargo to and receive cargo from the port facility. All traffic doing business at the port should receive an entry pass clearly delineating the access granted and the time and date for which the access is permitted; upon exiting the port, the pass should be recovered and recorded into a database. Port gate passes should provide a record of the cargo and transporting vehicle's driver, registration information, identifying numbers, cargo, and scale weight. This is one of the basic cargo security management mechanisms for port security. The gate pass is the controlling document that tracks the movement of container and vehicle traffic into, through, and out of the port. Procedures must exist for issuing clearly identifiable passes that, upon visual inspection, distinctly indicate the access and/or restricted access area to which the vehicle is destined to pick up cargo. Port gate pass procedures should be incorporated into the approved Port FSP and be in compliance with the requirements of local, state, and federal security regulations.

10.2.3 Cargo Security in Buildings

Specific security considerations may apply in cargo facilities located inside buildings and warehouses on the port facility. Cargo security breaches may occur due to doors being left or propped open. Security sweeps of cargo terminals, sheds, equipment facilities, and warehouses should be conducted at the beginning and end of operations, as well as at random times during operations shifts. Port security officers should have a clear reporting procedure that documents how and when the sweeps were conducted. If cargo terminal security staff have responsibilities for any aspects of the Port FSP, building sweeps should be jointly conducted with designated staff from all participating security organizations. Some areas of concern to be identified and mitigated are as follows:

- Open or unattended doors could be an issue in facilities without adequate heat or air-conditioning where terminal staff may be tempted to leave roll-up doors open for ventilation.
- Access to restricted waterside or dock areas must be controlled.
- Movements of terminal employees from nonrestricted to restricted areas should be monitored and controlled.
- Employee personal vehicle parking should be prohibited adjacent to and inside cargo buildings. Adequate signage should clearly specify restricted and prohibited parking regulations and be strictly enforced.
- Cargo-moving equipment, such as this forklift in Figure 10.5, should be secured at the end of operations, with the keys removed and secured in designated key control locations.
- Views of building and fence perimeters should be clear and unobstructed. Notice how the large equipment stored on the perimeter of the warehouse and fence line in Figure 10.6 obscures the views of the loading dock and fence line.

The Port FSO who develops good relationships with peers in the terminals and warehouses moving and storing cargo will enable collaborative risk assessments to

Figure 10.5   Forklift left unsecured in cargo operations area.

Figure 10.6   Cargo warehouse views blocked by equipment.

identify opportunities for effecting relatively simple solutions to eliminate potential problems. Mission-building activities to identify lapses in security, such as those depicted in the preceding figures, will go a long way toward instilling confidence in port users and security regulators that the facility is attentive to and desirous of a strong security posture. This does add value to the security component of the port facility in terms of decreased incidence of theft, lower insurance costs, and confidence in the organization as a whole.

References

Code of Federal Regulations. 2003a. Title 33, Navigation and Navigable Waters, Chapter I, Coast Guard, Department of Homeland Security, Part 104, Vessel Security, Subpart B, Vessel Security Requirements, Section 104.215, Vessel security officer. http://edocket.access.gpo.gov/cfr_2003/julqtr/33cfr104.215.htm (accessed July 28, 2008).

Code of Federal Regulations. 2003b. Title 33, Navigation and Navigable Waters, Chapter I, Coast Guard, Department of Homeland Security, Part 104, Vessel Security, Subpart B, Vessel Security Requirements, Section 104.255, Declaration of security. http://edocket.access.gpo.gov/cfr_2003/julqtr/33cfr104.255.htm (accessed July 28, 2008).

Code of Federal Regulations. 2003c. Title 33, Navigation and Navigable Waters, Chapter I, Coast Guard, Department of Homeland Security, Part 105, Facility Security, Subpart C, Facility Security Requirements, Section 105.265, Security measures for handling cargo. http://edocket.access.gpo.gov/cfr_2003/julqtr/33cfr105.265.htm (accessed August 1, 2008).

Fischer, Robert J., Edward Halibozek, and Gion Green. 2008. *Introduction to security*. Boston: Butterworth-Heinemann.

Hernandez, Salvador. 2007, September 19. Statement before the House Committee on Transportation and Infrastructure Subcommittee on Coast Guard and Maritime Transportation. Federal Bureau of Investigation, Congressional Testimony. http://www.fbi.gov/congress/congress07/hernandez091907.htm (accessed July 29, 2008).

International Atomic Energy Agency. 2006. Trafficking in nuclear and radioactive materials in 2005. http://www.iaea.org/NewsCenter/News/2006/traffickingstats2005.html (accessed July 30, 2008).

International Chamber of Shipping. 2001. Abstract: Guidance for ship owners, ship operators and masters on the protection of ships from terrorism and sabotage. National Criminal Justice Reference Service. http://www.ncjrs.gov/App/Publications/abstract.aspx?ID=193971 (accessed July 28, 2008).

Maritime Terrorism Research Center. 2008. MI6 said to have uncovered a maritime terrorism plot in the Caribbean. http://www.maritimeterrorism.com/2008/06/15/mi6-said-to-have-uncovered-a-maritime-terrorism-plot-in-the-caribbean/ (accessed July 4, 2008).

Murdock, Deroy. 2003, October 7. Seeing Greenpeace. National Review Online. http://www.nationalreview.com/murdock/murdock200310070839.asp (accessed July 31, 2008).

Pate, Anthony, Bruce Taylor, and Bruce Kubu. 2007. Protecting America's ports: Promising practices: A final report submitted by the Police Executive Research Forum to the National Institute of Justice. http://www.ncjrs.gov/pdffiles1/nij/grants/221075.pdf (accessed July 4, 2008).

Steamship Mutual. 2003. U.S. Customs 24-Hour Rule. BIMCO Voyages and Time Charterparty Clauses. http://www.simsl.com/Articles/BIMCO_US24_0303.asp (accessed July 4, 2008).

U.S. Customs and Border Protection. 2003. Enforcement of 24-Hour Rule Begins February 2. http://www.cbp.gov/xp/cgov/newsroom/news_releases/archives/cbp_press_releases/012003/01302003.xml (accessed July 4, 2008).

U.S. Customs and Border Protection. 2005, July/August. CBP's Container Security Initiative provides roadmap to international trade accord. U.S. Customs and Border Protection Today. http://www.cbp.gov/xp/CustomsToday/2005/Jul_Aug/csi.xml (accessed July 30, 2008).

U.S. Customs and Border Protection. 2007a. C-TPAT Overview. http://www.cbp.gov/xp/cgov/trade/cargo_security/ctpat/what_ctpat/ctpat_overview.xml (accessed July 30, 2008).

U.S. Customs and Border Protection. 2007b. CBP kicks off Secure Freight Initiative. U.S. Customs and Border Protection Today. http://www.cbp.gov/xp/CustomsToday/2007/apr_may/secure.xml (accessed July 4, 2008).

U.S. Department of Homeland Security. 2008. Container Security Initiative Ports. http://www.dhs.gov/xprevprot/programs/gc_1165872287564.shtm (accessed July 30, 2008).

U.S. Government Accountability Office. 2008. Supply chain security: U.S. Customs and Border Protection has enhanced its partnership with import trade sectors, but challenges remain in verifying security practices. Report to Congressional Requestors. GAO-08-240. http://www.gao.gov/new.items/d08240.pdf (accessed July 30, 2008).

U.S. National Nuclear Security Administration. 2008. Megaports Initiative. http://nnsa.energy.gov/nuclear_nonproliferation/1641.htm (accessed July 31, 2008).

Wise, Jeff. 2007, June. World's largest cruise ship pulls 360s with joystick. Popular Mechanics.com. http://www.popularmechanics.com/science/extreme_machines/4217987.html (accessed July 28, 2008).

Yen, H. 2008, May 26. Investigators find gaps in port security program. Associated Press. http://ap.google.com/article/ALeqM5gSxyAhQENdaNd3VWy4lMjk_mfP0gD90TPIMO0 (accessed May 29, 2008).

SAFETY AND EMERGENCY MANAGEMENT

11.1 Safety Management in the Port Facility

11.1.1 Occupational Safety and Health

The types of operations that occur day in and day out in modern port facilities include significant levels of industrial activities that lend themselves to risks of death, personal injury, and property damage. The transfer of containerized cargo between vessels and land conveyances, as illustrated in Figure 11.1, is just one example of the potential for danger that can occur from mishandling, poor supervision, ill-trained staff, defective equipment, and inadequate security practices. In 1970, the U.S. federal government enacted the Occupational Safety and Health Act. This act was designed to provide an environment of safe and healthful working conditions for employees by authorizing the enforcement of safety standards and providing for research, information, education, and training in the field of occupational safety and health (Legal Archiver.org 2008). Pursuant to the enactment of this legislation, the Occupational Safety and Health Administration (OSHA), an agency of the U.S. Department of Labor, was established in 1971.

According to OSHA statistics, in 2005 there were 4.2 million occupational injuries and illnesses among U.S. employees, approximating 4.6 cases per 100 employees. About 33 percent of work-related injuries occurred in goods-producing industries, and 67 percent in service sectors. In 2006, 5,703 employees lost their lives on the job, a fatality rate of 3.9 deaths per 100,000 employees (U.S. Department of Labor 2007). "The core function of any workplace safety and health program is to 'find and fix' hazards that endanger employees and to implement systems, procedures, and processes that prevent hazards from recurring or being introduced into the workplace. This element of a worker protection program has the most immediate and direct effect on injury and illness prevention" (U.S. Department of Labor 2001, par. 2). OSHA agency inspection priorities include the following:

- Reports of imminent dangers or accidents about to happen
- Fatalities or accidents serious enough to send three or more employees to the hospital
- Employee complaints
- Referrals from other government agencies

Figure 11.1   Cargo container movements in port facilities require focused consideration of safety requirements to prevent personal injuries and property damage.

- Targeted inspections that focus on employers who report high injury and illness rates
- Special emphasis programs that zero in on hazardous work such as trenching, or equipment such as mechanical power presses
- Follow-up inspections

Penalties for violating OSHA standards may include a fine of up to seventy thousand dollars, depending upon how likely the violation is to result in serious harm to employees. Penalties may be discounted if an employer has a small number of employees, has demonstrated good faith, or has few or no previous violations.

11.1.2 Port Facility Safety

In a recent study of port-related safety, the accident rate for direct businesses on ports in the United Kingdom was estimated to be 1.2 per one hundred employees on average, or 1.2 percent annually (Department of Transport 2005). Port facilities present unique challenges for safety management, given the diversity of operations they develop in interfaces among vessels, cargo, and land-based people and conveyances. Port infrastructure, plant, and equipment may be subject to safety management concerns in a variety of operational areas as follows (International Labour Office 2005):

- General safety issues related to the separation of people and vehicles, fire, traffic control, and pedestrian thoroughfares
- Cargo-handling processes, including operational layouts, edge protection, fencing, waterside ladders, and lifesaving equipment
- Shoreside access to vessels, including ramps, passenger walkways, landing stages, steps, walkways, and dockside ladders
- Access to terminal buildings, structures, and physical plant
- Terminal plant and equipment, including port-internal moving equipment, trailers, chassis, hand trucks, trolleys, and cargo platforms
- Ancillary equipment, including conveyors, electrical equipment, hand tools, machinery, mooring dolphins, and bollards
- Bulk cargo terminals, including solids, liquids, and gases
- Container terminals
- Passenger terminals
- Roll-on–roll-off terminals
- Warehouses and transit sheds
- Gatehouses and dock offices
- Port railways
- Tenders and work boats
- Personal protective equipment
- Lifting appliances, including cranes, forklifts, stackers, and loaders

11.1.3 Port Safety Officer

The primary role of the Port Safety Officer is to work collaboratively with, or as a component element of, the port security organization in managing the port facility's industrial safety and risk management programs. This will likely include responsibilities for vehicle accident prevention programs, as well as the development and maintenance of loss-control programs to prevent employee on-the-job accidents. Potential safety problems in port facilities can run the gamut from major incidents, such as a cargo container falling during crane transfers between port facility and vessels, to the routine, such as a passenger slipping on a waxed terminal floor. The nature of safety management is to consider the safety risks associated within a wide scope of potential vulnerabilities, from vehicle accidents, to equipment failure, to human error. The safety functions should include periodic inspections of port facilities, cargo operations, buildings, and equipment; preparation of reports detailing findings and recommendations; investigation of industrial accidents; and the provision of educational training courses for employees and supervisors to prevent on-the-job injuries. Given the complex nature of many multifunctional port facilities, the Port Safety Officer must have the ability to develop portwide loss-control program strategies as part of his/her engagement with users in large-scale port industrial operations. This is one reason why port management should seriously consider that the security and safety functions operate fluidly within a single organizational framework. It may be that many safety issues are also security issues and vice versa, which naturally should provoke a consolidated review and response from both security and safety.

The individual responsible for management of the port organization's safety program should have a combination of education and experience that provides a solid foundation for knowledge and skills in a variety of areas, including the following:

- Understanding how laws and regulations impact industrial safety in general and port facility operational safety and security in particular.
- Loss prevention practices, procedures, and techniques for a variety of employment situations and equipment operations.
- Development of loss control program mission, goals, and objectives.
- The ability to recruit and train competent support staff in implementing the port's safety and risk control programs.
- Safety equipment and safe driving methods applicable to varied types of vehicle operations and work areas.
- Familiarity with hazardous working conditions and equipment operations in various work environments.
- Accident prevention records and statistical measurements of accident frequency and severity.
- Hazardous materials risks and response protocols related to their storage and transportation in the port facility.
- Implementation and enforcement of loss prevention policies, procedures, and regulations.
- Use of vehicular and industrial accidents analyses to recommend prevention strategies.
- Computer programs applications to industrial safety functions.
- Analysis of the safety-related aspects of the port facility's plans, designs, and utility operations.
- Relationships with local, state, and national safety organizations.
- Relationships with U.S. Coast Guard command elements responsible for port facility security and marine safety.
- Relationships with local fire departments, first responder agencies, and emergency management organizations.
- Remain abreast of developments in the safety field, particularly as applicable to port facilities and the maritime sector.

As part of the Port Safety Officer's regular routine, he/she should be developing working relationships with port staff and organizational elements, particularly managers and supervisors, to strengthen an environment, or culture, of safety. Critical questions that the Port Safety Officer must pose to staff, either directly or indirectly through organizational communications and dialog, include the following:

- Who is responsible for safety?
- Does a sloppy loss-control program affect individual jobs? How?
- How can the safety record of the facility be improved by employees and supervisors?
- How can the safety record of the facility be improved by top management?
- What has been done in the past six months to improve the safety of the facility?
- How much authority do employees have to correct unsafe conditions?
- What supervisory safety training has been provided?

Port Safety Officers can convene meetings with other facility (e.g., terminals, vessels, companies) safety officers to review critical safety procedures and protocols, such as those concerning hazardous materials incident response and reporting. Include representatives from port security, coast guard, fire, and other first responders in these meetings. Follow up by conducting regular safety inspections with documentation and reports to senior management and managers from respective port elements. To develop a more effective deficiency identification and correction process, these inspections could be conducted jointly with port operations, facilities maintenance, and security to collaboratively identify and address safety and security deficiencies. Some examples of port operational safety deficiencies likely to contribute to increased safety risks, as well as provoke investigatory and enforcement action by the U.S. Coast Guard, OSHA, local fire marshals, or other concerned agencies, are as follows:

- Weeds, debris, and unnecessary clutter surrounding fire hydrants and fire-fighting equipment on vessel docks and cargo areas
- Inoperable or damaged fire- and utility-monitoring alarm systems
- Exposed wires, utility boxes, and junction boxes on terminal facilities and other buildings
- Hazardous materials, gas cylinders, and other industrial materials used in port operations (e.g., welding, repair, and machining) found unsecured, on docks, in cargo-operating areas, and in or adjacent to restricted areas within the port facility
- Fences, warehouse facilities, doors, windows, or machinery damaged by weather, criminal activity, or industrial accident, in states of disrepair or poor maintenance
- Waterside terminal, cargo, and dock locations cluttered with unused or unnecessary cargo pallets, machinery, debris, and so forth
- Trash and waste materials dumped on the ground or otherwise not deposited in containers designed for trash collection and removal
- Forklifts and other cargo-moving equipment being operated on port property without required portable fire extinguishers or other safety equipment required by law
- Blocked fire stairs and emergency exits

- Inoperable escalators and elevators not secured from public access
- Storage or maintenance closets and facilities left open, permitting tampering with hazardous materials contained therein
- Port trafficways with inadequate traffic controls and devices
- Inattention to personnel practices and use of safety equipment and materials in hazardous work areas (see Figure 11.2)

As waterfront facilities, ports in the United States are subject to the regulations provided in Title 33, CFR, Navigation and Navigable Waters, Part 126, Handling of Dangerous Cargo at Waterfront Facilities, which applies to the handling of packaged and bulk-solid dangerous cargo and to the vessels in those facilities. Port FSOs, and particularly Port Safety Officers and staff, should become thoroughly familiar with this and other relevant legislation regulating safety procedures and materials that can be stored and handled in port facilities.

11.1.4 Port Safety Committee

The establishment of a Port Safety Committee should be a security management priority in all port facilities. The committee structure is a useful method for communicating, assessing, and mitigating the safety and health issues in the port facility. The

Figure 11.2 The dockworkers servicing this vessel must have training in the safe and proper use of equipment, such as this water supply hose, while working in close proximity to the vessel and the edge of the dock.

committee is an organization in which both management and employee members representing a larger group participate in safety decisions affecting all port elements. In port facilities, the Safety Committee should have representatives from all port sectors and levels, including perhaps most importantly from the labor groups. It is an opportunity for port security managers to engage employees to participate in decision making related to their own well-being, security, and safety. While providing member organizations with a voice, it keeps meeting sizes manageable so that business can be conducted efficiently. The committee should be focused on creating and maintaining a safe and stable workplace for all port employees. It should be a nonadversarial, cooperative effort to promote safety throughout the port facility and to work together to identify and recommend solutions to health and safety problems.

A record of all Port Safety Committee meetings should be maintained. At a minimum committee reports should include dates and times of meetings; names of members present, excused, and absent; issues discussed; recommendations made; and people/groups responsible for action. Port Safety Committees should be focused on producing best practices revolving around port safety programs. Recommended objectives for a health and safety committee (National Ag Safety Database 2008) include the following:

- Study injury and disease statistics and trends
- Report unsafe and unhealthy conditions and practices, and recommended corrective action, to management
- Examination of safety and health audits
- Consider reports provided by government and insurance inspectors
- Consider reports by safety representatives
- Assist management in the development of job site safety rules
- Review the effectiveness of health and safety training of employees
- Review and assist in communication and promotion of health and safety matters in the workplace
- Carry out periodic safety and health audits to determine the effectiveness of programming

The American Association of Port Authorities (AAPA) is a major trade organization representing over 160 public port authorities in the United States, Canada, the Caribbean, and Latin America. AAPA has established a Risk Management and Safety Committee, which "monitors, collects and distributes information and data relating to port safety and risk management/insurance including the development of port safety awareness programs, training programs, fire protection programs and standards, and 'safe equipment' techniques. This also includes the ongoing review of all relative laws and regulations" (2008a, par. 1). AAPA also provides sample safety guidelines, which can be referred to by Port FSO and Safety Officers for developing port safety programs. These guidelines, provided to AAPA by the Maryland Port Administration (AAPA 2008b), include the following components:

- Management of a safety program, including policies, management responsibilities, accident preventability, the promotion of a safe employee environment for employees as part of everyday port activities, and consideration of the impacts on costs and operations
- Safety responsibilities, including those of port chief executives, managers, supervisors, line employees, and safety staff
- Record of accidents, including causes, definitions, impacts of near-misses, management systems failures, human error, and multiple causes
- Safety and health inspections, meetings, and committees
- Accident investigations, including categories and procedures

The federal and state governments in the United States and in many countries have regulations and guidelines concerning occupational safety and health programs. A comprehensive, mission-centered port facility safety program, focused on quality management, can reduce worker deaths, injuries, and illnesses and their associated costs. To further assist port security managers with developing their safety programs and complying with government standards, OSHA has published a booklet entitled Longshoring Industry, which is freely available on the U.S. Department of Labor's (2001) OSHA Web site. It provides a generic overview of safety and health standards concerning the marine terminal and longshoring industries, as contained in Title 29, CFR, Parts 1917 and 1918. Included in this publication are guidelines concerning marine terminal operations, cargo handling, personnel protection, gangways, working surfaces, vessels, and working conditions.

11.2 Emergency Management

11.2.1 Port Facility Interfaces with Homeland Security

The emergence of an emphasis on maritime security in general, and port facility security in particular, must be viewed within the context of a national emergency policy response to the terrorist attacks of 2001. Like many transportation facilities, ports have been required to implement contingencies and plans for the enhanced security risks associated with terrorism. The acquisition of more complex security technologies, as well as the deployment of additional emergency response and law enforcement assets (Figure 11.3), illustrates the complexities of the relationships between a port facility's security plan and the larger strategy for national and international security. On December 17, 2003, President George W. Bush signed Homeland Security Presidential Directive/HSPD-8, which established a national policy to strengthen the preparedness of the United States to prevent and respond to threatened or actual domestic terrorist attacks, major disasters, and other emergencies, by requiring a national domestic all-hazards preparedness goal (White House 2003a). Following HSPD-8, the U.S. National Response Plan was developed to foster unified management of domestic security incidents. It relied on integrating best practices and procedures from many

Figure 11.3   Police vehicles, like the ones at the entrance to this port facility, illustrate the increasing need to plan and prepare for emergencies at important transportation sites.

disciplines, including homeland security, emergency management, law enforcement, firefighting, and others, as the foundation for federal elements working together and coordinating with state, local, and tribal governments and the private sector during incidents (U.S. Department of Homeland Security 2005a). On March 22, 2008, the National Response Plan was replaced by the National Response Framework, which defined the principles, roles, and structures that frame how the United States will respond collectively in terms of a "national response doctrine" of coordination, specific authorities, and best practices. Five key principles reflect the overarching approach to incident and emergency response in the National Response Framework: engaged partnerships; a tiered response; scalable, flexible, and adaptable operational capabilities; unity of effort through unified command; and readiness to act (U.S. Department of Homeland Security 2008).

For the Port FSO and port management, the homeland security policy direction in the United States has clearly been for the federal government to aggressively engage not only local and state governments but increasingly the private sector in building an emergency operations and response capability to address domestic incidents threatening national security. Within the maritime sector, the Port FSP must be developed in concert with this policy direction, as established in federal policy statements, legislation, and administrative regulations. Predominant among these is the National Strategy for Maritime Security. Developed in 2005, it is the comprehensive U.S. government statement on its maritime security strategy as a global challenge to mitigate threats associated with hostile and illegal activities within the maritime domain. "Maritime security is best achieved by blending public and private maritime security activities on a global scale into an integrated effort that addresses all maritime threats. The new National Strategy for Maritime Security aligns all federal government maritime security programs and initiatives into a comprehensive and cohesive national effort involving appropriate Federal, State, local, and private sector entities" (White House 2005, par. 2). U.S. Federal law requires a National Maritime Transportation Security Plan to deter and minimize damage from a transportation security incident. In developing port-specific emergency operations and response policies and procedures, port security managers must remember that each facility's plan may play a component role in the larger national plan, as well as the area plans developed by each U.S. Coast Guard COTP in the particular areas they are responsible for. Because of this, it is essential that port-specific emergency operations and response plans are developed as practically as possible with cooperation from local U.S. Coast Guard port facility security staff. Although the staff will not likely prescribe port-specific procedures, they are in a position to ensure that port planning priorities and agendas are aligned with the risk assessments, strategies, and the larger area and national security plans. As with many aspects of port facility security, planning for emergencies must be managed collaboratively with those port users and government agencies that have interests and concerns in the stability of the port environment.

11.2.2 *National Incident Management System and Incident Command System*

Homeland Security Presidential Directive/HSPD-5 (White House 2003b) presaged the establishment of the National Incident Management System (NIMS) as the organizational structure for managing domestic incidents. Because the initial responsibility for responding to and managing emergencies is typically that of state and local government, there is a recognition that coordination of emergencies will likely require a federal response as additional personnel and resources are brought to bear on the problem. HSPD-5 established a policy that the U.S. federal government will provide assistance when state and local authorities' abilities to respond to emergencies diminish or when federal interests are involved. NIMS provides a framework for government, private sector, and nongovernmental organizations to collaborate and interrelate with each other in preparing for and responding to emergencies, wherever they occur. "NIMS was developed so responders from different jurisdictions and disciplines can work together better to respond to natural disasters and emergencies, including acts of terrorism. NIMS benefits include a unified approach to incident management; standard command and management structures; and emphasis on preparedness, mutual aid and resource management" (Federal Emergency Management Agency 2004, par. 1).

NIMS represents the U.S. government's efforts to formalize and operationalize a coordinated response to emergencies known as the Incident Command System (ICS).

ICS was first developed as a strategy to combat forest fires in California when systemic issues such as poor communications and resource planning demonstrated the need for better coordination of efforts to respond to emergencies (McEntire 2008, p. 243). It represents an organizational approach to emergencies and other incidents in which there is a unified command structure and common procedures and protocols for handling and directing communications, personnel, equipment, and other resources at the scene of an emergency. ICS is a philosophy of emergency response that has been adopted by many law enforcement, firefighting, and emergency response agencies in which the command of an incident is the responsibility of an on-scene leader or a team of leaders in a command post established to manage the incident. By establishing ICS as an emergency response and management approach, the ability of disparate agencies and private organizations to mobilize, respond, and cooperate in mitigating the problem is greatly improved.

The ICS structure is an ideal approach to emergency response because it enables the conditions for an effective response to be established by ensuring a manageable span of control, the ability to expand operations in a modular way, and particularly an assurance that participating agencies are focused on mission, goals, and objectives using a consistent and agreed to series of protocols. For port security managers, NIMS requirements and an ICS philosophy concerning emergency operations and response planning should be systemic components of the Port FSP. There is no more pronounced imperative for a unified approach to emergencies than an assurance that a coordinated response to port incidents and emergencies will be managed competently and in concert with national security priorities.

A major consideration for port facilities in their development of security infrastructure is funding. Compliance with NIMS must be demonstrated in order to continue to receive U.S. government federal preparedness funding. This includes significant federal funding programs for ports, including the Port Security Grant Program, which will consider the port facility's compliance with NIMS operating guidelines in terms of their integration with the national homeland and maritime security strategies. NIMS compliance requires that organizations review and update their SOPs, emergency operating procedures, and other protocols to ensure they are consistent with the U.S. government standards. Beyond the federal compliance issues, however, ensuring that port facility emergency operations plans are aligned with protocols similar to federal, state, and local first responder agencies only makes sense given that many different agency resources may be needed to mitigate port facility-related incidents. The U.S. DHS (2005b, p. 3) has developed a checklist that emergency planners can reference to ensure their emergency operations plans are consistent with NIMS concepts and terminology. It is useful for Port FSOs to use these guidelines in analyzing existing emergency operations and making plans to determine which components are included and which must be added or revised. When reviewing emergency operations plans for NIMS compliance, Port FSOs should consider if they:

- Define the scope of preparedness and incident management activities necessary for the local or tribal jurisdiction
- Describe organizational structures, roles and responsibilities, policies, and protocols for providing emergency support
- Facilitate response and short-term recovery activities
- Are flexible enough to use in all emergencies
- Describe its purpose
- Describe the situation and assumptions
- Describe the concept of operations
- Describe the organization and assignment of responsibilities
- Describe administration and logistics
- Contain a section that covers the development and maintenance of the emergency operations plan
- Contain authorities and references
- Contain functional annexes
- Contain hazard-specific appendices
- Contain a glossary
- Predesignate functional area representatives to the Emergency Operations Center/Multi-Agency Coordination System
- Include preincident and postincident public awareness, education, and communications plans and protocols

To ensure that port facility security emergency plans are not only NIMS-compliant but also current and updated regularly, the Port FSO should designate an NIMS coordinator for the port facility to be the liaison to both internal and external port elements responsible for emergency management. Since federal NIMS compliance requires completion of certain training, and since key members of the port management and security staffs will need to understand NIMS and ICS protocols, the NIMS coordinator can also manage the training and orientation requirements for the Port FSO. The National Integration Center, Incident Management Systems Integration Division, a component agency of FEMA, has a Web site with complete information on NIMS compliance training, standards, technology, and resource management available to Port FSOs and others at http://www.fema.gov/emergency/nims.

11.2.3 Elements of an Emergency Operations Plan

While much of a port facility's emergency operations planning will be driven by relevant international and federal, as well as state and local, government legal requirements, there are several basic elements recommended for inclusion (Fischer, Halibozek, and Green 2008), as follows:

- Designation of the authority to declare an emergency, order shutdown, and direct evacuation

- Establishment of an emergency chain of command
- Establishment of reporting responsibilities and channels
- Designation of an emergency headquarters or command post
- Establishment and training of emergency teams
- Establishment of specific asset-protection and lifesaving procedures
- Designation of equipment, facilities, and locations to be used in an emergency
- Communication of necessary elements of the emergency response plan to all affected personnel
- Communication with outside agencies
- Public relations and release of information

11.2.4 Role of the Port FSO in Emergencies

Under U.S. MTSA regulations for port facilities (Code of Federal Regulations 2003a), the Port FSO must ensure that security personnel respond to security threats or breaches of security to maintain critical facility and vessel-to-facility interface operations and be ready to evacuate the facility. The Port FSO is required to make official reports to various federal agencies concerning suspicious activities, breaches of security, transportation security incidents, and related public safety incidents. To provide timely information and details required by U.S. federal government regulations concerning security breaches and transportation security incidents, the Port FSO must be in possession of sufficient event details with which to make a complete report at the time of notification. In the event the incident involves a law enforcement agency, fire department, and/or other external agency response, copies of the relevant agency incident reports, if available, would be useful to comply with federal recordkeeping requirements. To ensure timely transmittal of official reports and information to the Port FSO, port security staff should be instructed to ensure that an on-duty port security supervisor responds to the scenes of incidents, assesses and gathers information, coordinates with responding agencies, and makes personal contact with the Port FSO to provide the necessary information to comply with reporting requirements.

The Port FSO must contact the U.S. National Response Center, by telephone or e-mail, and report activities that may result in a transportation security incident. The National Response Center (2008) is the U.S. DHS agency that serves as the national point of contact for reporting all oil, chemical, radiological, biological, and etiological discharges into the environment. It also takes terrorist/suspicious activities reports and maritime security breach reports. The National Response Center serves as the contact point for information on incidents, which it then conveys to the U.S. Coast Guard and other relevant federal agencies as part of the coordinated national response strategy to emergencies and incidents. Incidents that must be reported include breaches of security and transportation security incidents.

Breach of security. An incident that has not resulted in a transportation security incident but in which security measures have been circumvented, eluded, or violated is a breach of security. Some examples of a breach of security occurring in a port facility that would require reporting are as follows:

- Unauthorized or noncredentialed people located in restricted access areas
- People or vehicles deliberately avoiding port screening, inspection, or identification requirements
- Restricted access facilities discovered unsecured
- Vessels or cargo arriving at the facility without proper advance notice
- Port tenants subverting required security procedures (e.g., no security guard posted, damaged fence lines not repaired, doors left unlocked)
- Personal vehicles parked in restricted access cargo areas
- Cargo staged on common docks and wharves without required security
- Failure of security staff to perform required tasks

Transportation security incident. A security incident resulting in a significant loss of life, environmental damage, transportation system disruption, or economic disruption in a particular area is a transportation security incident. With respect to transportation security incidents, under MTSA, the Port FSO must ensure a report is made, without delay, to the cognizant U.S. Coast Guard District Commander and immediately begin following procedures established in the Port FSP. When contacting the National Response Center, the Port FSO or designee must be ready to provide as much of the following information as possible:

- Name and contact information of the reporting party
- Name and contact information of the suspicious or responsible party
- The location of the incident, as specifically as possible
- The description of the incident or activity involved (Code of Federal Regulations 2003b)

National Response Center reports of breaches of security and transportation security incidents are assigned incident numbers and will be referred to the U.S. Coast Guard COTP for the particular port facilities involved. Obviously, port facilities amassing relatively large numbers of incidents will receive more scrutiny from concerned federal officials. Port management would do well to develop a process for mitigating these incidents by addressing the underlying problems giving rise to them. Certainly, the Port FSO cannot predict and control every event; however, a continuing pattern of unlocked facilities, lax security patrols, or poor cargo management is an opportunity to identify the reasons for these breaches. There is then a responsibility to address the problems aggressively by meeting with the concerned elements and staff to collaborate on the management solutions, training, staff changes, or procedural devices that are needed to affect behavioral change. The incident reporting can be an effective tool for management to detect the changes in variance within the facility that are affecting the stability of the port. The system is essentially speaking to the security management if the management is willing to listen.

In guidance for emergency planning, as Port FSOs develop the Port FSP, the U.S. Coast Guard (2008, p. 11) provides recommendations on how to address security incident procedures. The plan should describe how port security will respond to security threats or breaches of security and safely continue critical facility and vessel-to-facility operations. It should describe evacuation and notification procedures in the event of a security threat or breach. The plan should also discuss the training given to port facility personnel on possible threats, on the need for vigilance, and on soliciting assistance in reporting suspicious people, objects, or activities. Finally, the plan should address its procedures in securing noncritical operations to focus response on critical operations in the event of a security threat or breach in security.

11.2.5 Hazardous Materials Incidents

A port-specific contingency plan for hazardous materials incidents, including oil spills, should identify the responsibilities of the port organization and concerned external agencies addressing preparations, mitigation, and response to safeguard the port and associated water assets. The plan should serve as a consolidated source of information for port employees and users responding to petroleum and other chemical spills, on docks, roadways, terminal yards, cargo storage and staging areas, and gantries throughout the port facility. The plan should complement existing local, state, federal, and international laws and treaties. Items to include in the plan are as follows:

- Jurisdiction
- General response procedures
- Port facility security and safety personnel procedures
- Equipment capabilities
- Contact information
- Responsible government agencies
- Additional resources that exceed the port facility's response capabilities

Concerns associated with hazardous materials in port facilities also extend to incidents occurring aboard vessels, including those docked or moored in port facilities and those transiting adjacent waters. Particularly in port facilities that serve large passenger vessels, such as this cruise vessel in Figure 11.4, aboard hazardous materials emergencies and their potential consequences (e.g., fire, contamination, injuries) will require the Port FSO to consider contingencies for safely managing vessel evacuations of large numbers of passengers. Plans for how the port facility will interface with vessels in managing aboard hazardous materials incidents, whether they are criminal/terrorist in nature, accidental, or the outcome of mishandling, must be addressed. The U.S. Coast Guard will play a major role in responding to vessel and port facility hazardous materials incidents. Given the potential for contamination to port facilities and their adjacent communities, consideration must be given to how hazardous materials involved in incidents will be managed, mitigated, and handled. In addition,

Figure 11.4 Large passenger vessels docked in port may have thousands of passengers and crew on board, who may need to quickly evacuate the vessel onto port facilities in the event of an onboard hazardous materials emergency.

many communities, particularly those adjacent to ports that handle high volumes of hazardous material cargo, will have a fire agency with a hazardous materials response capability. Shore-based first responder agencies should therefore also be consulted by port security managers during the planning process for these incidents.

Decisions about whether, where, and how compromised hazardous materials cargo will be off-loaded from vessels must consider legal requirements as well as the practical capabilities of the concerned port, vessel, company, and government agencies. In 2005, Operation Safe Port, a three-day hazardous materials exercise in San Francisco Bay, demonstrated the capability of a U.S. Maritime Administration Auxiliary Crane Ship to safely remove suspect or contaminated cargo containers from a vessel. In the simulation, a hazardous material or terrorist weapon threat detected inside one or more containers on board a vessel results in notifications to external resources and the movement of the vessel offshore or to the safest location away from the port complex. The purpose of the crane ship is to safely separate and remove the suspect container(s) to a second vessel or barge for investigation and disposition (Arrayan 2005). The exercise demonstrated the need for and use of specialized assets in responding to particular threats, and it emphasizes that each port facility must consider its unique operating conditions and capabilities in responding to similar hazardous materials scenarios. Working collaboratively with all responsible agencies to develop these response plans will help Port FSOs consider alternative methods for the management and safe removal of hazardous materials.

11.2.6 Port Facility Evacuations

The evacuation of any facility must be carefully planned in advance. A decision to have all people leave a building or other facility must be made, balancing the relative harm to people associated with the threat against the possible injuries or economic losses associated with moving large numbers of people at one time, as well as the interruption of business operations. Plans and detailed policies and procedures must take account of any reasonably foreseeable emergency or disaster that would affect the safety of people in the port facility. If there is no plan, it is the security or safety manager's responsibility to see that one is developed. Having a detailed plan of action ensures that the right people, equipment, and facilities will be available in a crisis. Evacuation plans should be carefully considered in terms of the various types of emergencies, alternative escape routes, staging areas for first responders and their equipment, and the prospects for the continuity of operations during prolonged periods of inaccessibility to necessary facilities. Conditions that may warrant total or partial evacuation from port facilities and property fall into the following categories:

- Fire: Includes fires to buildings, vessels, cargo containers, heavy equipment, and vehicles.
- Bomb Threat or Bomb Emergency: Includes receipt of credible threat, by telephone or other communication; the discovery of an actual or suspected explosive device; or an actual explosion. The development of specific bomb threat procedures and a bomb emergency plan is a necessary component of port security emergency management planning.
- Hazardous Materials Incident: Includes fuel or other toxic elements mistakenly or intentionally released in sufficient quantities to endanger life. Includes the following types of spills or incidents:
  - On board vessels, including cargo holds and fuel bunkers.
  - Suspected or actual cargo container leaks.
  - Reports of liquids, solids, fumes, or odors emanating from vessels, vehicles, buildings, or heavy equipment.
- Vessel Accident or Emergency: Includes emergencies on board vessels berthed or moored in port facilities.
  - Inbound or outbound vessels with onboard emergencies.
  - Vessels with onboard emergencies transiting the waters adjacent to the port facility that may impact port personnel and infrastructure.
- Severe Weather Events: May include hurricanes, tornadoes, blizzards, and so forth.

- Breach of Security: Any breach of security or incident that the Port FSO or official in command determines to be significant enough to warrant the partial or total evacuation of port facilities.
- Terrorist Incident: An unlawful use of force or violence to intimidate or coerce.
- Any other emergency or situation that, in the opinion of the Port FSO or other authorized port or government officials, is a threat to the safety and security of the port facility, including but not limited to criminal investigations, severe traffic crashes, airplane crashes, building collapse, civil disturbance/riot, earthquake, flood, sabotage, labor disputes, and power/water/communications failures.

In an emergency evacuation, people will typically do what they are conditioned, trained, or told to do. For example, building employees who normally arrive and depart their place of work by elevator will naturally gravitate toward the elevator during a building evacuation. Unless employees know where the stairs are, and how to find them in the dark, evacuation plans will be inadequate in protecting facility personnel from harm. Security managers must integrate personnel orientation and awareness programs, communications devices (e.g., employee newsletters, paycheck inserts), drills, and exercises as part of a regular program of preparing port employees for potential emergencies and evacuations. In port facilities with significant numbers of passengers, visitors, and guests who may be unfamiliar with the facilities and evacuation constraints, the Port FSO must assist port management in developing effective methods for educating the public. Pamphlets, signage, audio announcements, visual cues, placards, and maps are all effective devices in orienting people to evacuation routes and sheltering stations in the event of an emergency. By working directly with the vessels, companies, and terminals, the Port FSO can engage port internal organizations in developing facility-specific guidance for particular situations and unique threat conditions.

11.2.7 Emergency Information Management

Critical telephone numbers that may be necessary in an emergency must be readily available to responsible port security staff. These include telephone numbers for emergency police and fire (911), local police nonemergency, fire and rescue nonemergency, hazardous materials first responders, U.S. Coast Guard, National Response Center, U.S. Customs and Border Protection, port credentialing offices, port administrators, port security personnel, harbormaster, waterway pilots, and port berthing offices.

Emergency management planning must include the development and updating of port tenant and user contact lists for use in making emergency notifications. The basic information should include name, address, telephone numbers, e-mail addresses, and whom to contact in an emergency. Port tenants and users should be required to provide twenty-four-hour emergency contact information for their key personnel to port security. Improvements in computing and communications technology have spurred the development of automated emergency notification systems, which can quickly and simultaneously notify facility personnel in the event of an emergency. An example of this application is the emergency notification system implemented at Cleveland State University in Ohio (Security Solutions 2008). Prerecorded audio or live voice instructions can be transmitted to alert campus personnel in specific buildings or on individual floors about fire emergencies. The university plans to expand the system to alert students and faculty through voice and text messages to cell phones, personal data assistants, and laptops. The use of fixed and mobile public-address systems, emergency signaling devices, electronic message boards, visual monitors, and other message relay systems are essential in port facilities, where the need to quickly communicate instructions to large numbers of people is paramount. In considering systems applications, development must account for contingencies in the event of power failures and situations that may render communications technologies inoperative or severely limited. Reliance on any one type of technology (e.g., cell phones) as a primary communications device will likely leave the port security staff with limited communications alternatives when conditions render them inoperable. Advance planning and risk assessment are essential in developing redundant communications protocols.

Port-specific personnel and equipment records must also be kept in secure locations as part of the emergency management planning process. These records may include (Fischer, Halibozek, and Green 2008):

- Names and phone numbers of management personnel to be notified
- Names and information (e.g., assignments, location, phone numbers) of emergency forces
- Names and information of backup emergency forces
- List of emergency equipment and supplies, including type, location, quantity, backup, and outside support
- Building plans
- Mutual aid agreements
- Outside organizations (police, fire, hospital, and ambulance), locations, and phone numbers
- Emergency planning manual

The Port FSO must at all times ensure that, as required under U.S. MTSA port facility security regulations, the Port FSP and associated documents (e.g., building plans, communications protocols, vulnerability and security assessments, diagrams, security technology application documentation, credentialing records, and such) are maintained as sensitive security information in accordance with federal law.

11.2.8 Increases in MARSEC Levels

Emergency planning must address how port facility access controls will be strengthened and enhanced when increases in MARSEC levels occur. The MTSA guidelines for port facilities include requirements for the Port FSP to enhance measures for access control during periods of heightened risk. Incidents or threats of terrorism may require higher levels of scrutiny concerning the people, vessels, cargo, and vehicles accessing the port facility. It is important to have contingencies for strengthening access controls if the security levels at the port will increase. Some of these enhanced access control measures might include the following:

- New or additional background, criminal history, and terrorism watchlist checks for employees with qualified access to restricted areas
- Reverification of photo identification badges issued to port employees, vessel crew members, carrier employees, longshoremen, vendors, and visitors to ensure reliability of the credentialing systems
- Credentialing control mechanisms rechecked to ensure that existing port credentials have not been invalidated due to expiration, theft, misuse, or other reasons; paper-based or electronic stop lists, containing the list of invalid port credentials, revalidated and redistributed to port security access control staff daily
- Intrusion detection systems (e.g., video monitoring, remote sensors and alarms, computerized recording instrumentation) deployed to supplement or increase existing human resources' screening capabilities
- Pedestrian access controls enhanced to further restrict people from entering secure areas without a valid reason and authorization
- Visitor procedures enhanced to require escorts by port-credentialed staff in all restricted access areas
- Vehicle and pedestrian inspection and screening log information compared against reports of suspicious people and vehicles from law enforcement, as well as open-source threats concerning suspicious activities at other port and transportation facilities
- Reinsuring that all port security personnel know and understand the Port FSP-specified rates of vehicle, cargo, and pedestrian screening consistent with MARSEC levels and the port's threat posture
- Retraining and briefing all port security staff to ensure proper screening methodologies and use of tools and equipment

11.2.9 Continuity of Operations Planning

A Continuity of Operations Plan (COOP) must be developed to provide a method for the port facility to continue operations during emergencies and to gradually resume full operations, given the constraints of the emergency or situation affecting normal operations. A COOP should be an essential component of all business and operating systems that rely on continuous energy inputs, transformations, and outputs for sustainability. Port management must be assured that disparate conditions affecting operations, whether from an oil spill, a hurricane, a power failure, or an act of terror, do not unduly constrain the port from resuming operations in an orderly, progressive, and planned manner. To this end, the Port FSO must work together with counterparts in the shipping, cargo, and shore-based port business to synchronize COOP planning and to ensure that all parties have equitable access to the port to resume normal operations.

Federal Preparedness Circular 65, Federal Executive Branch Continuity of Operations (U.S. Department of Homeland Security 2004), provides guidance to U.S. government agencies in developing COOP contingency plans. As a resource for emergency planning in port facilities, it provides an effective structure for planning the resumption of port-essential functions during emergencies that disrupt normal operations. This circular suggests that COOP plans and programs include the following elements:

- Plans and Procedures: The continued performance of essential functions under all circumstances.
- Essential Functions: Those functions that enable agencies to provide vital services, maintain safety, and sustain the industrial/economic base in an emergency.
- Delegations of Authority: Ensure agency personnel know who has authority to make key decisions in a COOP situation.
- Orders of Succession: Ensure agency personnel know who has authority and responsibility if agency leadership is incapacitated or unavailable.
- Alternate Operating Facility: Prepare staff for the possibility of unannounced relocation of essential functions and personnel.
- Interoperable Communications: Availability and redundancy of critical communications and information systems.
- Vital Records and Databases: Agency personnel must be able to access necessary records and systems to conduct essential functions.
- Human Capital Procedures: Agency readiness issues, including designation of emergency employees, dismissal or closure procedures, media announcements, status of nonemergency employees, employee communications, pay and staffing flexibilities.
- Tests, Training, and Exercises: Plan, conduct, and document periodic tests, training, and exercises to demonstrate COOP viability and identify deficiencies.
- Devolution of Control and Direction: How an agency identifies and conducts essential functions during increased threat situations or in the aftermath of a catastrophic emergency.
- Reconstitution: Recovery from a catastrophic event and consolidating resources to return to full operations.

COOP Plans, as well as a general philosophical approach to plotting out anticipated emergency response and recovery activities in advance, will be indispensable in the period following emergencies. Because port facilities by nature must be able to accommodate the shifting needs of the maritime business, being ready with alternative methods of operations will demonstrate to port users that attention to good security management practices is a high priority.

References

American Association of Port Authorities. 2008a. Risk management and safety committee home-page: Mission. http://www.aapa-ports.org/Committees/content.cfm?ItemNumber=1079 (accessed August 3, 2008).

American Association of Port Authorities. 2008b. Sample safety guidelines provided by the Maryland Port Administration. http://aapa.files.cms-plus.com/PDFs/MPA_Safety_ Guidelines.pdf (accessed August 3, 2008).

Arrayan, Sabrina. 2005. Coast Guard contributes to Operation Safe Port in the battle against terrorism. U.S. Department of Homeland Security, U.S. Coast Guard. http://www.piersystem. com/go/doc/823/80655/ (accessed August 5, 2008).

Code of Federal Regulations. 2003a. Title 33, Navigation and Navigable Waters, Chapter I, Coast Guard, Department of Homeland Security, Part 105, Facility Security, Subpart B, Facility Security Requirements, Sec. 105.280, Security incident procedures. http://edocket.access. gpo.gov/cfr_2003/julqtr/33cfr105.280.htm (accessed August 5, 2008).

Code of Federal Regulations. 2003b. Title 33, Navigation and Navigable Waters, Chapter I, Coast Guard, Department of Homeland Security, Part 101, General Provisions, Subpart C, Communication (Port, Facility, Vessel), Sec. 101.305, Reporting. http://edocket.access.gpo. gov/cfr_2003/julqtr/33cfr101.305.htm (accessed August 5, 2008).

Department of Transport. 2005. Port employment and accident rates. Transport Statistics Bulletin: A Report by the Department of Transport, United Kingdom. http://www.dft.gov.uk/pgr/ statistics/datatablespublications/maritime/earates/portemploymentandaccidentsra5175 (accessed August 4, 2008).

Federal Emergency Management Agency. 2004. Welcome to the National Integration Center (NIC) Incident Management Systems Integration Division. http://www.fema.gov/emer-gency/nims/ (accessed August 5, 2008).

Fischer, Robert J., Edward Halibozek, and Gion Green. 2008. *Introduction to security*. Boston: Butterworth-Heinemann.

International Labour Office. 2005. Safety and health in ports. http://aapa.files.cms-plus. com/PDFs/ILO%20Code%20Of%20Practice%20-%20Safety%20In%20Ports%20 %282005%29.pdf (accessed August 3, 2008).

Legal Archiver.org. 2008. Occupational Safety and Health Act of 1970. http://www.legalarchiver. org/osh.htm (accessed July 10, 2008).

McEntire, David A. 2008. *Introduction to homeland security: Understanding terrorism with an emergency management perspective*. New York: John Wiley & Sons.

National Ag Safety Database. 2008. Objectives of a health and safety committee. http://www. cdc.gov/nasd/docs/d001601-d001700/d001652/d001652.html (accessed August 3, 2008).

National Response Center. 2008. NRC background. http://www.nrc.uscg.mil/nrcback.html (accessed August 5, 2008).

Security Solutions. 2008, May 1. The genesis of an emergency system. http://securitysolutions. com/enduser/schoolsuniversities/genesis_emergency_system_csu/index1.html (accessed July 4, 2008).

U.S. Coast Guard. 2008. U.S. Coast Guard Captain of the Port Memphis Facility Security Planning Guide. http://www.uscg.mil/d8/sector/lwrmsrvr/custs/facilities/ AMSFacilitySecurityPlan.pdf (accessed August 5, 2008).

U.S. Department of Homeland Security. 2004. Federal Emergency Management Agency, Directives Management System, Federal Preparedness Circular 65, Federal Executive Branch Continuity of Operations. http://en.wikisource.org/wiki/Transwiki:Federal_ Preparedness_Circular_65 (accessed May 30, 2008).

U.S. Department of Homeland Security. 2005a. Fact Sheet: National Response Plan. http:// www.dhs.gov/xnews/releases/press_release_0581.shtm (accessed July 4, 2008).

U.S. Department of Homeland Security. 2005b. Local and tribal NIMS integration: Integrating the National Incident Management System into local and tribal emergency operations plans and standard operating procedures. Version 1.0. NIMS Integration Center and Office of Grants and Training. Washington, DC: U.S. Department of Homeland Security.

U.S. Department of Homeland Security. 2008. National response framework: Frequently asked questions. http://www.fema.gov/pdf/emergency/nrf/NRF_FAQ.pdf (accessed August 4, 2008).

U.S. Department of Labor. 2001. Longshoring industry: Guidelines for workplace safety and health programs in the marine terminal and longshoring industries. http://www.osha.gov/ Publications/OSHA2232/osha2232.html (accessed July 10, 2008).

U.S. Department of Labor. 2007. OSHA facts August 2007. http://www.osha.gov/as/opa/ oshafacts.html (accessed July 10, 2008).

White House. 2003a. Homeland Security Presidential Directive/HSPD-8. http://www.mwcog. org/security/NCR/downloads/hspd8.pdf (accessed July 4, 2008).

White House. 2003b. Homeland Security Presidential Directive/HSPD-5. http://www.white- house.gov/news/releases/2003/02/20030228-9.html (accessed August 5, 2008).

White House. 2005. The National Strategy for Maritime Security. http://www.whitehouse.gov/ homeland/maritime-security.html (accessed August 4, 2008).

12

MANAGING TECHNOLOGY SOLUTIONS FOR PORT FACILITY SECURITY

12.1 Security Convergence in the Port Facility: The Role of Technology

At the Port of Miami in Florida, the development of innovative security technologies is changing the nature of how the port facility conducts business in the new homeland security environment. The optical character recognition devices illustrated in Figure 12.1 are just one example of how advances in technology, combined with port leadership's focus on enterprise security solutions, are enabling ports to adapt their business models to the new culture of port security. With a convergence of business, information technology (IT), and security operations, port facilities such as Miami are innovating new business models that embrace a strong integrative security approach to port management. In this particular application, the optical character recognition devices designed into the main cargo gate processing center are used to acquire the container, chassis, and truck license plate numbers of cargo-carrying vehicles as they pass through the array. The information is relayed to a remote command and control center staffed by port facility security staff for use in generating a gate pass. In conjunction with other IT applications, the port staff is not only able to record precisely who and what is entering the port facility, but can also verify the driver's and company's compliance with port security credentialing, business permitting, and insurance requirements. In addition, arrivals and departures are shared electronically with the port's cargo terminal facilities to confirm that the terminal is either expecting these individuals and shipments, or that they have received authorization to leave. Additionally, companies doing business at the port are encouraged to use a prepay option to facilitate collection of gate pass and scale fees without the need for traffic-delaying cash transactions. All of this is accomplished within minutes and without the need for the driver to exit the vehicle, and for the most part without a direct physical interaction with a posted security officer.

At the automated gate pedestal (Figure 12.2), truck drivers have the ability to electronically scan their issued port credential, including a biometric capability, and interact directly with the port's security and business enterprise systems. Much like a banking customer interacts with a bank using an automated teller machine, the driver inputs screen-requested information on a keypad and receives the necessary gate passes and vehicle documentation required for port admittance. Security management and business

247

Figure 12.1   Optical character recognition technology enables this port facility to automatically record the identifying information of cargo conveyances entering and departing its restricted access areas.

transaction processes are thus integrated to enable the facility to process cargo through-put more quickly and with less need for person-to-person interactions. Dynamic solutions like this one, designed to manage both increased cargo trade as well as increased port security requirements, are the outcome of emerging and growing business–security strategies that are using technology more creatively in security solutions.

An international survey of 8,200 IT and security executives in 2005 revealed that 53 percent of organizations have some level of integration between their physical and IT security divisions, up from 29 percent in 2003 (Hoffman 2006). This trend suggests that organizations are becoming more focused on implementing technology solutions that not only address their security needs, but also consider how their business enterprises can reflect improvements in their profit margins or, in the case of public entities, service productivity variables. In addition, there is a growing recognition from government officials responsible for homeland security policy that research and development of unique technological applications in the port security environment are becoming more and more vital as new ways are sought to protect against threats associated with import and export trade. For example, former U.S. Assistant Secretary of Homeland Security, Rear Admiral (retired) David M. Stone (2006) has suggested several new and developing port security technology applications that are becoming increasingly important in addressing homeland security plans in relation to threats from global terrorism:

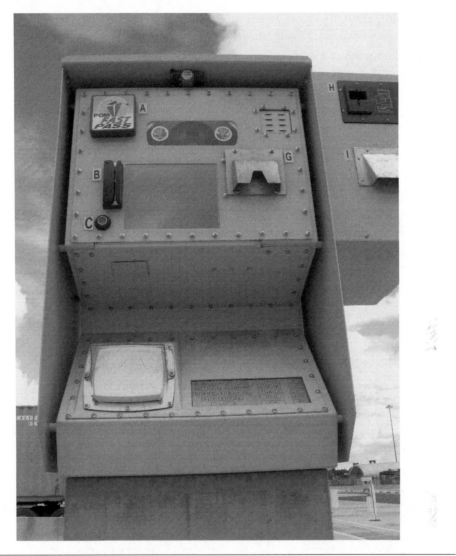

Figure 12.2 Automated gate pedestal at cargo entry processing facility enables truck drivers to interact with both port security and business processing systems without the need for physical, person-to-person transactions.

- X-ray and radiation portal monitoring equipment to scan cargo containers
- Intelligent video systems for monitoring cargo and activities in port terminals
- Crane-mounted sensors to scan containers during lifting and port–vessel transfer processes
- Radio frequency identification tags on cargo containers to track movement and location
- Intelligent device management to monitor changes in cargo container dynamics
- Maritime domain awareness systems incorporating diverse technologies to maintain situational awareness in the maritime sector

These technologies are in various stages of research, development, and implementation throughout the worldwide maritime sector and provide evidence that port security managers are faced with many complex technology alternatives when considering ways to implement Port FSPs.

12.2 Situational Awareness and Situational Readiness

The importance of understanding and managing technological capabilities in the port facility security environment stems from the need for the Port FSP to be properly positioned to address the identified risks. As a structure for mitigating threats, the FSP cannot just be a static document to be pulled off the shelf every now and then when emergencies occur, but an adaptable system for effecting behavioral change to impact and negate threats to the port. To do this effectively, port security managers must be in a position to completely understand the threat environment. Two concepts that emphasize the important relationship of technology management to port facility security planning are *situational awareness* and *situational readiness*.

12.2.1 Situational Awareness

The ability of the port security organization to acquire information and intelligence to support decision making is to a large extent a functional outcome of situational awareness. This is the dynamic of having sufficient information coming in from multiple sources and vectors to provide organizational leaders with current and accurate dimensions of problems, operating conditions, and resource capabilities. To be able to rationally consider alternative decision paths based on knowing the strengths and weaknesses in a given environment is what provides port security managers with an edge in developing risk mitigation strategies. Simply stated, situational awareness is, "knowing what is going on around you. Inherent in this definition is a notion of what is important" (Endsley 2000, p.2). Using an example from law enforcement, consider the situational awareness needs of an on-scene police commander managing a hostage situation with armed, barricaded subjects. As the commander considers the options, such as whether to engage in negotiations or proceed with a SWAT-style entry and rescue, factors bearing on the outcome must constantly be evaluated. The decision path must be driven by an ongoing stream of usable, accurate information about the environmental conditions. How many hostages are there? How many subjects? What kinds of weapons do they have? What is the layout of the interior scene? What resources are available to the subjects? To the police? What is the weather? Is it day or night? Can the police control utilities, food, and water? In situations like these, the police commander might benefit from technological tools and systems that would make the acquiring and processing of this information easier and faster. Are there listening devices that could be deployed to hear the subjects' conversations? Do the police have encrypted radios to ensure that their tactical planning conversations are not overheard by third parties? Does the commander have the ability to survey the scene from an aerial view? Or can infrared and audio sensors be deployed to obtain fixes on building occupants and their movements? Can the command post produce diagrams, maps, and written instructions for the responding police personnel? Thus, situational awareness is the perspective a decision maker is able to develop of a particular environment during a particular time. With the appropriate technologies available, an understanding of the extant conditions may enable the necessary systems and resources to be brought to bear on problems that must be solved. Similarly, the Port FSO can develop situational awareness within the port environment using an array of systems and devices, such as cameras, scanning devices, and computers. The key is in understanding the capabilities of available technology and in conceptualizing their integration in managing a comprehensive defense of the facility.

12.2.2 Situational Readiness

The second concept associated with technology management and security planning, situational readiness, at its core means being prepared for the unexpected. The port's development of emergency operations and response plans and systems is a process for ensuring the organization is ready to react and respond to particular events. For example, a plan for responding to bomb threats received in the facility is essentially a contingency plan for managing an extraordinary occurrence. Using information development processes to become aware of ancillary conditions (e.g., how many employees may need to be evacuated) enables security managers to preplan the structural components necessary to respond. The readiness component lies in using information to establish plans to prevent incidents, protect personnel and property, and respond to events or emergencies with the appropriate human and physical resources. Consider an example from the field of emergency management. A community facing a catastrophic weather event, such as an impending hurricane, must have contingencies in place to deploy resources and respond to public service needs as events unfold. As the storm approaches, the emergency management leadership is assembled in the Emergency Operations Center with representatives from police, fire, utility companies, sheltering agencies, and food distributors. What is the capability of the community's emergency services' communications systems to effectively receive and convey information and coordinate planning and response in the field? How will the emergency management director, city manager, or police or fire chief disseminate time-sensitive information to emergency workers and sheltering staff who may still be at home, in the field, or in offices scattered around the storm's projected path? What is the capability of the communications systems, (e.g., hard-wired telephony, cellular systems, two-way radios, electronic messaging)? The ability of an organization to be ready to face any number of extraordinary events speaks to its situational readiness. The Port FSO's ability to implement procedures for moving the port facility from MARSEC level

1 to MARSEC levels 2 and 3 will depend on his/her ability to communicate to any number of security staff, external law enforcement, terminal security managers, vendors, ships' agents, and so forth. Is the facility ready in terms of its communications protocols and systems?

12.3 Surveillance Systems

Increasingly, port facilities must consider security plan components that incorporate surveillance technology in one form or another. The specter of small-vessel threats (see Figure 12.3) to port infrastructure and shipping, as well as the need for situational readiness within all sectors of the target environment, truly necessitates some form of surveillance capability on, in, and around the port facility. One difficulty for many facilities may be in determining precisely what their actual environmental needs are in terms of the complexity of systems technology required. Port FSOs without the technical expertise themselves and without the ability to draw from internal port organizational resources will likely go to the outsourcing marketplace when considering surveillance technology. The use of an outside consultant to design plans and procure systems for surveillance may in fact be a wise decision. Having a resource with the right technical expertise and experience in port facility security would be an asset in helping to acquire systems that meet the port's threat environment appropriately. The

Figure 12.3   The small-vessel threat to larger, slow-moving vessels in port waters suggests an increased need for both shoreside and waterside surveillance systems.

caution is that the Port FSO must be wary of consultants eager to sell the port a Rolls Royce when it may really only need a dependable Chevrolet.

The Port FSO must be at the forefront of advancing a rational approach to security systems technology with port leadership and users. This means advocating that port security maintain a strong, layered foundation upon which technology is used smartly to add value to the overall threat mitigation function. The Port FSP should provide for a rational variety of technical systems, people, physical barriers, and so forth that integrate in a sound systems approach to prevent the threats that have been identified in the risk assessment phase. For example, when considering waterside surveillance, the port may have identified threats from vessels or covert underwater swimmers bearing explosive devices. The port may possess or have ready access to marine patrols, landside patrols, and external agency surveillance capabilities. The port's waterside surveillance system may not have to be so complex that it is designed and built disregarding the other systems and resources in place. The important question to answer when considering systems options is whether or not the experts the port has hired have factored in the various security layers the port already has, or is expected to have. The appointment of a systems integrator, a person with a functional understanding of port security, business, and technology, and how he or she interrelates, should receive important consideration from port leadership, especially when outsourcing complex surveillance systems development. The integrator should have the skills and abilities to work cooperatively with port staff, user agents, government regulators, outside consultants, and product representatives consistent with the specific port operations concerned.

Another important consideration lies in understanding the port's legal requirements for effecting varying levels of surveillance, especially in waters adjacent to the facility. To what extent are nonport facility authorities responsible for protecting waters that may not necessarily be within the port's jurisdiction? Many port facilities operate along rivers, lakes, and waterways that are patrolled by local, state, and federal law enforcement agencies. Notwithstanding the port's responsibility to secure its own infrastructure and protect the interests of its tenants and users, there may be external agency responsibilities to provide dedicated or shared levels of waterside protection, including surveillance, to the port facility. Identifying these resources and assets, as well as working collaboratively with the concerned agencies to develop consensus on the using and sharing of technology, is a strategy the Port FSO can use to continue building the layered security necessary in the facility.

When considering surveillance technology alternatives, it is helpful to have a fundamental understanding of the types of systems available and their capabilities. For the security professional with limited technical education and experience, it will be useful to attend trade shows, conferences, and product demonstrations that engage the port security trade sector in understanding technology solutions for port security. Two standard surveillance technologies that have potential for enhancing port facility security are *sonar* (an acronym for sound navigation and ranging), for deployment in the waters in and adjacent to ports, and *closed-circuit television (CCTV)*, which has applications for both surveillance and access control.

12.3.1 Sonar

Sonar is an acronym for *sound navigation and ranging*. Its modern development as a marine technology can be traced back to the 1800s, when scientists began to test the physical properties of sound transmitted through water (Science.jrank 2008). Sonar devices use energy to locate objects in the water and can calculate variables such as distance, direction of travel, speed, and size. As sound travels through water, the waves attenuate, or taper off, enabling instrumentation to record the changes and associate them with critical variables of interest. Vessels use sonar for a variety of purposes, including navigation, communications, vessel detection, and determining water depth. Its value as a modern surveillance technology was tested in submarine technology during World War I, and the world's navies, particularly the British, developed more advanced sonar applications during the interwar years. *Active sonar* systems, used to detect and calculate variables on underwater moving objects, use a transducer to send and bounce a sound signal off a target. This system is effective for determining distance variables, but the acoustic sounds produced may alert an adversary to the fact that it is being scanned with sonar. A *passive sonar* unit, which detects sound waves coming toward it, is useful for detecting noise from marine objects, including animals, but does not emit its own signal. Passive systems are good for listening when you don't want your adversary to know you are. The downside to passive sonar is that it cannot measure distance unless other passive listening devices are also employed (National Oceanic and Atmospheric Administration 2006).

The Port Security Grant Program (U.S. Office of State and Local Government Coordination and Preparedness 2005), a major source of funding for U.S. port facility security capital improvements and equipment needed to implement Port FSPs, identified several types of sonar technology eligible for funding to support the detection of underwater improvised explosive devices:

Imaging sonar produces a type of video imagery from pole-mounted systems placed over the side of a vessel or hand carried by a diver.

Scanning sonar systems are small systems that are mounted on tripods and lowered to the bottom of a waterway and produce 360-degree panoramic views of the surrounding area.

Three-dimensional sonar produces three-dimensional imagery of objects using an array receiver.

Side-scan sonar produces striplike side-view images from a device inside of a shell, which is towed behind a vessel.

Each of these types of systems has its own benefits and disadvantages associated with cost, technical expertise, maintenance, and flexibility of use. For example, side-scan sonar systems, which were first developed for use in locating mines during World War II, must be towed from or mounted on the hull of a vessel. These systems are useful for a variety of purposes, such as imaging large areas of the sea bottom, creating marine charts, identifying underwater objects, and locating debris items and obstructions on the seafloor that are hazardous to shipping. For example, the Port of Los Angeles is procuring an Underwater Explosive Detection System, designed to protect against underwater improvised explosive devices by integrating seabed image data that port survey operations collects by high-resolution multibeam sonar and making it available to port police dive units by point-and-click on a displayed map of the port (Maritime Terrorism Research Center 2008).

In another example, the ports in the state of Victoria, in southern Australia, recently purchased four side-scan sonar systems for use by the police boats servicing port facilities. For port security applications, side-scan sonar systems improve the port security capabilities to investigate underwater suspicious activity that may not be readily apparent from the surface (Victoria Ministry for Police and Emergency Services 2006). Because these systems may cost as much as twenty thousand dollars or more and require waterborne assets to deploy, smaller port facilities may not be in a flexible position to finance their purchase. One way to maximize cost savings using this technology would be to enter into cooperative agreements with other local port facilities and/or law enforcement agencies, or contract out with reputable private security agencies. Considerations associated with either proprietary or contract systems should include an acceptable rate of false alarms, as well as clear definitions and specifications in the contract and systems documentation. When considering portable sonar detection units, ensure an understanding of the size of the components, as well as what may be required to move and install them, including the need for any specialized vehicles, towing, storage, and maintenance equipment.

12.3.2 Closed-Circuit Television

CCTV refers to the use of one or more video cameras that can privately transmit video imagery of activity in a target environment directly to designated monitors. CCTV has a long history of security usage in many different types of facilities, employing a wide variety and sophistication of equipment, technology, and architecture. CCTV systems deployment in diverse private sector security applications, such as the retail and gaming industries, has led to their increased public sector use, particularly in law enforcement and homeland security applications. As a crime prevention and reduction strategy, CCTV systems have been developed in both large and small communities worldwide. Since 1998, Great Britain has funded 684 CCTV projects at a cost of over $300 million in a range of locations, including parking lots, town and city centers, and residential areas (Gill and Spriggs 2005, p. 1). Police agencies are using, or partnering with other public and private organizations to share, CCTV systems to monitor highway conditions, enforce traffic regulations, and surveil retail locations such as shopping malls, sports and amusement venues, and high-crime neighborhoods.

Within the transportation sector, CCTV systems may be developed and programmed to provide port facilities with some quite sophisticated surveillance capabilities to monitor vehicle movements, observe employee and passenger activities, inspect cargo transfer operations, and quickly detect and respond to security breaches. The Port of Richmond in northern California has used $2.5 million in U.S. port security grant funding to integrate eighty-two "intelligent" real-time surveillance cameras programmed to alert security and law enforcement officials to suspicious activities in the facility, thus enabling immediate response and investigation (Bulwa 2008). Many other port facilities have taken similar advantage of government funding to purchase and deploy various CCTV technologies in response to homeland security-driven policy requirements for port facilities. Beyond the opportunities for surveillance, CCTV cameras can be integrated with a port's access control system to provide an additional check and balance on ingress and egress activities. As surveillance tools, CCTV cameras (Figure 12.4) may be positioned in any number of port facility terminal interiors and exteriors, as well as on perimeter points, to relay images to security staff in a central location. Cameras may be stationary or have the ability to pan, tilt, and zoom, either as part of a programmed survey or manually by camera operators in remote locations. Depending on the configuration and sophistication of the equipment, CCTV cameras

Figure 12.4 Closed-circuit television cameras can be deployed in many interior and exterior locations to provide varying levels of surveillance capabilities.

Figure 12.5 Critical port infrastructure may require continuous video monitoring to alert port security to possible intrusions.

may enable the Port FSO to reduce the numbers of security personnel required at particular locations. This may also be a solution in threat environments where continuous monitoring of critical infrastructure is desired. For example, in Figure 12.5, this port facility's bridge supports are located in a restricted area that has been fenced to prevent access by land and water. A CCTV camera system with recording capabilities, designed to operate in this environment and monitored by a patrol force able to respond rapidly to suspicious activity, would add a significant layer of security for this important conduit.

Surveillance systems may be developed concurrently with existing or planned electronic access control systems to allow security staff to monitor and control access to specific restricted areas of the port. Cameras may be also positioned covertly to monitor entries and exits through access control points. System recording capabilities enable port security to maintain records of the vehicles and people entering and exiting the port facility. This type of information would be useful in conducting follow-up investigations concerning cargo theft, criminal activity, and unauthorized operations on port facility properties. With a capability of recording images of vehicle and cargo registration markings, the port facility could also develop a documentation system for validating and monitoring cargo entries and departures. CCTV-recorded information can be stored using a variety of media to document the release of specific containers to particular drivers. The ability to link individuals to specific cargo transactions provides a significant tool for port security and law enforcement in tracking the chain of custody of cargo.

Understanding the functionality of CCTV systems, including their various types, features, installation requirements, and transmission architecture, is crucial to the successful integration of this technology into the Port FSP. The Port FSO must work closely with product representatives, a systems integrator, and the port's IT and physical plant staff to successfully assess and identify the right choice of systems and devices, installation methods, and interfacing communications networks. Considerations for acquiring, developing, and managing CCTV technology in port facility security applications should include the following:

- Cameras: types, features (e.g., resolution, imaging), ambient or supplemental lighting requirements, digital requirements.
- Lenses: types, features, sizes.
- Monitors and accessories: selection, capabilities, and maintenance of CCTV options, such as screens, monitors, camera housings, pan-tilt-zoom mechanisms, and infrared illuminators.
- Equipment location and connectivity options: identifying facility locations and infrastructure capable of supporting CCTV applications. For example, high-mast lighting systems (Figure 12.6) in cargo container storage yards may be ideal positions for mounting cameras, assuming connectivity for power and desired image transmission resolution exists or can be retrofitted.
- System design and transmission issues: site surveys; utility requirements; environmental conditions; requirements for coaxial cable, fiber optics, and/or telephone networking; controlling signals; mounting of equipment; trenching and cabling; equipment testing and system debugging. Consider the capabilities and desires for incorporating video motion detectors and amplifiers. If integrating CCTV into a digital network, ensure understanding of terminology, different configurations, hardware and software requirements, and protocols.
- Camera operations in extreme conditions: capabilities and durability in extreme heat, cold, wind, and saltwater environments.
- Monitoring ranges: determine the desired and realistic operating ranges of cameras.
- Recording systems: understand capabilities and support for various recording system technologies (e.g., analog versus digital).
- Integration with existing and/or planned port-external surveillance systems: understanding the capabilities of surveillance resources existing or planned by external government and private security organizations. For example, what are the surveillance capabilities of the U.S. Coast Guard or local law enforcement? What are the opportunities for developing mutual aid agreements and cooperative resource-sharing and funding initiatives?

Figure 12.6   High-mast lighting systems can integrate CCTV applications for surveillance of facility activity.

- Maintenance and troubleshooting of components: cameras, lenses, switchers, transmission systems, monitors, accessories, and recording systems. Before investing deeply in complex technology, develop an understanding of the abilities of port facility staff to maintain, service, and repair surveillance equipment. What type of special training, tools, diagnostic equipment, and spare parts will be provided by vendors for maintenance and upkeep? If maintenance and service will be outsourced, plan for budgeting these expenditures during the initial design and procurement processes.
- Security staff orientation and training: consider the training program and materials necessary for educating the security staff to operate, monitor, and integrate CCTV into existing security protocols. Will the vendor pro-

vide on-site support and staff for training? Determine the responsibility for developing or providing a systems operations manual.

- Intelligent video: consider the capabilities and applications for intelligent video analytics that employ software to interpret and assess monitored activity in a target environment as part of a programmed threat assessment. For example, intrusions in a monitored environment can be programmed to alert security patrols to respond. CCTV applications may program various cameras to target intrusions and relay signals as the intruder moves through the environment. Alarms, alerts, instant messaging, and notifications to external police and emergency response agencies can also be developed. Applications should consider installation, configurations, integration, wired versus wireless systems, and network transmission capabilities.

As with all technologies being considered for port security solutions, CCTV may provide a significant level of situational awareness to enable the Port FSO to have excellent command and control of the target environment. Given the advances in this technology over the past few years though, port management must be aware of industry trends and be cognizant that systems and components developed for today's threat environment could be outmoded within three, five, or ten years. The ability to recruit and develop internal staff, or have ready access to external CCTV and IT, is crucial to understanding and implementing this complex technology.

12.4 Computer and Information Security

Security measures in the port facility must be developed to restrict access to information, particularly information stored in computer systems and devices used in furtherance of the Port FSP. Controlling access to information is also an important consideration for managing port access control systems, which depend on confidential databases to determine access authorizations and restrictions within the facility. Security plans and critical facility information related to security measures in place must be protected from compromise and unauthorized disclosure. The potential for the conversion of the port's proprietary and security information to criminal or other illicit purposes must receive considerable attention from port security planners and managers. Procedures may include physical and electronic storage systems, limited distributions of plans and procedures to select individuals, placing Security Sensitive Information disclaimers on correspondence and internal documents, and limiting communications to only those with a need to know.

12.4.1 Cyberterrorism

Terrorism has generated many definitions, but according to the U.S. CFR, it is ". . . the unlawful use of force and violence against people or property to intimidate or coerce a government, the civilian population, or any segment thereof, in furtherance of political or social objectives" (Federal Bureau of Investigation 2001, par. 3). The term *cyberterrorism* has evolved to refer to electronic terrorism, or information war, or the use of IT by terrorists for the purpose of promoting a political agenda. Targets for cyberterrorism might include a port facility's communications networks, utility systems, computer hardware, computer networks, access control systems, surveillance architecture, and information storage and retrieval systems. The anonymous nature of communications using IT systems suggests the technology is an ideal structure for use by terrorists and other criminals. The ability to transmit plans, coordinate activities, and launch incursions into computer-controlled systems must be assessed as a risk to port facilities, especially those with significant reliance on IT systems engaged in critical security operations.

The threats to national security associated with cyberterrorism are receiving intensified attention from the U.S. government. For example, the U.S. Department of Defense's Defense Advanced Research Projects Agency (DARPA) recently reported to Congress that "cyber warfare will be a major and growing part of future operations." DARPA is responsible for developing technological options for the military through research projects that look for military applications for recent technological innovations. DARPA advised Congress that it has been developing technologies to secure Department of Defense computers and networks to be "disruption-tolerant and, when attacked, self-reconstituting. As the U.S. military adopts network-centric warfare, terrorists and other nation-states are likely to develop and employ malicious code to impede our ability to fight efficiently and effectively. The ever-growing sophistication of the malicious code threat has surpassed the ability of normal commercial markets to address this problem" (Tether 2008, pp. 17–18). In other words, the federal government is taking the position that the threats to national security from electronic warfare are so strong that it is unlikely that the private sector alone will be able to effect the necessary defenses that will be required. Certainly, port security managers must be cognizant of the limitations of the facility's own capabilities concerning the security of IT systems and infrastructure. As with any complex organizational system, managing security for the IT components of the Port FSP will require focused collaboration with systems experts and staff, and access to resources that can bridge gaps between the stability of the IT networks and the threats facing the port facility.

At the law enforcement level, the FBI is providing $3 million to fund initial operations of a cybersecurity research center, the National Center for Digital Intrusion Response, at the University of Illinois at Urbana-Champaign. The mission of the research is to determine the capabilities that are necessary to detect and investigate cyber attacks, to develop new tools, and to ensure that FBI agents in the field can use them effectively (Dizzard 2007). This is a timely initiative given growing concerns and reports of incursions and attacks on corporate and government IT infrastructures worldwide. A recent IT security study conducted by the Computing Technology Industry Association (2008) indicated information security is a widespread concern among IT professionals responsible for information security in their organizations. "The percentage of their IT budget that companies dedicate to security is growing year after year. In the U.S., companies earmarked 12% of their IT budget in 2007 for security purposes, up from only 7% in 2005. The bulk of these dollars are used to procure security-related technologies" (par. 4). Other reports of IT systems' vulnerabilities, such as those associated with certain wireless communications protocols (Espiner and Meyer 2008), and increases in the numbers of computer hackers accessing legitimate commercial Web sites to launch attacks into third-party client and customer networks (Higgins 2008) suggest the risks associated with IT security are in fact real and growing. Clearly, government agencies are increasing their levels of policy concern and funding to support increased government efforts to mitigate the threats associated with the use of computers and IT as a terrorist methodology. Port facilities that depend on complex computing architecture to network their surveillance, credentialing, access controls, communications, and related systems must seriously consider these increasing risks. Tapping into government assistance and expertise, as well as private sector resources, to fund and develop security protections for these IT systems must receive a high priority in planning and budgeting for facility security. The opportunities for collaboration with the port facility's client base should also be explored and cultivated. Global corporations that ship cargo and passengers are also aware of and worried about these threats to their own IT systems. Given the value of partnering, resource sharing, developing new research, and innovating new protection mechanisms, the Port FSO and port management must aggressively partner with their clients in protecting each others' IT assets.

12.4.2 Employee Education for IT Security

A significant component of protecting the port facility's IT network from infiltration and compromise must be in developing computer and information systems security protocols and educating employees to adhere to them. In one example of lax IT security procedures, U.S. government inspectors posed as help desk employees working on a computer network problem. They telephoned Internal Revenue Service managers and staff, requesting their log-in names and advising them to change passwords. Out of one hundred employees contacted, thirty-five (over one-third) provided this secure information over the telephone (Pratt 2006). IT security failures are not limited to the unwitting release of secure information. According to Microsoft (2007), "during the second half of 2007 there was a 300% increase in the number of Trojan downloaders and droppers detected and removed" (p. 6). The term *Trojan*, derived from the mythical story of the Trojan horse, refers to malicious software (e.g., malware, virus, worm) disguised as desirable software but designed to conceal its true, harmful nature. Trojans may be downloaded onto a user's computer and/or networked systems in a variety of ways, for example, by clicking links embedded in e-mails. A program hidden in the malware, ostensibly providing some desirable product such as a screensaver, may actually launch hidden commands, prompts, and protocols designed to harm, incapacitate, or extract secure information from the user's devices, systems, and databases. Employee downloading of malware, in addition to the risks of loss of sensitive data through carelessness, theft, or accidents related to portable media (e.g., thumb drives, disks, laptop computers), suggests that employment training and enforcement of facility/organizational procedures related to computer and IT systems are essential priorities for port security managers.

Following are recommendations for enhancing port facility employees' attention and adherence to IT security:

- Educating employees about the importance of protecting employee and client personal data and proprietary, classified, and confidential information
- Providing employees with basic awareness training concerning computing systems and capabilities, networking, hardware, and software
- Alerting employees to IT system vulnerabilities, including piracy and unauthorized use of software, susceptibility of hardware to environmental conditions and theft, attacks from remote hackers, and losses attributable to illegal or improper access to databases
- Training on various forms of Internet fraud schemes, for example, telemarketing, investment scams, and identity theft
- Educating employees about the integration and use of malware protection and security firewalls into the facility's IT networks
- Developing security procedures for the removal of portable computing devices and media from the facility while traveling or conducting field work
- Instituting reporting and accountability mechanisms in response to lost or compromised information systems data and materials

Focused attention to and adherence with employee security precautions and procedures contributes to building another layer of facility security within the port.

References

Bulwa, Demian. 2008, May 15. Richmond installs 'smart' crime cameras. SFGate. http://www.sfgate.com/cgi-bin/article.cgi?f=/c/a/2008/05/14/BAIL10MF8V.DTL (accessed August 24, 2008).

Computing Technology Industry Association. 2008. Summary of "trends in information security: A CompTIA analysis of IT security and the workforce" survey information. Comp TIA Research. http://www.comptia.org/sections/research/reports/200804-SecuritySummary.aspx (accessed August 24, 2008).

Dizzard, W. P. 2007, August 20. FBI launches cybersecurity project. *Government Computer News*. http://www.gcn.com/online/vol1_no1/44898-1.html (accessed February 28, 2008).

Endsley, Mica R. 2000. Theoretical underpinnings of situation awareness: A critical review. In Endsley, M. R. and D. J. Garland, (Eds.). 2000. *Situation awareness analysis and measurement* Mahwah, NJ: Lawrence Erlbaum Associates. http://www.satechnologies.com/Papers/pdf/SATheorychapter.pdf (accessed August 11, 2008).

Espiner, Tom, and David Meyer. 2008, April 23. Bluetooth security dangers ignored, say experts. ZDNet.co.uk. http://news.zdnet.co.uk/security/0,1000000189,39397480,00.htm (accessed August 24, 2008).

Federal Bureau of Investigation. 2001. Terrorism 2000/2001. FBI Publication No. 0308. http://www.fbi.gov/publications/terror/terror2000_2001.htm (accessed August 11, 2008).

Gill, Martin, and Angela Spriggs. 2005. Home Office research study 292: Assessing the impact of CCTV. Home Office: United Kingdom. http://www.homeoffice.gov.uk/rds/pdfs05/hors292.pdf (accessed August 18, 2008).

Higgins, Kelly Jackson. 2008, May 21. Hack-and-pier phishing on the rise. Dark Reading. http://www.darkreading.com/document.asp?doc_id=154558&f_src=darkreading_information-week (accessed August 24, 2008).

Hoffman, Thomas. 2006. Security convergence: Physical and information security are slowly beginning to come together. *Computerworld Security*. http://www.computerworld.com/securitytopics/security/story/0,10801,108571,00.html (accessed August 24, 2008).

Maritime Terrorism Research Center. 2008, June 17. Port security news today. http://www.maritimeterrorism.com/2008/06/17/port-security-news-today/ (accessed August 24, 2008).

Microsoft. 2007. Microsoft security intelligence report, July through December, 2007: Key findings. http://download.microsoft.com/download/f/f/d/ffd1f8b8-afcc-4ed1-a635-2caa-8b96ac2f/KeyFindings_MS_Security_Report_Jul-Dec07.pdf (accessed August 24, 2008).

National Oceanic and Atmospheric Administration. 2006. Sonar. Ocean Explorer. http://www.oceanexplorer.noaa.gov/technology/tools/sonar/sonar.html (accessed August 9, 2008).

Pratt, Mary K. 2006, April 17. Employee security training: Beyond posters: Your employees need more than slogans. Here's how to get them to take security seriously. *Computerworld Security*. http://www.computerworld.com/action/article.do?command=viewArticleTOC&specialReportId=100&articleId=110494 (accessed August 24, 2008).

Science.jrank. 2008. Sonar: Historical development of sonar. http://science.jrank.org/pages/6289/SONAR-Historical-development-SONAR.html (accessed August 9, 2008).

Stone, David M. (2006). Port security: Top threats and technology trends: A look at reducing security risks of ports worldwide using today's newest technologies. Securityinfowatch.com. http://www.securityinfowatch.com/article/article.jsp?id=7481&siteSection=306 (accessed August 11, 2008).

Tether, Tony. 2008. Statement by Dr. Tony Tether, Director, Defense Advanced Research Projects Agency, Submitted to the Subcommittee on Terrorism, Unconventional Threats and Capabilities, House Armed Services Committee, United States House of Representatives, March 13, 2008. http://www.darpa.mil/body/news/2008/hasc3-13-08.pdf (accessed August 11, 2008).

U.S. Office of State and Local Government Coordination and Preparedness. 2005. FY 2005 Port security grant program: Change or revision to the PSG05 application kit. ODP Information Bulletin No. 173, June 03, 2005. http://www.ojp.usdoj.gov/odp/docs/info173.htm (accessed August 11, 2008).

Victoria Ministry for Police and Emergency Services. 2006, April 10. Port security water-tight: New police boat fleet. Victoria, Australia Department of Premier and Cabinet. Media Releases. http://www.dpc.vic.gov.au/domino/Web_Notes/newmedia.nsf/b0222c68d27626e2ca256c8c001a3d2d/cf0e8c699446e1eeca25714c007c0d3e!OpenDocument (accessed August 11, 2008).

13

SYSTEMIC MANAGEMENT FOR A SECURE AND VIABLE PORT FACILITY

13.1 Collaborations between Port Security and Law Enforcement Operations

The terrorist threat in the early twenty-first century is testing the basic political values and structures of democracy, and in particular, criminal justice roles and processes in controlling deviance in society. Terrorism and the emergence of homeland security are changing the character of local policing, not only in the United States, but around the world. Many local police agencies now have some type of homeland security bureau or unit in their tables of organization. With this growing homeland security role, the usual attention to traditional crime and disorder has been expanded to include terrorist investigations and intelligence efforts, weapons of mass destruction training, infrastructure security deployments, emergency operations planning, and new personal protective and tactical equipment and armaments (much of it funded by federal grant dollars). Intelligence gathering and analysis operations, formerly concerned perhaps with traditional organized crime and narcotics smuggling, have been expanded to include intelligence geared toward identifying homegrown terrorists, working with federal agencies in joint task forces, and illegal immigration. Within this new construct of policing, port authorities and facilities must work cooperatively with their local police agencies to integrate the appropriate level of law enforcement service into the Port FSP and security regimen.

Law enforcement agencies and port security organizations must agree on the appropriate combinations of police officers and civilian port security officers, consistent with normal governmental budget cycles and mutual aid agreements. The local police agency with jurisdictional responsibilities for law enforcement and public safety duties at the port facility must necessarily work cooperatively with the port security agency, as well as with the other security and public safety agencies with port responsibilities. Developing formal working agreements between port authorities and law enforcement agencies will ensure mutual understanding and acceptance of each agency's component port security roles and responsibilities. Collaborations and discussions between ports and police agencies should occur to address a number of organizational and management issues.

13.1.1 Administrative and Coordinating Roles of Police Units in Port Facilities

Administrative and coordinating police responsibilities may include access capabilities into port cargo and restricted areas, high-visibility and directed police patrols, and administration of various special events and emergency response programs. Supervision and administration of law enforcement operations may be the responsibility of a senior command officer assigned to the port. This person may report via a distinct chain of command to the police department, or to a port administrator in some jurisdictions. In any event the police command officer should collaborate directly with the Port FSO/Security Administrator and other concerned federal, state, and local law enforcement agencies to achieve port security objectives, including port-specific operational and tactical procedures and training in compliance with government regulations and standards. The port facility police commander may be responsible for the management, direction, and control of the deployed law enforcement contingent and resources at the port, including the following:

- All police services at the port including those within cargo terminal and private business leaseholds
- Implementation of additional police services upon notification of MARSEC level increases for the port, or of arriving vessels with a higher security level than the facility or with specific security needs
- Assisting in the development and maintenance of port-specific SOPs and training curricula for all police personnel assigned to the port (e.g., evacuation procedures, bomb threat procedures)
- Distribution of procedures to all personnel assigned to the port and assurance that assigned personnel are familiar with them, as well as with applicable federal, state, and local port security requirements
- Implementation of all law enforcement requirements as required by federal and state regulations, and the necessary inspections and controls to ensure continued compliance with security standards
- Active collaboration with the Port FSO in the notification of appropriate agencies and individuals, under routine and emergency conditions, of security breaches and transportation security incidents, including the National Response Center in compliance with U.S. MTSA and Coast Guard regulations
- Acting as liaison to appropriate police department elements for deployment of additional police resources necessary for continuity of port operations under heightened threat assessments and/or MARSEC alert levels
- Acting as liaison with port users, such as ferry, cruise, and cargo operations security managers and contract security services operating at the port
- Assisting or recommending modifications to the Port FSP as needed and identified by the police command and/or the Port FSO

- Participating in security awareness training to promote the encouragement of and vigilance in interactions with port management, staff, employees, vendors, and visitors, and to meet requirements for recognition and reporting of suspicious people, vehicles, and activities as well as dangerous goods or potential threat devices
- Participating in activities with the port and other federal, state, and local law enforcement agencies that have operational responsibilities at the port, and the development and implementation of drills and exercises to test the FSP and integrated security-police procedures
- Reviewing and reporting budgetary needs to maintain adequate law enforcement presence at the port facility through the Port FSO on a continuing basis
- Coordination of appropriate levels of police operational, investigative, and administrative personnel
- Maintenance of interoperable interagency communications capabilities

13.1.2 Incident Investigations: Suspicious Activities

The security function in the port facility is enhanced when the organizations responsible for port security and for investigating actual or potential incidents of crime work harmoniously to mitigate situations involving suspicious activities. It is difficult to predict which people or vehicles entering a port facility may pose a threat to safety; thus it is critical for the Port FSO to work with assigned law enforcement staff to identify and establish guidelines for security and police staff, and to make plans to protect against threats from suspicious activity. The parameters for the investigation of suspicious activity should be developed collaboratively with law enforcement, and in concert with the port's risk assessment practices. On its public Web site, Port Everglades (2008), in Broward County, Florida, has articulated a number of parameters addressing unusual activities that can begin a discussion in planning jointly for investigating suspicious activity in the port facility, including the following:

- Unknown people or workers trying to access facilities
- Individuals without required identification credentials
- Unknown people or vendors loitering for extended periods of time
- Unknown people photographing facilities in and around the port
- Telephone calls or e-mails inquiring about security, personnel, or procedures
- Vehicles or small vessels loitering, photographing, taking notes, or drawing sketches
- Bomb threats
- Theft of vehicles, vehicle passes, personnel identification, uniforms, or procedural documents

- Low-flying general aviation aircraft operating near facilities
- Unknown people attempting to gain information about facilities
- Suspicious packages

Security officers observing or called to investigate suspicious vehicles and people may not have the legal authority that a police officer has in stopping vehicles and in detaining or arresting individuals. The value of port security and law enforcement working together on these issues is in planning cooperative investigatory practices that will ensure suspicious activity reports are mitigated completely and efficiently.

13.2 Systemic Management of Port Security: A Case Study of the Port of Miami

Security and safety at seaports is a responsibility of all entities with a vested interest in ensuring a port's continued development and viability. In applying the concept of *layered security*, port administrators must develop a systemic approach that co-opts a variety of organizational resources, processes, and systems to build an interconnected security program. Interagency cooperation and leadership are the keys to synchronizing security efforts across the diverse group of actors at seaports. In a systemic approach to port security management, energy is channeled to reducing conflicts and maximizing the resources from varied public and private sector organizations. The reality is that port facility security is not the responsibility of only one entity, but involves many international, national, state, and local organizations over which the port authorities themselves often have no direct control:

- Customs and border protection
- Police, fire, and emergency medical services
- Immigration and agriculture agencies
- Coast Guard and harbor authorities
- Transportation and utility regulating bodies
- Employer groups, stevedores, and labor unions
- Cargo terminal operators
- Passenger cruise and ferry lines
- Vendors, suppliers, and customers

To emphasize the importance of adopting a systemic approach to managing port security, it is illustrative to examine the experience of the Port of Miami, Florida, during a period of organizational change before and after the September 2001 terrorist attacks, and in response to increased governmental regulation and oversight of seaport security.

13.2.1 *Overview of the Port of Miami*

Located just east of downtown Miami in Biscayne Bay between the Atlantic Ocean and the Intracoastal Waterway, the Port of Miami is a 528-acre facility constructed on

Dodge and Lummus Islands, two spoil islands developed for commercial maritime use in relatively shallow Biscayne Bay. With both passenger cruise and cargo operations, as well as an assortment of corporate and government offices, warehouses, stevedoring companies, travel agencies, and food and beverage concessions, the Port of Miami is a significant multiuse port and an economic engine in South Florida. In terms of maritime infrastructure, the port has 3.6 miles of linear berth space; 441,317 square feet of commercial office space; and nine passenger terminals, two of which were newly constructed and became operational in 2007. The Port of Miami is nominally marketed as the "cruise capital of the world" by virtue of its proximity to the Caribbean and its high volume of cruise passenger traffic. In 2001, cruise passenger volume amounted to 3.4 million (Port of Miami 2007a). In 2006, more than 3.7 million cruise passengers transited the port, an increase of 3.5 percent from 2005. On the cargo side, the Port of Miami has four transit cargo sheds with a combined total of 468,000 square feet. The port operates both roll-on–roll-off and gantry crane operations, with ten cranes, including two new super post-Panamax, ship-to-shore luffing-boom cranes. In 2006, the port handled nearly a million TEUs* (Port of Miami 2007b). The Port of Miami is a significant component of the economy of Miami-Dade County, with an economic impact of $17 billion a year, with over 176,000 jobs directly or indirectly related to port activities (Port of Miami 2008). As many as one hundred thousand jobs are directly or indirectly related to port activities (2003).

The Port of Miami is owned and operated as a landlord-tenant seaport by the Board of County Commissioners of Miami-Dade County, Florida, and is managed by the Miami-Dade Seaport Department, an element of county government. Administration and management is provided by a port director who reports administratively to the mayor of Miami-Dade County and to the county manager. At the port, county government provides the land, utilities, support structures, and systems in contractual lease arrangements with cruise lines, cargo terminal operators, and a variety of maritime, travel, and related businesses, which effectively enable the port to operate as one of the major multiuse, cruise, and cargo ports in the United States and in the world. Although the Port of Miami is an element of county government, its budget is not funded by Miami-Dade County's general operating fund. Instead, all operating expenses are funded by revenues generated by the port's cruise, cargo, and ancillary commercial enterprises. This is significant because, unlike many other ports that receive some type of public funding, the Port of Miami must be self-sustaining as an entrepreneurial organization. As such, when overhead costs, such as security, increase, there is an opportunity cost to the commercial enterprises at the port. This became painfully apparent in the

---

* A TEU, or Twenty-foot Equivalent Unit, is a common standard of measurement in containerized shipping equating to a twenty-foot cargo container, that is, a volume equivalent to that occupied by one ISO (International Organization for Standardization) twenty-foot container.

aftermath of September 11, as homeland security policy issues advanced to the top of the national political agenda.

13.2.2 *Security Organization at the Port of Miami*

Prior to and since September 11, security at the Port of Miami has been the responsibility of a variety of public agencies and private organizations. The Miami-Dade Police Department, effectively the sheriff's office, is the largest law enforcement agency in Miami-Dade County and has local police jurisdiction at the Port of Miami. The Miami-Dade Police Department provides traditional law enforcement services to the port, which include patrol and investigative services, as well as specialized law enforcement and security services consistent with the Port FSP, pursuant to working agreements and budgetary arrangements between the police department and the seaport department, which are collateral departments in the county's organizational structure.

Civilian port security personnel, employed by the Seaport Department, provide a variety of security and ancillary services including credentialing; access-gate control for pedestrians, commercial, and private vehicles; parking enforcement; traffic control; revenue collection; random routine security patrols; and administrative services to the port. Specific functions requiring security staffing depend on time of day, vessel arrivals and departures, number of cruise ships in port, number of terminals in use, special events, volume of traffic, and exigent circumstances. In addition to the civil service police and security personnel employed by Miami-Dade County, additional port security is provided by the entities that lease facilities at the port to conduct cruise, cargo, and ancillary operations. For example, when the terminals are in active use, passenger terminal security, is provided by private security services contracted by the cruise lines that use the Port of Miami as a home port or port of call for its passenger cruise services. Though other lines also use the Port of Miami, there are primarily three major cruise lines that operate cruises worldwide, principally to the Caribbean: Royal Caribbean Cruises Ltd. (which also has its corporate offices at the Port of Miami), Carnival Cruise Lines, and Norwegian Cruise Lines. Similarly, the three major cargo terminal operators, APM Terminals, the Port of Miami Terminal Operating Company, and Seaboard Marine, all have either proprietary or contracted security services in the cargo container yards and related facilities and warehouses.

Law enforcement elements of both the U.S. and State of Florida governments have a significant presence at the Port of Miami. The U.S. DHS deploys staff from the U.S. Coast Guard, U.S. Customs and Border Protection, and U.S. Immigration and Customs Enforcement in support of a number of federal law enforcement and port security missions and responsibilities. The U.S. Coast Guard in particular plays a significant oversight role ensuring port compliance with the MTSA of 2002 and other federal legislation. The Florida Department of Law Enforcement has statutory authority for ensuring the port's compliance with the statewide minimum standards for port security, which apply to all of the state's fourteen deepwater seaports. In addition, marine patrol elements of the Florida Fish and Wildlife Conservation Commission provide waterborne law enforcement and security services to the port in a contractual arrangement prompted by the MTSA's requirements for a waterborne security component to the Port FSP.

The Miami-Dade Police Department's responsibilities and involvement in seaport security operations became an increasingly significant component of the Port of Miami's security regime beginning in 1997. At that time, to comply with new local statutory requirements regarding the possession of identification credentials for people who desire access to restricted areas of the seaport, the Port of Miami established the Seaport Identification (ID) Section, which became responsible for administering provisions of Miami-Dade County Ordinances, Chapter 28-A, Seaport Security and Operations, and later in 2001, Florida Statute 311.12, Seaport Security Standards. The processing of applications for Port of Miami Seaport ID cards, including a fingerprint-based criminal history check, to people desiring access to port restricted access areas constituted the primary function of the ID Section.

The police department's staffing and management of the Seaport ID Section was originally authorized in 1997 by the Miami-Dade County Manager. The original, statutorily required function specifically assigned to the Miami-Dade Police Department, via Chapter 28-A, was the authentication of Seaport ID card applicant fingerprints. With the passage of Florida Statute 311.12, this requirement essentially became moot because the new state law required the port to transmit Seaport ID card applicant fingerprints electronically and directly to the Florida Department of Law Enforcement. Although the police department was no longer required to authenticate ID card applicant fingerprints, it continued to provide the Port of Miami with staff and managerial oversight for the Seaport ID Section. Organizationally, the staffing and operation of the ID section was under the authority of police department, and the administration and infrastructure was under the purview of the port director.

Also in 1997, Miami-Dade County government implemented a plan to establish an enhanced police presence at the port to coordinate what was then viewed as the parallel duties of seaport law enforcement and security under the umbrella of one management system. Under the 1997 plan, the police department assumed the overall management of the Port of Miami civilian port security officers, supervisors, and support staff. The police department established the Seaport Operations Section at the port, assigning a police captain to oversee the previously established Seaport ID Section, a dedicated port facility police contingent, and the port's civilian security staff. Between 1997 and 2001, the captain of the police department was collaterally a de facto staff member of the Port of Miami, reporting to the port director. The organizational structure reflected the captain as the chief of security, who directly supervised Miami-Dade Seaport Department employees, yet also continued to report organizationally through the police department's chain of command.

In the aftermath of September 11, Miami-Dade County government assigned a police major to the port and increased the size of the law enforcement contingent. A decision was made to transfer all port civilian security staff to the command, control, and authority of the Miami-Dade Police Department. All port security officers, supervisors, and support staff were organizationally reassigned to the police department. This included the establishment of police department chains of command, personnel files, and the issuance of police uniforms to security personnel. In effect, the police department now managed and operated port security. This organizational structure continued to function until 2005, when the security personnel, operations, and credentialing functions were reassigned back to the Seaport Department. Since then, the Miami-Dade Police Department has continued to perform traditional law enforcement functions, as well as specialized police and security functions as specified in the Port FSP. Because the police department was in command and control of both law enforcement and security operations at the Port of Miami in the aftermath of September 11 and the enactment of the MTSA, it participated directly in the development of the Port FSP, in cooperation with the Port FSO, who was employed by the Seaport Department and reported administratively to the port director. In effecting compliance with both federal and state seaport security regulations, Miami-Dade Police Department staffing was deployed in a variety of key security positions, such as cruise terminal security and vehicle screening checkpoints. With the 2005 organizational restructuring, the continued use of police staff in some of these security functions contributed to an increasing financial burden for the Port of Miami in funding security operations.

13.2.3 Legal and Financial Constraints: Port of Miami Security after 9/11

The MTSA established a number of new security parameters for seaports, including Miami's. As enacted in the CFR (2003), MTSA required, among other things, that vulnerability assessments of U.S. seaports be conducted to determine the nature and type of threat or risk for each particular port facility. Based on the assessment, ports now had to develop FSPs to mitigate the threats. These FSPs became subject to review and oversight by the U.S. Coast Guard, which has primary federal responsibility for regulating port security. This legislation essentially required that seaports be part of a national maritime transportation security planning system. Because seaports are a vital link in the nation's economic and transportation systems, the absence of a comprehensive standard of security among the nation's seaports represented a significant vulnerability. For security at the Port of Miami, the focus of much effort in the aftermath of September 11 was the development of an FSP that would provide effective security, comply with MTSA, and continue to serve the business interests of the port's clients.

Collaterally, in the State of Florida, the enactment of Florida Statute 311.12, Seaport Security Standards, represented a comprehensive effort at the state level to enhance security at the state's fourteen deepwater seaports. Designed to address the general threat of crime and narcotics trafficking through the state's seaports before September 11 occurred, the statute adopted a complex set of prescriptive standards for seaport security addressing access control, personnel, cargo security, parking, fencing, lighting, and a host of other security infrastructure issues. A significant component of the standards requires each seaport to develop an access control credential, issued pursuant to a fingerprint-based criminal history check. Applicants with specified crimes in their past are prohibited from accessing restricted areas of the seaport. Each seaport is subject to an annual unannounced inspection by the Florida Department of Law Enforcement, which is statutorily authorized to determine and report to the state legislature each seaport's compliance or noncompliance with the standards.

The Port of Miami's interfaces with the U.S. Coast Guard in relation to the federal MTSA requirements and with the Florida Department of Law Enforcement in relation to the state's standards for seaport security are heavily driven by regulatory compliance activity. Compliance requires significant expense of resources in terms of coordination, documentation, correspondence, operations, personnel, and training. For example, a significant security expense at the Port of Miami has been the provision of waterborne security patrols, which became required under federal MTSA provisions but were not provided directly by the U.S. Coast Guard. The options available were limited to constructing agreements with state and/or local law enforcement marine patrols or developing a proprietary or contract marine patrol capability. In 2005, the Port of Miami elected to contract, at a significant expense, with the marine patrol component of the Florida Fish and Wildlife Conservation Commission, a State of Florida law enforcement agency, to effect compliance with MTSA. Again, the operational expenses associated with this plan component, such as personnel costs, came from port revenues. Although federal port security grant funds became available for many security resources, personnel and other regular operating costs are typically not funded through grants.

Many operational decisions at the Port of Miami are driven by statutory requirements and external concerns about security. For example, a cargo terminal operator's need to shift cargo operations from one berthing location to another in some cases may not be done until the U.S. Coast Guard or Florida Department of Law Enforcement review an amended FSP provision. Constraints such as these dictate that Port of Miami security personnel, private security contractors, law enforcement officials, and federal/state regulators work cooperatively to effect FSP revisions and amendments, and minimize delays that translate into increased operating costs to elements of the maritime transportation system. The writing and submittal of FSPs and amendments, with concomitant review by federal, state, and local regulating entities, can be heavily bureaucratic, with threats of penalties for noncompliance. The costs and constraints necessitated by the need for increased security after September 11 placed a responsibility on Port of Miami management to better coordinate all of the tenants' activities. Obtaining tenant compliance may require changes to operating agreements, local ordinances, tariffs, and/or leases, which in some cases takes time and requires additional staff and resources. Increased security has affected all aspects of operations at the port. While working toward full compliance with federal and state port security regulations in developing an effective FSP, the port must continue to integrate security with port operations, which requires significant investments in capital infrastructure.

The Port of Miami's annual security operating expenses, for the most part the costs attributed to both police and civilian security personnel, more than quadrupled since September 11, surpassing $11 million in fiscal year 2005, and $18 million in fiscal year 2007 (Port of Miami 2007b). In fiscal year 2005, the security infrastructure budget exceeded $55.4 million, six times higher than its 2001 estimate (Port of Miami 2007b). One of the biggest challenges the Port of Miami has faced is funding security-related operational costs.

Miami has one of the highest security budgets of any port in the state; percentage-wise, it is probably the highest in the country. The port is working on modifying its existing security plan to reduce the overall cost in the range of $4 to $5 million, at least as a start. "One of the port's goals is to integrate the various security systems, such as electronic scanning equipment and CCTV cameras with the Port's Communications, Command, and Control (CCC) center. This requires very close communication and coordination with the port's business partners, who also spend millions of dollars in their individual security systems. 'We need to think as one and have all the systems integrate with the CCC,' said port director Bill Johnson" (Port of Miami 2007b, pp. 31–32). Thus, senior port leadership recognizes the value that security can add to the port's overall security and business posture, and is emphasizing the collaborative, systemic approach required to obtain the cooperation of its valued stakeholders.

To meet its security infrastructure needs for funding assistance, the Port of Miami has aggressively applied for security grants from state and federal programs. By 2005, the port had received in excess of $17 million in federal funds and had also been successful in getting more than $9.4 million in State of Florida commerce grants funds reallocated for security projects (Port of Miami 2005). Although these are among the highest of such awards across the nation for seaports, the grant funding does not provide for day-to-day operational expenses, such as personnel, which must come from revenues generated by cruise and cargo operations.

*13.2.4 A Systemic Approach to Port Security: Lessons Learned in
Addressing Constraints at the Port of Miami*

As discussed previously, historically the global maritime industry has been subject to relatively little regulation concerning vessel and port facility security. That paradigm has changed significantly with increasing levels of criminal activity, piracy, international smuggling, and global acts of terrorism. Recognized international standards for port security have only emerged within the past decade. With this heightened sense of urgency, measures aimed at neutralizing seaports' vulnerabilities to criminal activity have become more focused. The role of security at port facilities is driven by two primary imperatives: (1) developing measures aimed at neutralizing vulnerability to criminal activity and security threats, and (2) affecting the nexus between the port and those who would commit crime and terrorism. Key to this effort is developing a layered approach to security, that is, a variety of tools that, when interrelated, provide a strong defense against terrorism and crime. Port security is enhanced through the development of multiple security systems and processes. Physical security measures, combined with access controls, present a multidimensional security barrier. The intention is that if one layer of security fails to detect an unwanted threat, another layer will work to identify and neutralize the threat.

A review of the experience at the Port of Miami in addressing these imperatives since September 11 suggests that a sound approach to managing security and developing a layered Port FSP, one that is both security-effective and cost-efficient, is to use a systemic approach. The theoretical model for this strategy has previously been discussed within the context of Katz and Kahn's (1978, pp. 20–21) view of the organization as an energic input–output system. Organizational outcomes are the result of the transformation of behavioral energy within the system. Developing patterns of energy exchange (i.e., people's activities) that focus on the desired output is the key to affecting productivity. In the case of the Port of Miami, the port stakeholders are the people and groups who have an interest in the security and continued successful operation of the port. As stakeholders, port users have a vested interest in ensuring that the seaport remain safe, secure, and able to operate effectively to achieve its goals and objectives. In this systemic approach to security, port management's focus of behavior has been an effort to energize the system to achieve cooperative leadership, coordination, and the integration of disparate positions and interests.

What port security managers can learn from the Port of Miami experience is that there is a viable strategy for maximizing a collaborative, systemic approach to port facility security. This strategy is based on three fundamental management activities:

1. Developing cooperative leadership among those having an interest in port security and operations
2. Improving communications among the stakeholders
3. Identifying appropriate security technologies and methods that, when used collaboratively, will mitigate both the security threats and the financial impact of compliance with federal and state port security regulations

The responsibility for port security must be shared by all who have an interest in efficient and effective port security and operations: the federal and state governments, local law enforcement, passenger cruise and ferry lines, cargo terminal operators, shipping lines, stevedores, employees, labor groups, vendors, port management, and the transportation industry. Seaports must develop complementary relationships among users and stakeholders. Cooperation is essential in identifying and mitigating threats to the security of seaports. It is also essential that all stakeholder groups have a basic understanding and buy into the port security program.

One method that the Port of Miami has used effectively in developing and strengthening these relationships is the establishment of an Executive Security Steering Committee. This committee is cochaired by the port director and the U.S. Coast Guard COTP and is comprised of senior officials from port administration, law enforcement, and government. The benefit of this committee is that it shares information relevant to port security resulting from threat assessments conducted by law enforcement agencies. The Port of Miami uses this process to develop and refine its FSP, communicate with port users, and work in a coordinated fashion to develop plans and strategies to address and neutralize identified threats and vulnerabilities. Ports must develop partnerships to protect against security threats. Working cooperatively with stakeholders and appropriate governmental agencies, port management can tap into and use the combined resources of many organizations to improve intelligence gathering, threat assessments, risk-based decision making, and response planning. In addition, since port management must coordinate and integrate each stakeholder's role to optimize the port's security posture, the communications must extend to all port users. To accomplish this, another Port of Miami approach that has capitalized on this strategy is the organization of a variety of working committees and task forces, which help to bridge the communication gap that so often results in conflict. Some of these initiatives have included the following:

- Port Safety Committee. Employees and managers of concerned port user organizations are invited to work collaboratively with port safety and security staff to identify and mitigate threats to individual safety and health.
- Port Users Security Committee. Chaired by the Port FSO with representatives from law enforcement, proprietary and contract security companies, and major port cargo and cruise tenants, the Port Users Security Committee meets regularly to communicate and share information on access control issues, security threats, special events, operational constraints, and planning.
- Capital Improvements Development Staff Meetings. Information and updates on capital improvements to port infrastructure (e.g., new roadways, buildings, facilities, wharf construction) are shared in regular meetings attended by senior port leadership, law enforcement, port security, information technology, and private contracting staff. Security and operational issues and concerns are surfaced. Plans for mitigation are developed and tasked. This enhances the collaborative approach by front-loading security concerns into the design stages of development projects.
- Strategic Weather Advisory Team. The U.S. Coast Guard Sector Miami command staff established a Strategic Weather Advisory Team, a working group of key leaders in port operations, waterway management, law enforcement, and security. The purpose of this group was to assemble in advance of impending severe weather (e.g., a hurricane or tropical storm) and function as the

coordinating team and communications vehicle for managing port operations before, during, and after a severe weather event. The model worked effectively to streamline communications and coordinate government-business interfaces and port operations in the management of severe weather events.

- Labor Relations Working Groups. Port leadership established several Labor Relations Working Groups comprised of leaders from port labor organizations, unions, stevedores, cruise lines, cargo terminals, port operations, marketing, and administration. The purpose of these meetings was to identify and resolve conflicts related to cargo and passenger terminal operations involving the port's unionized and itinerant labor.
- Port Community Meetings. Port leadership established quarterly meetings to which members of all port user and tenant organizations were invited to participate. At these meetings, representatives from port operations, administration, and security addressed tenant and user questions and concerns related to operational and security issues.
- Port Administrative Working Group. Representatives from port-internal departments (e.g., security, maintenance, media relations, IT, and personnel) meet regularly to review and discuss operational and security issues affecting port business and the FSP. Issues related to safety hazards, physical plant maintenance, restricted area access, physical security, and credentialing were discussed and tasked out for necessary action and follow-up.

Seaport administration has the responsibility for coordinating and integrating each stakeholder's interests into the decision-making processes that drive the port's operational directions. Without systemic efforts such as these to coordinate and integrate each stakeholder's role, the port's security posture will not be optimized. The port's leadership in maximizing stakeholder participation is crucial to the safe and secure environment seaports must maintain.

13.3 The Challenge of Collaboration in Managing Port Security

In 2007, the U.S. Government Accountability Office convened a forum of national and international experts for a dialog on applying risk management to homeland security. Participants included federal, state, and local officials and risk management experts from the private sector and academia. Participants identified three key challenges: (1) improving risk communication, (2) political obstacles to risk-based resource allocation, and (3) a lack of strategic thinking about managing homeland security risks (Rabkin 2008). It is a telling observation that, six years out from the paradigm-shifting September 11 terrorist event, a government-coordinated forum of security and risk management experts essentially identified traditional management practices as the primary functional component necessary for reducing threats to homeland security. The discussion in previous chapters has consistently advocated collaboration as being at the crux of effecting rational and effective port facility security practices. As the Government Accountability Office forum identified, it is precisely those elements of collaboration that lead to productive organizational outcomes, i.e., communications, a rational approach, and strategic thinking.

In this final chapter, the discussion concludes to emphasize the port security manager's responsibility to develop a collaborative agenda. The construction of a sound managerial approach to the port security organization must include a concerted strategy to identify and move several important port stakeholders in the direction of a shared vision of port security. Recognizing that the port represents an important resource for both market-based and government-based community members, the port security manager becomes a central player in structuring a Port FSP that meets the goals and objectives of not only the port itself, but those of the diverse interests that have responsibilities and vested interests in a safe and secure port. These interests include two major categories of stakeholders: (1) the government officials and their staffs that have responsibilities for public safety, law enforcement, and homeland security; and (2) the business forces that need and desire an economically competitive, well-organized, and efficient port facility attuned to the evolving needs and dynamics of the maritime community. In all forums, meetings, and discussions of port security, the key conversation that will evolve will center around what the port facility is doing to protect its people and assets, and how those security solutions will affect the business. This discussion will occur in an environment where port facility usage is changing dramatically.

Port facilities that have traditionally been oriented to a relatively narrow market of maritime interests now must entertain solicitations for the capital development of their facilities across a wide spectrum of commercial interests. As new markets develop and grow in many corners of the world, the need for port facilities to adapt to changing economic conditions will increase. Consider the following case in point. The Suape Port and Industrial Complex in the State of Pernambuco, Brazil, about 50 miles south of Recife, is in a period of sustained growth. Due to its strategic location in northeastern Brazil, it is poised to become a major conduit for South American trade to all corners of the world. More than seventy companies, representing $1.7 billion in investments, are in various phases of development at the port, which is experiencing record growth. In 2007, it reported a general load-handling increase of 89%, and a 19% increase in net revenue over the previous year (Suape Complex 2008). Suape is an example of a multiuse port in a period of expansion and development. It is attracting investors due to its strategic location, availability of natural resources, and focus on economic sustainability. As ports around the world like this continue to grow, their strategic importance to the local, regional, national, and global economies will increase. Threat assessments and security planning will become an increasingly important component of ports' overall capital development plans. The ability of the port organization to successfully merge the business interests with the security needs will increasingly require leaders who understand the inherent value of working cooperatively with their customers, employees, and governments to achieve desired outcomes.

The intersections of government and business in managing port security interests may occur in a number of commercial enterprises. Major roadways or railways running into, out of, and adjacent to port areas may not only service the port facility but also provide necessary conduits for travel for the surrounding community. Seaport protection activities may extend to ports' interfaces with multimodal transportation systems. Major highways, state roadways, and rail lines often connect directly to seaports due to the need to have efficient networks to transport people and commodities to and from seaports. Activities at the seaport may impact its state, county, and city. Seaports often become the focal point for community activities and events. Due to their waterfront locations adjacent to major metropolitan areas, private and public sector interests often use seaports to produce films, concerts, festivals, international trade events, and maritime domain activities designed to develop new trade and commerce. Port activities may also impact neighboring states or countries that depend on the port for trade and tourism. The security of a particular segment of the maritime industry, such as passenger cruises, depends on secure ports across the spectrum. Security incidents, or breaches that impact one port of call, may seriously impact activities at other ports within a region.

Collaborative approaches that capitalize on the expertise residing in the many organizations vested in secure port facilities can engage interested stakeholders in partnerships that can achieve both security and economies of scale.

References

Code of Federal Regulations. 2003. Title 33, Navigation and Navigable Waters, Chapter I, Coast Guard, Department of Homeland Security, Part 105, Facility security. http://www.access. gpo.gov/nara/cfr/waisidx_03/33cfr105_03.html (accessed August 30, 2008).

Florida Statutes. 2006. Seaport security standards. Section 311.12. http://www.leg.state.fl.us/statutes/index.cfm?App_mode=Display_Statute&Search_String=&URL=Ch0311/SEC12. HTM&Title=-%3E2006-%3ECh0311-%3ESection%2012#0311.12 (accessed June 5, 2007).

Katz, Daniel, and Robert L. Kahn. 1978. *The social psychology of organizations.* 2nd ed. New York: John Wiley & Sons.

Port Everglades. 2008. Security is everyone's business. http://www.broward.org/port/security_partners.htm (accessed August 31, 2008).

Port of Miami. 2005. Port of Miami overview. Miami-Dade County, FL: Port of Miami, Office of Communications.

Port of Miami. 2007a. Cruise statistics. Miami-Dade County, FL: Port of Miami. http://www. miamidade.gov/portofmiami/cruise_stats.asp (accessed March 10, 2007).

Port of Miami. 2007b. Official directory. Miami-Dade County, FL: Port of Miami. http://seaportsinfo.com/portofmiami/PORT OF MIAMI2007.pdf (accessed March 11, 2007).

Port of Miami. 2008. Port directory. Miami-Dade County, FL: Port of Miami. http://seaportsinfo.com/portofmiami/POM2008.pdf (accessed August 30, 2008).

Rabkin, Norman. 2008. Testimony before the Subcommittee on Transportation Security and Infrastructure Protection, Homeland Security Committee, House of Representatives. Risk Management: Strengthening the use of risk management principles in homeland security. Washington, DC: General Accountability Office. GAO-08-904-T. http://www.gao.gov/new.items/d08904t.pdf (accessed August 16, 2008).

Suape Complex. 2008. Suape port and industrial complex. http://www.suape.pe.gov.br/ingles/index.asp (accessed August 31, 2008).

Glossary and Organizational Resources

The following glossary and organizational resources provide the port security manager with a foundational understanding of maritime, seaport, and security terminology, and a compendium of public and private sector organizational resources and publications to assist in understanding the maritime transportation sector, developing port facility security plans, and researching current issues and trends of interest to port officials, stakeholders, and organizations.

American Association of Port Authorities (AAPA): AAPA is trade association representing deepwater public port authorities in the United States, Canada, Latin America, and the Caribbean. It provides a variety of education and training programs for its membership, conducts research, distributes newsletters, and provides public relations and information services for port professionals. http://www.aapa-ports.org

American Journal of Transportation: A U.S.-based periodical that provides shippers, carriers, transportation intermediaries, and logistics professionals with news and events in international trade and transportation. http://www.ajot.com

American Society for Industrial Security (ASIS International): ASIS International is an organization for security professionals with more than thirty-six thousand members worldwide. Founded in 1955, the organization provides programs and services focused on improving effectiveness and productivity in the security profession through education and materials that address broad security interests. http://www.asisonline.org

Area Maritime Security Committee (AMSC): An AMSC is convened by a U.S. Coast Guard Captain of the Port (COTP) in his/her capacity as the Federal Maritime Security Coordinator responsible for development of the Area

Maritime Security Plan. AMSC members may include representatives from government, law enforcement, emergency management, security, the maritime industry, and port elements with a vested interest in maritime and port security planning. The membership engages in planning and coordinating activities in compliance with U.S. federal legislation and the National Strategy for Maritime Security.

Automated Secure Vessel Tracking System™ (ASVTS): A secure vessel tracking, open-architecture system that uses satellite transmissions and other information to identify and track the locations and movements of vessels. http://asvts. com/about.htm

Biometrics: Methods for uniquely recognizing humans based upon one or more physical traits, such as through the use of fingerprints, voiceprint identification, and retina scans.

BNICE: A commonly used acronym in military and homeland security used to categorize weapons of mass destruction: Biological, Nuclear, Incendiary, Chemical, and Explosives.

Breach of Security: An incident that has not resulted in a transportation security incident, in which security measures have been circumvented, eluded, or violated.

Break-Bulk Cargo: Noncontainerized general cargo, such as iron or machinery, marked for individual consignees, which may be stored in boxes, bales, pallets, or other units to be loaded onto or discharged from ships or other forms of transportation.

Bunkering, Bunkers: The process of supplying a vessel with fuel.

Captain of the Port (COTP): The local U.S. Coast Guard officer exercising authority for the COTP zones required by the U.S. Maritime Transportation Act of 2002, and described in Section 33 of the U.S. Code of Federal Regulations.

Caribbean Central American Action (CCAA): CCAA is a private organization that promotes private sector-led economic development in the Caribbean Basin and the Western Hemisphere. It conducts policy-oriented programs in the financial services, transportation, energy, agriculture, apparel, intellectual property rights, tourism, telecommunications, and information technology sectors. http://www.c-caa.org

CBRNE: A commonly used acronym in military and homeland security used to categorize weapons of mass destruction: Chemical, Biological, Radiological, Nuclear, and High Yield Explosive.

Center for International Trade and Transportation (CITT): Established at California State University, Long Beach, CITT is a multidisciplinary center for multimodal transportation studies and integrated logistics research, education, training, policy analysis, and community outreach. http://www.uces. csulb.edu/CITT

Centers for Disease Control and Prevention (CDC): CDC is an agency of the U.S. Department of Health and Human Services responsible for public health protection in the United States. http://www.cdc.gov

Certain Dangerous Cargo: Certain dangerous cargo refers to specific materials as defined in Title 33, U.S. Code of Federal Regulations, Part 160. These include, but are not limited to, explosives, blasting agents, poisonous gases and materials, oxidizing materials, certain radioactive and fissile materials, flammables, caustics, and environmentally hazardous materials.

Citizen Corps: The U.S. Department of Homeland Security coordinates Citizen Corps, a network of volunteers who work with federal entities, state and local governments, first responders, and emergency managers. The program, a component of USA Freedom Corps, enables citizens to participate in local community efforts involved in homeland security planning and emergency preparedness. http://www.citizencorps.gov

Closed-Circuit TV (CCTV): CCTV refers to the ability to deploy one or more video cameras that have the ability to privately transmit video signals of activity in a target environment directly to designated monitors.

Code of Federal Regulations (CFR): The codification of the general and permanent rules published in the Federal Register by the executive departments and agencies of the U.S. Federal Government. It is divided into 50 titles that represent broad areas subject to Federal regulation. http://www.gpoaccess.gov/cfr

Command and Control System: A system established by an organization's leadership to manage staff and resource activities associated with the organization's mission, as well as with singular events causing disruption to normal operations. Command and control systems, such as the Incident Command System, are used to coordinate the activities of responding external personnel and agencies to ensure unity of command and mission-directed response.

Commercial Vehicle Inspection Station: A location designated by a port facility where vehicles making deliveries of provisions to cruise and cargo vessels may be inspected and screened prior to delivery.

Community Emergency Response Team (CERT): The CERT Program is administered by U.S. Federal Emergency Management Agency's Community Preparedness Division as a training program to prepare individuals to assist themselves and their community in the event of a disaster. Training includes topics such as disaster preparedness and response, fire safety, light search and rescue, and disaster medical operations. http://www.citizencorps.gov/cert

Company Security Officer (CSO): The International Ship and Port Facility Security (ISPS) Code defines the CSO as the person designated by a company for ensuring that a ship security assessment is carried out; for ensuring that a ship security plan is developed, submitted for approval, implemented, and maintained; and for liaison with port facility security officers and the ship security officer.

Container: A box made of aluminum, steel, or fiberglass used to transport cargo by ship, rail, truck, or barge. Common dimensions are 20' x 8' x 8' (called a TEU or twenty-foot equivalent unit) or 40' x 8' x 8'.

Container Security Initiative (CSI): CSI is an antiterrorism program developed by the U.S. Customs and Border Protection shortly after the September 11, 2001, terrorist attacks. CSI identifies high-risk cargo containers that pose a potential risk for terrorism by deploying U.S. Customs and Border Protection officials and equipment in foreign ports to prescreen and evaluate containers before they are shipped, as early in the supply chain as possible, using various technologies, such as x-ray, gamma ray, and radiation detection devices.

Container Terminal: A crane-equipped facility where container vessels dock to discharge and load cargo containers.

Containerization: A shipping system that uses standard sized cargo-carrying containers that can be interchanged between trucks, trains, and vessels for easy transport.

Counterterrorism: Offensive strategies, tactics, and plans used by government agencies, military forces, law enforcement agencies, and private sector organizations to mitigate the threat of terrorism by reducing the chances that individuals or groups can successfully wage campaigns of terror in pursuit of their organizational goals.

Crime Prevention through Environmental Design (CPTED): The design and effective use of the built environment to reduce the fear and incidence of crime and to improve the quality of life.

Critical Infrastructure: Assets, systems, and resources deemed essential by government for continued organizational, economic, and social stability. Critical infrastructure may refer to material objects such as roads, highways, dams, and bridges; production processes such as agriculture and utilities; public services such as police, fire, and medical; and commercial enterprises such as banking, transportation, and fossil fuels.

Criticality: In calculating the risk associated with a specific asset, criticality refers to the value, impact, or cost of any asset, should it be lost as a result of natural or other forces.

Cruise Lines International Association (CLIA): Organized in 1975 to promote the passenger cruise industry, CLIA represents twenty-four major cruise lines serving North America. In 2006 CLIA merged with the International Council of Cruise Lines, an industry trade organization which focused on regulatory and policy development processes of the cruise industry. http://www.cruising.org

Customs-Trade Partnership against Terrorism (C-TPAT): C-TPAT is a voluntary U.S. government–business initiative administered by the U.S. Customs and Border Protection designed to build cooperative relationships between U.S. Customs and Border Protection and business interests in the international supply chain. Businesses that agree to ensure the integrity of their security practices and verify the security guidelines of their business partners within the supply chain are eligible for reduced numbers of and priority processing in U.S. Customs and Border Protection inspections.

Declaration of Security: An agreement reached between a ship and either a port facility or another ship with which it interfaces, specifying the security measures each will implement.

Demurrage: In the maritime sector, demurrage refers to the excess time taken for loading or unloading a vessel due to the acts of shippers or ports, which results in a fee levied by the shipping company upon the port or supplier that is assessed daily after the deadline.

Dirty Bomb: A radiological dispersal device that uses a conventional explosive to disperse radioactive material.

Dry Port: A facility used to store cargo containers or break-bulk cargo.

Electronic Trace Detector: A system or device that can be deployed to detect traces of volatile chemical substances in the air.

Escort: Port facility security access control systems and plans may include provisions for visitors and other nonport-credentialed individuals to be accompanied at all times by a port-credentialed individual who has access to the specific areas of the facility being accessed.

Explosive Detection System: Various technologies that can be deployed to detect the presence of explosive materials in the environment.

Facility Security Assessment: Under the U.S. Maritime Transportation Security Act (MTSA), a Facility Security Assessment refers to the analysis that examines and evaluates the infrastructure and operations of a port facility taking into account possible threats, vulnerabilities, consequences, and existing protective measures, procedures, and operations.

Facility Security Audit: Under MTSA, a Facility Security Audit is an evaluation of a security assessment or security plan performed by an owner or operator, the owner or operator's designee, or an approved third-party, intended to identify deficiencies, nonconformities, and/or inadequacies that would render the assessment or plan insufficient.

Facility Security Officer (FSO): The person designated as responsible for the development, implementation, revision, and maintenance of the Port Facility Security Plan (FSP) and for liaison with the U.S. Coast Guard Captain of the Port (COTP), and Company/Vessel Security Officers.

Facility Security Plan (FSP): The plan developed to ensure the application of security measures designed to protect the port facility and its servicing vessels or those vessels interfacing with the facility, their cargoes, and persons on board at the respective MARSEC levels.

Federal Bureau of Investigation (FBI): An agency of the U.S. Department of Justice responsible for protecting against terrorist and foreign intelligence threats, enforcin the criminal laws of the United States, and for providing criminal justice services to federal, state, municipal, and international agencies. http:// www.fbi.gov

Federal Emergency Management Agency (FEMA): An agency of the U.S. Department of Homeland Security responsible for the reduction of loss of life and property and protection from hazards including natural disasters, acts of terrorism, and man-made disasters. http://www.fema.gov

Federal Maritime Security Coordinator: The U.S. Coast Guard official in each area designated by the U.S. Secretary of Homeland Security to develop an Area Maritime Security Plan and coordinate activities required by the National Transportation Security Plan.

Fishing Port: A port primarily used to service and manage a fleet of vessels engaged in the fishing industry.

Force Multiplier: Added organizational devices or capabilities that improve the chances of mission success.

Government Accountability Office (GAO): The GAO is the independent, non-partisan agency that provides investigative and advising services for the U.S. Congress. GAO audits federal agency operations; investigates allegations of illegal and improper activities; reports on government programs; performs policy analyses; and issues legal decisions and opinions. http://www.gao.gov

Hazardous Materials: Also referred to as HAZMAT or dangerous goods, hazard-ous materials are solids, liquids, or gases that can injure or harm living organ-isms and cause damage to property and/or the environment.

HAZMAT: An acronym for hazardous materials.

Homeland Security: Homeland security refers to a governmental initiative to pro-tect the people and territory of the U.S. from injury and damage caused by internal and external threats. Also, the federal agency created pursuant to the U.S. Department of Homeland Security Act of 2002, the primary mission of which is to help prevent, protect against, and respond to acts of terrorism on U.S. soil.

Homeland Security Advisory System (HSAS): HSAS is a U.S. government advi-sory system that guides protective measures pursuant to the receipt of threat information. When combined with vulnerability assessments, HSAS employs a color-coded threat-level system to communicate with the public to reduce the likelihood or impact of an attack.

Homeland Security Presidential Directive (HSPD): Issued by the President of the United States, HSPDs establish national public policies related to U.S. home-land security.

Homeport, U.S. Coast Guard: The web portal administered by the U.S. Coast Guard designed to communicate with the public and with maritime and port interests concerning federal legislation, regulations, and programs related to maritime domain awareness and maritime security. http://homeport.uscg.mil

Immigration and Customs Enforcement (ICE): An agency of the U.S. Department of Homeland Security that includes the law enforcement arms of the former Immigration and Naturalization Service and the former U.S. Customs Service to enforce U.S. immigration and customs laws. http://www.ice.gov

Incident Command System (ICS): A set of common procedures for organizing agency personnel, facilities, equipment, and communications at the scene of extraordinary incidents threatening public safety. ICS protocols enable police, fire, security, and other responders to organize their activities in a systematic manner that expands to meet incident requirements.

Information Security Officer (ISO): The individual designated within an organization responsible for establishing standards for and managing information security.

INFOSEC: An acronym for information security.

Inland Port: A port located on a lake, river, or canal that may have access to larger bodies of water.

Institute of Shipping Economics and Logistics: A research and consulting organization headquartered in Bremen, Germany, that concentrates on maritime research and development projects, client-related information services, and statistical market analyses. http://www.isl.org

Intermodal: Refers to transportation systems that are interconnected or involve more than one method of transport.

International Association of Airport and Seaport Police: A nonprofit organization of representatives from police and other enforcement agencies associated with the transportation industry, particularly the movement of passengers and cargo at airports and seaports. http://www.iaasp.net

International Chamber of Commerce (ICC) Commercial Crime Services: ICC Commercial Crime Services is a membership organization based in the United Kingdom that provides the corporate sector with the information and resources concerning illegal activity in the global marketplace. It conducts investigations upon evidence or suspicion of fraud, and assists victims of fraud in recovering losses. http://www.icc-ccs.org

International Maritime Organization (IMO): Based in London, the IMO is a worldwide convention on maritime issues established in 1948 pursuant to an international conference in Geneva. The IMO represented the first major international initiative to establish cooperation among governments concerning regulations affecting international shipping. http://www.imo.org

International Organization for Standardization: Based in Geneva, the ISO is a developer and publisher of international standards and a network of the national standards institutes of 157 countries. http://www.iso.org/iso/

International Ship and Port Facility Security (ISPS) Code: The ISPS Code is a comprehensive set of measures implemented in 2004 to enhance the security of ships and port facilities, developed and agreed to by member countries of the International Maritime Organization in response to the perceived threats to ships and port facilities after the September 11, 2001, terrorist attacks in the United States.

INTERPOL: Based in Lyon, France, INTERPOL is an international police organization, with 186 member countries created in 1923 to facilitate cross-border police cooperation in combating international crime. http://www.interpol.int

Intrusion Detection System: A system designed to monitor a target environment and alert users on attempts to overcome or subvert the physical defenses established to protect it.

Joint Harbor Operations Center (JHOC): Operations center established by U.S. Coast Guard sector commands designed to provide centralized command, communications, and monitoring capabilities in tracking the movements of vehicles and detecting threats in port facilities and adjacent waters. Also communicates threat information and coordinates responses with participating local, state, and federal agencies with interests in maritime domain awareness and security.

Joint Terrorism Task Forces (JTTF): Located in approximately a hundred cities, JTTF is a multiagency initiative of the U.S. Department of Justice and the Federal Bureau of Investigation that employs small units of combined federal, state, and local law enforcement investigators, analysts, linguists, and other specialists to gather intelligence on, investigate, and respond to potential terrorist threats and incidents. http://www.usdoj.gov/jttf

Journal of Commerce: A weekly news magazine that reports on international trade and logistics. http://www.joc.com

Landlord-Tenant Port: A port organizational structure in which the entity owning a port facility provides the land, utilities, support structures, and systems in contractual lease arrangements with port tenants or users, such as passenger cruise lines and cargo terminal operators. Revenues raised through lease payments and usage fees are used to support port operations and development.

Longshoreman: A dockworker or laborer who is employed in activities related to the loading and unloading of vessels in a port facility.

Manifest: The list of passengers or cargo on a vessel or other conveyance.

Marine Safety and Security Team (MSST): Antiterrorism teams comprised of members of the U.S. Coast Guard whose job it is to protect the interests and assets in local maritime jurisdictions.

Maritime Administration (MARAD): An agency of the U.S. Department of Transportation whose programs promote the use of waterborne transportation and integration with other segments of the transportation system and the viability of the U.S. merchant marine. http://www.marad.dot.gov

Maritime Domain Awareness: The collection of information, intelligence, and knowledge within the maritime domain that affects port and ship security and safety.

Maritime Security (MARSEC) Level: The level set to reflect the prevailing threat environment to the marine elements of the U.S. national transportation system, including ports, vessels, facilities, and critical assets and infrastructure located on or adjacent to waters subject to the jurisdiction of the United States.

Maritime Transportation Security Act of 2002: U.S. legislation enacted in 2002 that addresses the port security efforts of the U.S. Coast Guard and other agencies in the U.S. maritime domain. The law requires vessel and facility security plans to be developed, submitted to, and approved by the U.S. Coast Guard, and incorporated into a National Maritime Security Plan that includes incident response plans.

MARSEC Level 1: The level for which minimum appropriate security measures shall be maintained at all times. It generally applies when Homeland Security Advisory System (HSAS) Threat Conditions Green, Blue, or Yellow are set.

MARSEC Level 2: The level for which appropriate additional protective security measures shall be maintained for a period of time as a result of heightened risk of a transportation security incident. It generally corresponds to HSAS Threat Condition Orange.

MARSEC Level 3: The level for which further specific protective security measures shall be maintained for a limited period of time when a transportation security incident is probable, imminent, or has occurred, although it may not be possible to identify the specific target. It generally corresponds to HSAS Threat Condition Red.

Memorial Institute for the Prevention of Terrorism (MIPT): MIPT was established pursuant to the 1995 bombing of Oklahoma City's Alfred P. Murrah Federal Building and engages in research, study, programs, and reporting on terrorism. http://www.mipt.org

National Counterterrorism Center: Established by the President of the United States in 2004, and later codified in the Intelligence Reform and Terrorism Prevention Act, the National Counterterrorism Center is the primary U.S. government entity for conducting strategic operational planning, and integrating and analyzing all intelligence pertaining to terrorism and counterterrorism. http://www.nctc.gov

National Criminal Justice Reference Service (NCJRS): NCJRS is a federally funded resource offering justice and substance abuse information to support research, policy, and program development. http://www.ncjrs.gov

National Incident Management System (NIMS): NIMS was developed by the U.S. government to enable emergency responders from different jurisdictions and disciplines to work together to respond to natural disasters and emergencies, including acts of terrorism. NIMS is based on a unified approach to incident management; standard command and management structures; and emphasis on preparedness, mutual aid, and resource management. http://www.fema.gov/emergency/nims

National Integration Center (NIC) Incident Management Systems Integration Division: Established in the U.S. Department of Homeland Security to provide direction and oversight of the National Incident Management System (NIMS), including the development of compliance criteria and implementation activities at federal, state, and local levels, it provides guidance and support to jurisdictions and incident management and responder organizations as they adopt the system. http://www.fema.gov/emergency/nims

National Nuclear Security Administration (NNSA) Megaports Initiative: The NNSA Megaports Initiative is a part of the U.S. layered strategy to prevent terrorists from acquiring, smuggling, and using nuclear materials to develop a weapon of mass destruction or radiological dispersal device in attacks against the United States or its allies. http://www.nnsa.energy.gov/nuclear_nonproliferation/1641.htm

National Response Center (NRC): The NRC is the U.S. Department of Homeland Security's national point of contact for reporting all oil, chemical, radiological, biological, and etiological discharges into the environment. It also takes terrorist/suspicious activities reports and maritime security breach reports. The NRC serves as the contact point for information on incidents, which it then conveys to the U.S. Coast Guard and other relevant federal agencies as part of the coordinated national response strategy to emergencies and incidents. http://www.nrc.uscg.mil/nrc

National Response Framework: The National Response Framework is a comprehensive all-hazards approach established by the U.S. federal government to manage domestic incidents with a unified national response to disasters and emergencies.

National Response Framework Resource Center: Provides information, documents, guides, and resources for understanding and working within the National Response Framework. http://www.fema.gov/emergency/nrf

National Strategy for Maritime Security: The U.S. government's documented strategy and supporting plans to promote global economic stability and protect legitimate activities while preventing hostile or illegal acts within the maritime domain. http://www.whitehouse.gov/homeland/4844-nsms.pdf

National Transportation Safety Board: An independent U.S. government agency responsible for investigating aviation, marine, rail, highway, and pipeline accidents. http://www.ntsb.gov

National Vessel Movement Center: Mandated by Title 33, U.S. Code of Federal Regulations, Part 160, the National Vessel Movement Center was established to track notice of arrival information from ships entering U.S. ports. http:// www.nvmc.uscg.gov

Naval Criminal Investigative Service (NCIS): NCIS is the U.S. Navy's law enforcement and counterintelligence element that works with local, state, federal, and foreign agencies to counter and investigate terrorism, espionage, computer intrusions, and many other criminal offenses. NCIS is the Navy's primary source of security for U.S. Navy personnel and assets. http://www. ncis.navy.mil

Navigation and Vessel Inspection Circular (NVIC): Issued by the U.S. Coast Guard, NVICs provide detailed guidance about the enforcement or compliance with certain federal marine safety regulations and U.S. Coast Guard marine safety programs. NVICs do not have the force of law, but do assist in complying with laws under the Coast Guard's jurisdiction. Noncompliance with an NVIC is not a violation of law but may be interpreted as an indication that there is noncompliance with a law, regulation, or policy. http://www. uscg.mil/hq/g-m/nvic

Ninety-Six-Hour Advance Notice of Arrival (96-Hour Rule): A U.S. requirement established after the September 11, 2001, terrorist attacks, enforced by the U.S. Coast Guard, which mandates that foreign-flagged vessels and foreign and domestic commercial vessels entering the U.S. from a foreign port provide a 96-hour advance notice of arrival.

Occupational Safety and Health Administration (OSHA): An agency of the U.S. Department of Labor established pursuant to the Occupational Safety and Health Act in 1971 responsible for the prevention of work-related injuries, illnesses, and deaths. http://www.osha.gov

Office of Naval Intelligence (ONI): ONI provides intelligence on the capabilities of foreign naval powers, global maritime intelligence integration in support of the War on Terror, and maritime domain awareness for homeland security. http://www.nmic.navy.mil

Panamax: The term used in the shipping industry referring to vessels that are the maximum dimensions of those capable of transiting the locks of the Panama Canal.

Personal Protective Equipment (PPE): PPE refers to devices used to protect individuals from injuries or illnesses resulting from contact with hazardous materials or other workplace hazards. Depending on the type of hazard, PPE may include but is not limited to goggles, face shields, hard hats, gloves, vests, earplugs, and respirators.

Pilot: An individual with knowledge of local waters responsible for safely guiding vessels into and out of local ports and waterways.

Piracy: Generally, piracy refers to illegal acts of violence or detention for private gain by the crew or passengers of a private ship or aircraft, and directed against another ship or aircraft or persons or property on board, on the high seas or outside the jurisdiction of any state.

Ports and Waterways Safety System (PAWSS): The PAWSS Vessel Traffic Service project is a national transportation system administered by the U.S. Coast Guard under the authority of the Ports and Waterways Safety Act of 1972 that collects, processes, and disseminates information on the marine operating environment and maritime vessel traffic in major U.S. ports and waterways. http://www.navcen.uscg.gov/mwv/vts/PAWSS.htm

Port Identification Card: An identification credential issued by a port facility authorizing access to one or more specific port locations pursuant to procedures and regulations established by the port-governing authority and concerned local, state, federal, and international regulatory agencies.

Port Security Grant Program: This U.S. government program provides grant funding to port areas for the protection of critical port infrastructure. Funds are intended for projects that protect against terrorism by enhancing risk management capabilities, domain awareness, training and exercises, and capabilities to prevent, detect, respond to, and recover from attacks involving improvised explosive devices and other nonconventional weapons.

Port Security Training Exercise Program (PortSTEP): A 2005 U.S. Transportation Security Administration (TSA) program organized to develop port security exercise and evaluation services and solutions for maritime and port security organizations. The TSA worked with the U.S. Coast Guard to provide support, planning, and other services for a series of port security training exercises, between August 2005 and October 2007, working through the Area Maritime Security Committees. PortSTEP included a mix of tabletop and functional exercises geared around managing a transportation security incident in the maritime domain.

Probability: In conducting risk assessments, probability refers to the likelihood that a particular event or occurrence will compromise security of a target environment.

Radiation Portal Monitor (RPM): A detection device that uses passive, nonintrusive means to screen trucks and other conveyances for the presence of nuclear and radiological materials. RPM systems can detect various types of radiation emanating from nuclear devices, dirty bombs, special nuclear materials, natural sources, and isotopes commonly used in medicine and industry.

Radio Frequency Identification (RFID): An automatic identification method incorporating radio wave technology.

Radiological Dispersal Device: Also called a dirty bomb, a radiological dispersal device combines radioactive material with conventional explosives such that when detonated, the explosive force would cause the radioactive material to be dispersed over a wide area.

RAND Corporation: A nonprofit organization that conducts research and provides analysis in many disciplines affecting public policy. http://www.rand.org

Red Teaming: A structured process whereby a team, taking the perspective of an opponent or adversary, challenges existing plans, operations, concepts, organizations, and capabilities in determining weaknesses associated with prevailing systems and structures.

Restricted Access Area (RAA): In a target environment, the RAA refers to those locations for which special authorization and credentialing documents are required to gain access.

Risk Management: A process whereby decision makers assess threats to a target environment, allocate resources, and take actions under conditions of uncertainty.

River Port: A river port handles vessels trafficking on rivers, such as barges and transport vessels that are capable of operating in shallower waters.

Roll-On–Roll-Off: Vessels that have built-in ramps that allow the cargo to be efficiently transported onto and off of the vessel.

Safety of Life at Sea (SOLAS) Convention: SOLAS, the International Convention for the Safety of Life at Sea, was first adopted in 1914 in response to the *Titanic* disaster. In succeeding iterations, the SOLAS Convention represents a comprehensive international treaty addressing the safety of the world's merchant ships.

Seaport: A seaport refers to a port primarily used for ocean-going vessels.

Seaports Press Review: A publication that reports on ports, logistics, shipping, and maritime transportation. http://www.seaportspr.com

Security and Accountability for Every Port Act (SAFE Port Act): U.S. legislation enacted in 2006 that addresses programs related to port security, including facility security requirements, the Transportation Worker Identification Credential, interagency operational centers, the Port Security Grant Program, the Container Security Initiative, foreign port assessments, and the Customs-Trade Partnership against Terrorism.

Security Breach: An incident that has not resulted in a transportation security incident, in which security measures have been circumvented, eluded, or violated.

Sensitive Security Information (SSI): SSI is a term referenced in the U.S. Maritime Transportation Security Act of 2002. Under Title 49 of the Code of Federal Regulations, Part 1520, the U.S. Transportation Security Administration has the authority to designate as SSI any information obtained or developed in carrying out security requirements that would be detrimental to the security of transportation if that information was disclosed.

Stevedore: A person or organization employed in the loading or unloading of ship-borne cargo. The term originated in Spain (estibador) and Portugal (estivador), meaning "a man who stuffs," and entered English-speaking countries through its use by sailors.

Tariff: A tax on goods levied upon trade across borders; also generally can refer to fixing a price on goods and services.

Transportation Intermediaries Association: A professional organization of third-party logistics industry intermediaries doing business in domestic and international commerce. http://www.tianet.org

Transportation Security Administration (TSA): An agency of the U.S. Department of Homeland Security responsible for security of the U.S. transportation systems. http://www.tsa.gov

Transportation Security Incident: A security incident resulting in a significant loss of life, environmental damage, transportation system disruption, or economic disruption in a particular area.

Transportation Worker Identification Credential (TWIC): The TWIC is a common federal identification credential for all dockworkers, truckers, merchant mariners, other port workers requiring unescorted access to secure areas of MTSA-regulated facilities and vessels, and all mariners holding U.S. Coast Guard-issued credentials. The U.S. Transportation Security Administration, which administers the TWIC program, will issue workers a tamper-resistant credential containing the worker's biometric (fingerprint template) to allow for a positive link between the card itself and the individual.

Twenty (20)-Foot Equivalency Unit (TEU): TEU is an abbreviation for twenty (20)-foot equivalent unit and is a standard of measurement used in the cargo containerization industry. Most shipping containers used today are forty feet long and are therefore equivalent to two TEUs.

Twenty-Four (24)-Hour Rule: The 24-hour rule requires sea carriers and nonvessel-operating common carriers to provide U.S. Customs and Border Protection with detailed descriptions of the contents of sea containers bound for the United States 24 hours before the container is loaded on board a vessel. The rule allows U.S. Customs officers to analyze the container content information and identify potential terrorist threats before the U.S.-bound container is loaded at the foreign seaport.

Urban Area Security Initiative (UASI): The UASI program is a U.S. grant program that provides financial assistance for multidisciplinary planning, operations, equipment, training, and exercises in high-threat, high-density urban areas.

U.S. Coast Guard: An element of the U.S. Department of Homeland Security, the U.S. Coast Guard is a military branch involved in maritime law, mariner assistance, and search and rescue. The U.S. Coast Guard has broad roles in homeland security, law enforcement, search and rescue, marine environmental pollution response, and the maintenance of river, intracoastal, and offshore aids to navigation. http://www.uscg.mil

U.S. Customs and Border Protection: An agency of the U.S. Department of Homeland Security, U.S. Customs and Border Protection has broad roles in homeland security and responsibilities for securing and facilitating trade and travel, and enforcing U.S. immigration and drug laws. http://www.cbp.gov

U.S. Department of Homeland Security (DHS): The federal agency created pursuant to the U.S. Department of Homeland Security Act of 2002, the primary mission of which is to help prevent, protect against, and respond to acts of terrorism on U.S. soil. http://www.dhs.gov

Vulnerability: Vulnerability refers to how prone a particular person, asset, system, function, or process is to injury, death, damage, loss, or disaster.

Weapons of Mass Destruction (WMD): Weapons designed or fabricated to kill large numbers of people or cause major damage to property and the environment (see BNICE, CBRNE).

World Cargo Alliance: A global network of independent international freight forwarders. http://www.worldcargoalliance.com

World Customs Organization (WCO): The WCO is an intergovernmental organization focused on customs matters, including the development of global standards, procedures, trade supply chain security, the facilitation of international trade, the enhancement of customs enforcement and compliance activities, anti-counterfeiting and piracy initiatives, public–private partnerships, integrity promotion, and sustainable global customs capacity building programs. http://www.wcoomd.org

Select Bibliography

Booz Allen Hamilton. 2005. *Convergence of enterprise security organizations.* Alexandria, VA: American Society for Industrial Security (ASIS) International.

Broder, James F. 2006. *Risk analysis and the security survey.* 3rd ed. Amsterdam: Elsevier.

Carter, David L. 2008. *Intelligence fusion and the information sharing environment: Implications for policy and research.* A paper presented at the 2008 annual meeting, Academy of Criminal Justice Sciences, Cincinnati, OH. East Lansing, MI: Intelligence Program, School of Criminal Justice, Michigan State University.

Chalk, Peter, Bruce Hoffman, Robert Reville, and Anna-Britt Kasupski. 2005. *Trends in terrorism: Threats to the United States and the future of the Terrorism Risk Insurance Act.* Center for Terrorism Risk Management Policy. Santa Monica, CA: Rand Corporation.

Clifford, Mary. 2004. *Identifying and exploring security essentials.* Upper Saddle River, NJ: Pearson Prentice Hall.

Collins, Pamela, Truett A. Ricks, and Clifford W. Van Meter. 2000. *Principles of security and crime prevention.* 4th ed. Cincinnati: Anderson Publishing.

Curtis, George E., and R. Bruce McBride. *Proactive security administration.* Upper Saddle River, NJ: Pearson Prentice Hall.

CW Productions Ltd. 2006. *The United States Department of Homeland Security: An overview.* In: Richard White and Kevin Collins (eds.). Boston: Pearson Custom Publishing.

Ellis, James O. (ed.). 2007. *Terrorism: What's coming: The mutating threat.* Oklahoma City, OK: Memorial Institute for the Prevention of Terrorism.

Fischer, Robert J., Edward Halibozek, and Gion Green. 2008. *Introduction to security*. 8th ed. Boston: Butterworth-Heinemann.

Frittelli, J. (ed.). 2003. Port and maritime security: Background and issues. New York: Novinka Books.

General Accountability Office. 2007. *Port risk management: Additional federal guidance would aid ports in disaster planning and recovery.* GAO-07-412. Washington, DC: U.S. General Accountability Office.

Gibbs Van Brunschot, Erin, and Leslie W. Kennedy. 2008. *Risk balance and security.* Los Angeles: Sage Publications.

Gray, J., M. Monday, and G. Stubblefield. 1999. *Maritime terror: Protecting your vessel and your crew against piracy.* Boulder, CO: Paladin Press.

Greenberg, Michael D., Peter Chalk, Henry H. Willis, Ivan Khilko, and David S. Ortiz. 2006. *Maritime terrorism: Risk and liability.* Center for Terrorism Risk Management Policy. Santa Monica, CA: Rand Corporation.

Hersey, P., and K. H. Blanchard. 1988. *Management of organizational behavior: Utilizing human resources.* Englewood Cliffs, NJ: Prentice Hall.

Homeland Security Institute. 2007. *Report of the DHS National Small Vessel Security Summit.* HSI Publication Number RP07-12-01. Arlington, VA: Homeland Security Institute.

International Labour Office. 2005. *Safety and health in ports.* Geneva: International Labour Office.

Jackson, Brian A., Lloyd Dixon, and Victoria A. Greenfield. 2007. *Economically targeted terrorism: A review of the literature and a framework for considering defensive approaches.* Center for Terrorism Risk Management Policy. Santa Monica, CA: Rand Corporation.

Katz, Daniel, and Robert L. Kahn. 1978. *The social psychology of organizations.* New York: John Wiley & Sons.

Lyndon B. Johnson School of Public Affairs Policy Research Project on Port and Supply Chain Security, Leigh B. Boske (Project Director). 2006. *Port and supply chain security initiatives in the United States and abroad: Prepared for the Congressional Research Service.* Austin, TX: University of Texas at Austin.

McEntire, David A. 2008. *Introduction to homeland security: Understanding terrorism with an emergency management perspective.* New York: John Wiley & Sons.

McNicholas, Michael. 2008. *Maritime security: An introduction.* Boston: Butterworth-Heinemann.

Mintzberg, Henry, and James Brian Quinn. 1992. *The strategy process: Concepts and contexts.* Englewood Cliffs, NJ: Prentice Hall.

O'Brien, Thomas. 2007. *The who, what, when, where, and why of port security: A resource guide for your use today and in the future.* California State University, Long Beach: Center for International Trade and Transportation.

Ortmeier, P. J. 2005. *Security management: An introduction.* 2nd ed. Upper Saddle River, NJ: Pearson Prentice Hall.

Ortmeier, P. J. 2009. *Introduction to security operations and management.* 3rd ed. Upper Saddle River, NJ: Pearson Prentice Hall.

Pate, Anthony, Bruce Taylor, and Bruce Kubu. 2007. *Protecting America's ports: Promising practices: A final report submitted by the Police Executive Research Forum to the National Institute of Justice.* Washington, DC: Police Executive Research Forum.

Richardson, M. 2004. *A time bomb for global trade: Maritime-related terrorism in an age of weapons of mass destruction.* Singapore: Institute of Southeast Asian Studies.

Sennewald, Charles A. 2003. *Effective security management.* Boston: Butterworth-Heinemann.

Stohr, Mary K., and Peter A. Collins. 2009. *Criminal justice management: Theory and practice in justice-centered organizations.* New York: Oxford University Press.

Sweet, Kathleen M. 2006. *Transportation and cargo security.* Upper Saddle River, NJ: Pearson Prentice Hall.

Tyson, Dave. 2007. *Security convergence: Managing enterprise security risk.* Amsterdam: Elsevier.

U.S. Department of Justice. 2005. *Assessing and managing the terrorism threat.* NCJ210680. Washington, DC: Bureau of Justice Assistance.

Vasu, Michael L., Debra W. Stewart, and G. David Garson. 1998. *Organizational behavior and public management.* 3rd ed. New York: Marcel Dekker, Inc.

Waldron, Jonathan, and Andrew W. Dyer. 2005. *Maritime security handbook: Implementing the new U.S. initiatives and regulations.* Lantham, MD: Government Institutes.

Werther, William B., and Keith Davis. 1996. *Human resources and personnel management.* 5th ed. Boston: Irwin McGraw-Hill.

White, Jonathan R. 2009. *Terrorism and homeland security.* 6th ed. Belmont, CA: Wadsworth Cengage Learning.

Willis, Henry H., and David S. Ortiz. (2004). *Evaluating the security of the global containerized supply chain.* Santa Monica, CA: Rand Corporation.

Appendix A

Facility Security Audit Scope of Services for Outsourcing

AUDIT OF PORT OF _____ FACILITY SECURITY PLAN

SCOPE OF SERVICES

INTRODUCTION-BACKGROUND

The Port of _____, hereinafter referred to as the port facility, is required to comply with and implement portions of the maritime security regime required by the Maritime Transportation Security Act of 2002, as codified in 46 U.S.C. Chapter 701. A requirement of this federal law is that the port facility has and maintains an approved Facility Security Plan (FSP). Title 33 CFR, Navigation and Navigable Waters, Chapter I, Coast Guard, Department of Homeland Security, Subchapter H, Maritime Security, Part 105, Maritime Security: Facilities, Section 105.415, Amendment and Audit specifies a requirement for an annual audit of the FSP.

The port facility is requesting the services of a qualified firm to audit the port's FSP in accordance with 33 CFR 105. Specifically, 33 CFR 105 states the Facility Security Officer (FSO) must ensure an audit of the FSP is performed annually, beginning no later than one year from the initial date of approval, and attach a letter to the FSP certifying that the FSP meets the applicable requirements of 33 CFR 105. Unless impracticable due to the size and nature of the company or the facility, personnel conducting internal audits of the security measures specified in the FSP or evaluating its implementation must:

1. Have knowledge of methods for conducting audits and inspections, and security, control, and monitoring techniques;
2. Not have regularly assigned security duties; and
3. Be independent of any security measures being audited.

If the results of an audit require amendment of either the Facility Security Assessment or FSP, the FSO must submit, in accordance with 33 CFR 105, Section 105.410, the amendments to the cognizant U.S. Coast Guard Captain of the Port for review and approval no later than 30 days after completion of the audit and a letter certifying that the amended FSP meets applicable requirements of this part.

SERVICES REQUESTED

Annual Audit Requirements:

1. Commence a regulatory compliance audit of the port facility FSP as required by 33 CFR 105 no later than _____ (Date).
2. Perform and complete the regulatory compliance audit of the port facility FSP as required by 33 CFR 105.
3. Generation of compliance letters to the U.S. Coast Guard on behalf of the port facility FSO, no later than _____ (Date).
4. Provide the port facility with recommendations for enhancing port security to comply with 33 CFR 105.

PERFORMANCE SPECIFICATIONS

1. Personnel conducting audits must:
   a. Have knowledge of methods for conducting audits and inspections, and security, control, and monitoring techniques.
   b. Not have regularly assigned port facility security duties.
   c. Be independent of any security measures being audited.
2. The firm shall adhere to auditing standards, regulations, and guidelines applicable in the State of _____, and will conduct the audit in accordance with these requirements existing, or as may be pronounced during the period or term of this audit engagement.
3. The audit report shall contain an opinion of the auditor on the security conditions at the port facility.

Index